Innovating Genesis

Microgenesis and
the Constructive Mind in Action

A volume in
Advances in Cultural Psychology

Series Editor:
Jaan Valsiner, *Clark University*

Advances in Cultural Psychology

Jaan Valsiner, Series Editor

Innovating Genesis

Microgenesis and
the Constructive Mind in Action

edited by

Emily Abbey
Ramapo College of New Jersey

and

Rainer Diriwächter
California Lutheran University

Information Age Publishing, Inc.
Charlotte, North Carolina • www.infoagepub.com

Library of Congress Cataloging-in-Publication Data

Innovating genesis microgenesis and the constructive mind in action / edited by Emily Abbey and Rainer Diriwdchter.
    p. cm. -- (Advances in cultural psychology)
 Includes bibliographical references.
 ISBN 978-1-59311-909-6 (pbk.) -- ISBN 978-1-59311-910-2 (hardcover) 1. Ethnopsychology. 2. Personality and culture. 3. Cognition and culture. I. Abbey, Emily. II. Diriwdchter, Rainer.
 GN502.I5555 2008
 155.8--dc   222008008112

Printed in the United States of America

CONTENTS

PART III: SYMBOLIC SELF-SOOTHING

PART IV: DAYDREAMS

PART V: EARLY DEVELOPMENT OF SUBJECT-OBJECT RELATIONS

FOREWORD

Genesis of Methodological Innovation

Cultural psychology is currently in a phase of rapid growth. Innovating Genesis is an example of how the most central aspect of any science—its methodology—undergoes revolutionary transformation. Yet in this book we see careful continuity with the past of the discipline. The orientation to study processes of emergence was well prepared by the *Ganzheitspsychologie* tradition in early twentieth century. If we all have learned something about the world since then it is the inevitable quality of the whole that transcends its parts. Scientists have tried to grasp the general notion of such wholes—yet recurrently regressing to the easy illusion that one can reduce the complexities of the *in vivo* events to the scrutinizes in vitro. By looking to the history of how holistic ideas might help our present investigations, this book demonstrates how contemporary science has something to learn from its own history.

Finding history to be of relevance for the future may at first glance be surprising—in so many sciences the researchers prefer to either ignore their history—which indeed entails a myriad of failed constructs among episodic solutions—or treat it as a museum of "hero" scientists who are recognized as "pioneers" in their fields—without further delving into how they actually worked. We all seem to know more about Albert Einstein's violin than about his failed efforts to solve basic scientific problems—prior to the successful solution of the one for which he became famous. Scientists create their breakthroughs through a sequence of searches, misunderstandings, false starts, new starts that mostly turn out to be unproductive, and (maybe) finally solve the problems they have set for themselves. The whole history of their effortful pursuits is a rich realm from where new pursuits can sail off to look for new undiscovered domains of human understanding.

However, the regular orthodoxy of passing on knowledge from generation to generation in science abhors its own history. It is an act of communication between different social institutions all of which have their vested interests in the outcome of the negotiations of the role of sciences within societies. It is such institutional presentation that leads a science to circumscribing the narratives about its history—presented in textbooks—to specific genres of how such history is to be socially presented. Thus, the official histories of most sciences tend to be stories of sequences of glory. In such stories the scientists of the past emerge on the scene as positive heroes who—after some puzzlement and difficulties— get the upper hand over the demons of ignorance.

Psychology is no different from that—its recurrent teaching of courses under label of its "history and systems" guarantees the glorious "museum status" for historical scholarship. By glorifying individual psychologists of the past—the fate of Lev Vygotsky, or of Jean Piaget, is a good example— the creative ideas of the glorified personage can be stopped from further growing. Instead, we may find a new social network that follows the "guru figure," evaluates the "fit" of the different followers to the "true teaching," and uses such social discourse for creating one's own social capital. Science—in the sense of *Wissenschaft*—vanishes, while the vanity of success in the social enterprise of science proliferates. The result can be alienation of a given science from its subject matter—in hailing a success story we may forget which basic problems are not yet solved in the given science.

In terms of intellectual breakthroughs in any science, ignoring of history can backfire—what looks like a series of failed conceptual reconstructions at some historical period may turn into an intellectual goldmine if carefully reanalyzed. The case of *Ganzheitspsychologie* in this book is but one of such forgotten tracks that provide us with new innovations. This book fills a gap in the current series as it brings back together the crucial psychological phenomena—that are constantly in movement, in transformation—with the microgenetic methodological orientation. This entails relocating the methodological focus of cultural psychology from the study of outcomes of psychological processes—such as a decision already made, or a rating given on a rating scale, or a "yes, I agree" answer given in an interview or questionnaire—to the intricate investigation of the psychological processes through which such outcomes are reached. Such processes are rich in detail, dynamic, and filled with cultural organizers—signs—that human beings bring to bear upon the self-organizing processes of the *psyche*. *Innovating Genesis* is a book that continues along the lines of focusing on cultural-psychological processes. Thus, the tensions in relationships between the self and the other (in L. Simão and J. Valsiner, *Otherness in Question*, Information Age Publishing [IAP], 2006) as well as Ernest E. Boesch's focus on the eternal dynamics of *Heimweh* and *Fernweh* (in W. Lonner & S. Hayes, *Discovering Cultural Psychology*, IAP, 2007) pave the way to the different contributions that can be found in this current book. Cultural psychology is currently on the forefront of the social sciences toward overcoming the scaffolds of the outcomes-oriented research methods that have dominated psychology for half a century.

The editors of this volume—Emily Abbey and Rainer Diriwächter— have achieved something we rarely see among the junior scholars in our discipline—freedom from the normative orthodoxy of contemporary psychology. Knowing tolerates no orthodoxies—and innovative science requires all the creative impulses that human lives entail. Psychologys methodology needs a serious overhaul—restoring the central feature of phenomenology in its center, and looking for new dynamic approaches to the solution of old problems. The editors of this volume have managed to bring together a creative international team of scholars whom they have guided to be on target of the content matter of the book—innovating the genesis of the methods for the study of psychological emergence.

Chapel Hill, NC-Worcester, MA
September 2007
Jaan Valsiner
Series Editor

EDITORS' INTRODUCTION

Emily Abbey and Rainer Diriwächter

As outlined by Henri Bergson (1913), human lives are continuously developing into novel forms, making the study of emergence centrally important for any science of the human mind and behavior. From its historical predecessor *Völkerpsychologie* to its modern enactment, cultural psychology has long been concerned with just such a focus—tasked itself with understanding that which is in motion and transforming. Within this orientation, the primacy of the formed and stable has been surpassed as researchers better appreciate the unstable and semiformed, as well as the ambiguity and uncertainty imbuing human lives on account of continuous change. Yet work in this area will continue to be productive only as long as researchers find ways to deal with the methodological challenges such a focus presents.

Any researcher faces something of a quandary when he or she tries to understand emergence—inquiry of this nature requires explaining that which is not yet in existence using only two pieces of information: what is known, and what is expected (Valsiner, 2001, p. 53). In facing this quandary, traditional methods of research in psychology—those capturing only "snap shots" in time— are of little use. Such traditional methods erase rather than maintain the time sequence of the data, and cannot make visible the specific conditions through which novelty is produced. Thus, it is to this basic methodological difficulty in cultural psychological research—or any other that accepts the irreversible nature of human lives—that this book responds. What methods allow the researcher contact with the process of transition? How can one access those shifts and movements through which the appearance of new forms can be better understood? In sum, our goal in this volume is to provide answers to the deceptively simple question: what methods can be used to study phenomena as they emerge?

HISTORICAL FOUNDATIONS AND EMERGENT METHODS

Early efforts to answering this question can be traced to the first portion of the twentieth century and the tradition of *Ganzheitspsychologie* (see Diriwächter & Valsiner, 2008). The method—in English often referred to as a "microgenetic method"—involves understanding emergence by treating "forms" as merely boundary states within the ongoing transformation process, and instead of seeing the transition of forms X → Y → Z as simple progression of separate forms (X, Y, Z), highlighting transition moments (e.g., between X and Y or Y and Z), whether in the development of visual percepts (e.g., see Wohlfahrt, 1925/1932) or general meaning-constructs (such as micromelodies, see Werner 1925; or the role of symbols, see Werner, 1954).

Such an orientation provides the foundation from which one can begin to answer our present question, yet any researcher is not well-advised to take the practices used by another researcher and simply apply that method to his or her own research program. Of course, such an orientation is potentially not uncommon to the extent that researchers see *methodology as consisting of a personal "tool box" of ready-to-use methods* (Branco & Valsiner, 1997; Diriwächter & Valsiner, 2005) that are "brought in" to the research process at a particular moment for use in collecting empirical data. In contrast, however, we view *methodology as a cycle, wherein axiomatic assumptions, theory, phenomena and method are all united with one another* (Branco & Valsiner, 1997; Diriwaechter & Valsiner, 2005; Valsiner, 2000). In this latter understanding, the researcher does not use preconstructed methods, but rather, *the construction of his or her method is influenced by other aspects in the research cycle*—most directly by phenomena on the one hand, and theory on the other (Valsiner, 2000, p. 64). On this understanding, our central question in this volume cannot be answered through history alone: methods are themselves emergent, coming into being alongside the particular researcher's project.

Contributions to This Volume

The five studies discussed in this volume, thus, are all possible answers to the above question, for in each there is the story of a researcher trying to understand emergence using methods that have been *adapted* given his or her particular project. As well, consistent with our orientation, commentaries are provided following each chapter, serving to provide still further expansion of ideas. We start our journey with a contribution that addresses the interests of early microgenetic researchers: visual actual genesis. In Part I, Lothar Kleine-Horst revisits the early works of *Aktualgenese* and expands on them by introducing his own research findings. His discussed methodology and proposed "theory of man" is then subsequently commented upon in Brady Wagoner's contribution.

Our second topic of discussion elevates the "meaning-making-process" to a higher sphere of cognitive events. In Part II, Nicole Capezza and Jaan Valsiner address our affective self-regulations in the context of mediated experiences. Their crucial contribution toward a better understanding of human decision making that can lead to a violent or nonviolent outcome places the emphasis on semiotic mediation. The semiotic regulatory construction is examined across national boundaries (United States and Estonia) and their proposed methodology to study the microgenesis of particular gun-violence addresses the emerging arenas for action. Their proposal to examine this phenomenon not from a linear-causal perspective but from a systemic transformational one (that emphasizes semiotic regulators) is further commented upon in Gyuseog Han's contribution. This discussion should prove particularly fruitful for scholars interested in microgenesis within the social psychology field.

It should be clear that the process of microgenesis is multifold. In Part III we find Valerie Bellas and James McHale making sense of their own investigative approach. It is rare that one finds a self-analysis of a researcher's constructive processes. Bellas and McHale explore the emerging properties of meaning making for a researcher who is examining toddler-parent dyads. From the moment of data dissection, to generating questions and subsequently establishing models of analytic investigation, Bellas and McHale highlight the struggles a researcher must go through in trying to understand phenomena. In that regard, we can gain additional insight of the constructive research process through Carla Cunha's contribution that emphasizes the dialogical nature of the task at hand. The days of the "un-biased" or "neutral" researcher are over. All research involves a state of ambiguity that—microgenetically speaking—is transformed to concrete statements through a process of negotiation.

In Part IV, Stacey Pereira and Rainer Diriwächter take a closer look at the qualitative nature of daydreams. That is, how daydreams emerge and transform both in terms of content as well as the daydreamers self-reference. In this regard, the methodology used is twofold: both written and vocal expressions were examined in order to "capture" the emergence of new forms. The subsequent commentary by Jeanette Lawrence and Agnes Dodds examines this methodology as well as implications regarding the qualitative transformation of daydreams and the dichotomy (e.g., dream-awake) which it entails.

Lastly, in Part V Christiane Moro and Cintia Rodriguez discuss their research that examines the meaning-making process through triadic interactions. The central theme in this contribution involves the production of signs in general and ostensions in particular. The child is examined both as an interpreter and producer of signs, whereby these signs are meaningful only if understood within the context of social others. This issue is reflected upon by Selma Leitão's subsequent commentary. Furthermore, critical thoughts are also devoted to the methodology in addressing the researcher's approach toward understanding the role of linguistics and general semiotic activity while constructing meaning.

Our hope is that the following discussions will provide food-for-thought to the interested scholar, which in return will lead to much fruitful labor.

REFERENCES

Bergson, H. (1913). *Time and free will*. London: George Allen.

Branco, A. U., & Valsiner, J. (1997). Changing methodologies: A co-constructivist study of goal orientations in social interactions. *Psychology & Developing Societies*, 9(1) 35-64.

Diriwächter, R., & Valsiner, J. (Eds.). (2008). *Striving for the whole: Creating theoretical syntheses*. Somerset, NJ: Transaction.

Diriwächter, R., & Valsiner, J. (2005, December). Qualitative developmental research methods in their historical and epistemological contexts [53 paragraphs]. *Forum Qualitative Sozialforschung/Forum: Qualitative Social Research* [Online Journal], 7(1), Art 8. Retrieved December 30, 2005, http://www.qualitative-research.net/fqs-texte/1-06/06-1-8-e.htm

Valsiner, J. (2000). *Culture and human development*. Thousand Oaks, CA: Sage.

Valsiner, J. (2001). *Comparative study of human cultural development*. Madrid, Spain: Fundacion Infancia y Aprendizaje.

Werner, H. (1925). Studien über die Strukturgesetze IV: Über Mikromelodik und Mikroharmonik [Studies on structural laws IV: On micromelodies and microharmony]. *Zeitschrift für Psychologie*, 98, 74-89.

Werner, H. (1954). Change of meaning: A study of semantic processes through the experimental method. *Journal of General Psychology*, 50, 181-208.

Wohlfahrt, E. (1932). Der Auffassungsvorgang an kleinen Gestalten. Ein Beitrag zur Psychologie des Vorgestalterlebnisses. *Neve Psychologische Studien*, 4, 347-414. [Dissertation, Leipzig-1925].

PART I

MICROGENESIS OF VISUAL GESTALT PERCEPTION

CHAPTER 1

FROM VISUAL ACTUAL GENESIS AND ONTOGENESIS TOWARD A THEORY OF MAN

Lothar Kleine-Horst

Visual actual genesis (microgenesis) is the process of stepwise differentiation of visual experience. Visual actual lysis is its counterprocess, that is, a stepwise dedifferentiation of visual experience. Both processes are basic facts of perception, but ignored by mainstream science. The aim of this chapter is, first, to report methods and results of experimental research on this domain, second, to describe, according to the "Empiristic theory of visual gestalt perception" (Kleine-Horst, 2001), the ontogenesis of the visual gestalt factor hierarchy, the actualization of which leads to visual actual geneses, and third, to demonstrate a way to reach to a theory of man, by enlarging the symmetries found.

Innovating Genesis: Microgenesis and the Constructive Mind in Action, pp. 3–40

3

METHODS AND RESULTS OF
VISUAL ACTUAL-GENETIC/ACTUAL-LYTIC RESEARCH

Laboratory Methods for Producing Visual Actual Geneses and Actual Lyses

The only systematic research on visual actual genesis was published between 1932 and 1940. In his 1925 doctoral thesis, Erich Wohlfahrt (1932), student of Friedrich Sander (the cofounder of the genetic Ganzheitspsychologie), presented the results of his actual-genetic experiments. With the help of a slide projector, he projected patterns on to a projection screen so that they were seen as bright figures in an almost darkened room. In the beginning, the patterns were optically reduced in size greatly. In each further experiment, the pattern was projected while being successively increased in size at intervals of 25%. Seven subjects, trained in self-observation (i.e., introspection), described what they perceived verbally and graphically. In the beginning, these figures were so small that the subjects perceived mostly bright patches with sharp, and often circular borders only. It was only after the pattern was enlarged somewhat that the subjects were able to make further distinctions: here, the originally unitary outer contour of the figure became divided into several segments and then inner contours emerged. Finally, after the stimulus had reached a certain size, the perception was completely differentiated, and the figure was perceived as it would be under "normal" perceptual circumstances.

This process, this development of perceptual configuration, from a diffuse-holistic configuration to the final percept, the "endgestalt," through several intermediate percepts was termed in 1928 *Aktualgenese* by Friedrich Sander (1962a), "actual genesis" by Kragh (1955) as in this contribution, and "microgenesis" by Werner (1956). Sander was familiar also with the counterprocess of actual genesis, which he termed *Morpholyse*, and which is termed "actual lysis" in this contribution. Figure 1.1 shows an actual-genetic series of visual percepts, the stages 3 to 8 of which were also depicted by Sander (1962a, p. 101) (incidentally, the only actual-genetic series he has ever published). Wohlfahrt numbered the line-ends and corners of the stimulus so that he could indicate which line of the prepercepts had led to a given line in the prepercept. The series in Figure 1.1 has been expanded according to the courses often reported by the subjects, as in one third of the cases a "completely undifferentiated bright patch" was seen at first, which "was usually sketched as a small filled-in circle" (Wohlfahrt, 1932, p. 364) (stage 2 in Figure 1.1). It can be clearly "seen" that the perceptual development follows certain rules. As

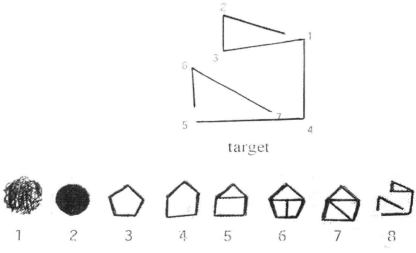

Figure 1.1.   An actual-genetic series of the target, with stages 2 to 8 reported by Wohlfahrt (1932), and stage 1 reported by Butzmann (1940), according to Kleine-Horst, 2001, Figure 6.4.

outlined in stage 3, the percept has already differentiated itself into a figure consisting of an inner field separated from its outer field by a border. This contour is no longer a single contour as in stage 2, instead it consists of five lines and is insofar more "veridical." On the other hand, it is not fully adequate to the final percept, which consists of seven lines. And it is also inadequate in another respect as the lines of the final percept are of unequal lengths, whereas stage 3 shows lines of equal lengths. After the size of the stimulus had increased further, the regularity of the contour disappeared in favor of more stimulus adequate line length differences, as shown in stage 4. Wohlfahrt reported that, after the outer contour had developed a particular form, the inner fields usually occurred as "dark nuclei" connected by "bridges" which later became inner contours (stages 5 and 6).

One sees in Figure 1.1, on the one hand, this general *development to adequacy* just described, that is, predominantly the successive occurrence of new features, in a certain sequence. One sees, on the other hand, also the *tendency to Gestaltetheit*, that is, the temporal preference of often nonveridical but more "regular" forms over the veridical, but possibly "irregular" forms. Thus earlier stages are usually "simpler" than later stages; the percepts are initially more regular than when the stimulus is stronger, or a line is first formatively linked perpendicularly (second contour in stage 6) rather than veridically at a nonright angle (stage 7).

The target is also easier to see formatively closed (stages 1 to 7) than veridically open (stage 8). However, in the sequence shown there are also some deviations to these rules; they will be described (and explained) in section 3.

Butzmann (1940), another of Sander's students, investigated visual actual geneses in peripheral vision. He used a Zeiss projection-perimeter, with which he projected the target at first on a peripheral area, far from the fovea, the center of sharpest sight. In a number of steps, he projected the target nearer to the fovea, so that more detail was perceived by the subject. The subjects reported percepts even simpler than the first percepts of Wohlfahrt's subjects. Butzmann described the percepts that appeared in the first phase as follows:

> There remains more or less an impression of brightness, regarding which one can neither say where it is bound nor whether it is bound at all. It is something that possesses an extension. To some degree, it even merges in the ground so that a clear ground-figure differentiation is impossible. (p. 148)

This contourless "impression" has been introduced in Figure 1.1 as stage 1. Sander's students Hausmann (1935), Dun (1939), and Mörschner (1940) chose tachistoscopic procedures, by which the subjects were exposed to the targets initially in very short periods, which were then successively expanded. Mörschner did not project meaningless patterns; he used sets of consumer goods, one set containing, for example, a ruler, a pair of compasses, a protractor and a tweezers.

All experimenters came to the same, or similar, results: The actual genesis is conditioned by two endogenous processes, one toward an increase in object adequacy (working the stronger, the stronger being the stimulus), and one toward an increase in regularity, symmetry, straightness, and closedness, for example, caused by "gestalt tendencies" (which work the stronger, the weaker being the stimulus). Thus the effect of gestalt tendencies decreases as the effect of the stimulus increases. It is that primary course, the development toward object adequacy, that is, veridicality of a percept, that defines perceptual actual genesis, through which a very new insight into perception was expected, whereas the effect of the gestalt tendencies was already known.

Sander (1962a, pp. 111-112) distinguished between two types of actual genesis: the "hologenous" and the "merogenous" actual genesis. The hologenous actual genesis is a holistic perceptual experience beginning with a holistic percept that reveals stages of increasing differentiation, as shown in Figure 1.1. The merogenous actual genesis begins, contrastingly, with several single percepts, already having ended its own hologenous actual geneses, and uniting to form a holistic cognitive and as such mental experience, which also reveals stages of increasing differentiation.

Since Mörschner (1940) worked with visual stimuli, which however came from real, concrete objects rather than meaningless patterns, he observed connections of (perceptual) hologenous and (mental) merogenous actual geneses: With the improvement of the objects' perception, the objects' cognition also improved.

In this contribution, pure visual actual geneses and visual actual lyses will be referred to only, that is, without consideration of the visual patterns' possible meaning as representing any certain object.

There are studies carried out in different conditions where entire contour sections were observed to disappear. A small apparatus that effected a "stabilization" of retinal images was constructed and mounted on the cornea; in fact, the eyes are constantly subject to spasmodic motion, which is not (or not entirely) to be voluntarily suppressed. As a consequence of this motion, images of the environment constantly "whisk" back and forth across the retina. This motion, termed *physiological nystagmus*, is apparently absolutely necessary for normal vision. If the motion is compensated for by an optical system—such as the apparatus mentioned above, so that despite eye movement every stimulus impinges on the same retinal location—then one can no longer perceive anything after a short time. At the beginning of this process, which eventually leads to the complete breakdown of visual perception, a disappearance of contour sections was observed (Evans & Piggins, 1963; Pritchard, Heron, & Hebb, 1960). Using another method, the images were produced by short light flashes (intermittent illumination), so that the percepts appeared before any eye movement could influence them. With this different method, but using the same target used by Evans and Piggins. Piggins (1970) found similar percepts. Every disappearance of a target's line, or a group of lines, is a step in an actual-lytic process.

Negative Afterimages

Afterimages are a good example for a natural kind of visual experience; this is why even Aristotle was aware of them; they can be investigated without the aid of any equipment, that is, with the naked eye. An afterimage can be seen following a brief intense illumination of the eye, for example, when looking into the sun: After having closed the eyes, one sees a bright copy of the sun. This kind of phenomenon is called a "positive afterimage," whereas those afterimages that present themselves in complementary colors are called "negative afterimages."

The latter are important for research on visual actual genesis and actual lysis, and are easily produced by fixating on a black pattern for about 20 seconds and then focusing on a point on a white sheet of paper, or simply by closing the eyes. However, no research of interest has been done on actual genesis and/or actual lysis using patterned negative afterimages—only very little research has been done at all. In his experiments, Rothschild (1923) closed his eyes after having focused on a design of white woolen threads on a dark background for 20 to 40 seconds and reported the observed changes in the pattern's form. In later years, some papers on afterimages have been published, but there was seldom one reporting any changes of their form. Nobody obviously was (and is) interested in the many different forms that one single patterned afterimage could establish. Popular research topics have instead been referring to such aspects as binocular rivalry, line length, orientation, all of them predominantly quantitative studies, the results of which suitable to be measured, or counted.

However, negative afterimages are an important medium for studying visual actual genesis and actual lysis. If one fixes one's eyes on a certain point on a black "ring with cross" (as seen in Figure 1.2, target X), which is also used in the stabilization experiments using equipment, for 10 seconds, and then focuses upon a mark on a blank sheet of white paper, negative afterimages of the target will appear, that is, bright images in a darker outfield with more or less the same or similar structure as the target. When the paper with the pattern ring with cross is swiftly replaced with a blank sheet, one usually first sees the complete target configuration, which then varies between states of lesser and greater differentiation, until the afterimage fades and completely disappears. Diffuse illumination was used, as direct sunlight or artificial light weakened the effect (Kleine-Horst, 2001, Figure 6.15).

Figure 1.2 shows 12 negative afterimages, using this method, depicted here with inverse brightness polarity. A tiny cross indicates the point of fixation. The arrows indicate those afterimages, which have been observed to follow one another at least once. In most cases, several afterimages can be observed after each inspection phase. Figure 1.2 shows series of afterimages according to both actual-lytic and actual-genetic processes, that is, sometimes the differentiation decreases, sometimes it increases, but ultimately the afterimage wanes completely, as can be seen in image L. These 12 afterimages are but a part of a total of 72 different afterimages that six subjects were able to produce (Kleine-Horst, 2001, Figures 6.18, 6.20). Note the often-occurring central-peripheral alternation, from C to D (and back), for instance.

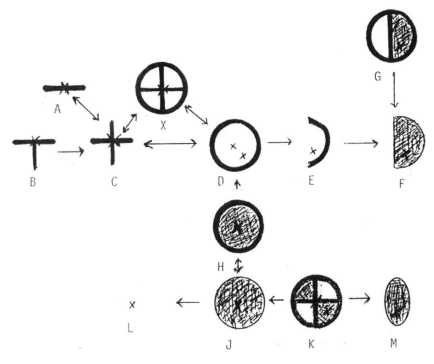

Figure 1.2.   Series of afterimages from the target in X (Kleine-Horst, 2001, Figure 6.15)

Actual Lysis of a Percept Through Concentrative Withdrawal of Attention

Attention is another domain for establishing actual lyses: "with time," attention directed toward a particular object wanes. An increase in the attention directed toward a single object corresponds to a decrease in the attention directed toward all other objects. This process can be designated "concentrative withdrawal of attention." Percept decomposition through concentrative withdrawal of attention will be introduced and interpreted in the following observation experiment; this experiment can also be performed by untrained subjects. Some individual differences are however possible and the same subject may observe different sequences of percepts when the experiment is repeated.

Thus I shall report my observations. The object observed was the pattern depicted in Figure 1.3 target a. It consists of eight compartments and is an "ambiguous figure," as known in the traditional psychology.

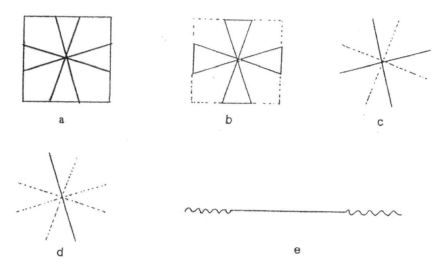

Figure 1.3.   The actual-lytic disintegration of the Maltese cross by concentrative-withdrawal of attention (according to Kleine-Horst, 2001, Figures, 6.7–6.10).

When one looks at it, one often sees a winged cross or the Maltese cross. It was not my concern to observe and investigate these changes of the ambiguous figure; instead, I wanted to become acquainted with what happens when I stare at the center of the figure. I wanted to simulate the situation given in the experiments in which the retinal images were stabilized by an apparatus, or in the afterimage situation. Thus I stabilized the images exclusively by rigidly fixating the center of Figure 1.3 target a. As the center itself is extended to a certain degree and thus provides much room for deviation from a chosen point of fixation, I chose a tiny inhomogeneity within the black center as a focus. When attention is focused on the center of a figure, it is withdrawn from more peripheral locations of the figure, so that a complex figure decomposes into less complex figures, as is to see in Figure 1.3.

At first, I saw the Maltese cross (Figure 1.3 target b). After a short time, the percept began to change in form: it lost in complexity, and finally disappeared—nice case of visual actual lysis. In the first stage, I saw the Maltese cross disintegrate into two crosses, one of which apparently located behind the other (Figure 1.3 target c). In the next stage, I saw four straight lines, staggered in depth (Figure 1.3 target d). During further fixation, the end of the lines became "waved," and then increasingly faded while becoming shorter (Figure 1.3 target e). Finally, for a fraction of a second, the figure disappeared completely, that is, I no longer perceived the color black, but rather only the white of the paper. We now cast our attention back to the two deviations from a pure actual-genetic sequence in the Wohlfahrt series depicted in Figure 2.1. When the stimulus increased in size from stage 4 to stage 5, a first inner contour appeared, which is an increase in complexity of the percept as a whole. The form of the outer contour, however, fell back into more inadequate regularity, that is, perpendicular line connections, after the percept had already reached a more adequate (veridical) state in stage 4. This developmental regression toward less veridicality is what is called actual lysis. A further special regression is to be observed within the general progression from stage 5 to stage 6, where a second inner contour appears. Here the outer contour changes its form a further step toward regularity, as it regresses to stage 3. These actual-lytic regressions can be accounted for due to the withdrawal of attention from the outer contour, as the subject's attention is occupied when suddenly a nonexpected inner contour appears. Actual lysis of a percept increases not only through a decrease in the strength of the stimulus, but also through a decrease in directing attention to the source of the stimulus.

Actual-Genetic Series of Extrasensory Percepts

Another domain of visual actual-genetic and actual-lytic stages is extrasensory perception (ESP). One would expect that the experimenters would ask their subjects to sketch their visual percepts—but for some unknown reason only very few did. The most well known was Upton Sinclair (1930), who got his "sensitive" wife to sketch 290 extrasensorily perceived patterns, the targets drawn by himself, and enclosed in an opaque envelope. He was not a scientist, but a writer. Kotik (1908, p. 19) reported that J. Shuk had also published a number of such drawings, as well as Schrenck-Notzing. I recollect to have read somewhere, that a Chinese scientist has also done it. I know of nobody except Bender (1935), who got his subject to sketch her clairvoyant images; however, Bender's targets were letters, and his only subject knew this.

Tischner (1920) got a sensitive subject to extrasensorily perceive a scissors, and then only verbally but not graphically describe her percepts. In order to form a picture of what she really might have seen, I made some drawings according to her descriptions (see the letters in the following text and in Figure 1.4) and discovered a nice actual-genetic series. At first, the subject assumed the target to be metallic, and said:

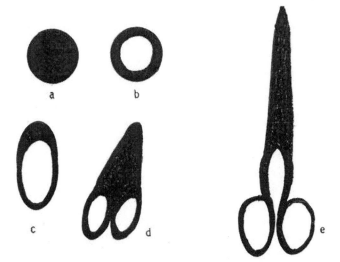

Figure 1.4. Actual-genetic ESP series of a scissors, sketched according to Tischner's (1920) subject's verbal report (Kleine-Horst, 2004, Figure 1.14).

Now it is round and shining (a).... It is so shiny. Now it is like a ring (b).... It is once again metal—like glass or metal, shiny. Round and yet long (c).... As if it were a scissors—at the bottom there are two round things and then it is stretched into a longer form (d).... It must be a scissors (and then immediately afterwards with an expression of certainty on the subjects face:) .... It is a scissors (e). (p. 21)

Ryzl (1982) took an iron scissors with crossed ("open") blades which lay behind an opaque umbrella as an ESP target. His subject was put under hypnosis. The perception began in this case, however, with the perception of the crossed scissor blades.

J. B. Rhine used in his still famous and still employed experiments five cards, each with a simple optical pattern, for ESP purposes especially designed from the perception psychologist Zener (Zener cards). The analysis of the experiments, however, was carried out while completely ignoring the possible visual impressions of the subjects. The subjects knew what the cards looked like and needed only to guess which of the cards was in front of them. In other words: the Zener cards experiment is nonsense; such guesswork experiments are possible with two cards, one blank and the other with the scribbles of a toddler while asking the subject: "Is there something on the card or not?"

The experiments with a scissors have also motivated me to choose a scissors as one of the targets in my ESP experiments. I used as subjects, however, not "sensitives" but "people like you and I." The subjects had not been in a particular state of consciousness such as hypnosis, trance, or sleep, instead they were awake and alert. The subjects were, for example, presented with an opaque envelope that contained the target as a black drawing on white paper. They were asked to close their eyes, receive images that appeared, and then copy precisely what they had seen onto a sheet of paper, with their eyes open. They repeated this procedure for approximatley 8 minutes, at which point I stopped the experiment. Thus every subject sketched a number of different "clairvoyant images" from one and the same target (Kleine-Horst, 1989).

The scissors, one of about 50 targets, was either as a drawing enclosed in an opaque envelope or as a real object enclosed in a carton. In all cases an open scissors was presented. Most of the sketched clairvoyant images of the scissors could be assigned to one of four certain similarity classes (A, B, C, or D), as Figure 1.5 shows.

The similarity classes contain images that have the following appearance:

(a) Wholly or partially a single/ double contoured scissors.
(b) A pair of ellipses (1) or circles (2), also bows (3) or symmetrical rolls(4), joined together either diagonally (1, 2) or lengthwise (4, 5).
(c) A single or double contoured ellipse or circle with a single or double contoured appendage.
(d) V-form objects (1, 2, 3), also multiplied (4, 5). Clip-like objects bent inwards (5, 8) (also at the beginning in 6), further, knife-like objects (7).

Another important target in my experiments was the ring with cross, the same used in both the afterimage and in the retinal stabilization procedure experiments. Most of these ESP percepts occurred as static single images and show great similarity to actual-genetic/lytic percepts, produced by other methods. Only few subjects produced several consecutively occurring ESP percepts that formed an actual-genetic series with increasing differentiation, including also some actual-lytic stages of decreasing differentiation, as seen in Figure 1.6. A number of subjects were asked to indicate the "extrasensory visual focus" of the clairvoyant image with a tiny "x," and several were able to do so, as shown in Figure 1.6 target D. Many "clairvoyant images" of the ring with cross resemble the negative afterimages of the same target (Kleine-Horst, 1989). Seventy-two different individual afterimages of the ring

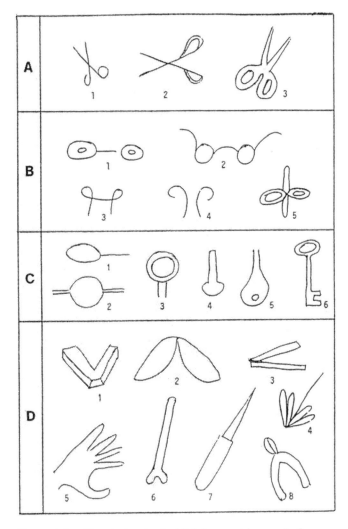

Figure 1.5.   Twenty-two typical "clairvoyant images" of an
open scissors, each assigned to one of four similarity classes
(From Kleine-Horst, 2004, Figure 1.16).

with cross have been produced and sketched (Kleine-Horst, 2001,
Figures 6.18 & 6.20), and are assigned to eleven "similarity classes,"
most of them well defined (Kleine-Horst, 1994). 119 of 271 (43,9%)
clairvoyant images of the same target can be assigned to the same
classes as the afterimages (Kleine-Horst, 2001, Figures 6.19 & 6.21).

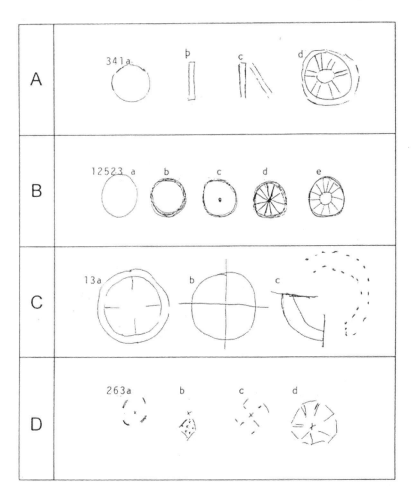

Figure 1.6. Series of actual-genetic / actual-lytic stages of clairvoyant images of the "ring with cross"; in D with central "clairvoyant focus" (Kleine-Horst, 2004, Figure 1.22).

EMPIRISTIC THEORY OF VISUAL GESTALT PERCEPTION

The Ontogenesis of the Gestalt Factors Conditioning the "figure in its outfield" Percept

The Empiristic theory of visual gestalt perception (ETVG) (Kleine-Horst, 2001) accounts for visual actual genesis. This theory describes the visual system of gestalt perception as a 10-level hierarchy of 26 gestalt factors. Figures 1.7 and 1.9 show the 15 gestalt factors referring to static, two-dimensional perception. Eleven further gestalt factors are responsible for time, movement, and depth perception. Actual genesis of a visual percept is the result of superthreshold actualization of the gestalt factor hierarchy "from the bottom up," and actual lysis of a visual percept occurs through the deactualization of the hierarchy "from the top down."

A particular gestalt factor, when actualized by sensory stimuli, in association with the directing of attention to the stimulus source, produces "its" particular gestalt quality, as will be shown in the following. Symbols will be assigned to the factors as well as to the qualities produced by the factors. As the ETVG is available in English and the basic principles are also in the Internet at http://www.enane.de/cont.htm, the reader is referred to these publications for further details. Thus only a rough outline of the structure of the visual system is required here.

According to the ETVG (see Figure 1.7), visual perception proceeds in the following ways: Photons—as optical sensory stimuli—impinge the retina's photoreceptors ("y" in the world of vital matter, VM). The receptors become "excited," that is, they produce vital, bodily functions (VF). Functions are not matters, but rather entities of their own, that belong to a manner that is different from the material manner of being. Visual functions are such, for example, in that they allow humans (and other living beings) to perceive brightnesses and colors, in a certain way. But perceiving does not have to mean "experiencing"; (subjective) experience is not possible on the physical level, as the body does not comprise the phenomenal manner of being. Genes condition everything that happens on this biological, physical, vital evolutionary level in the domain of perception. So a frog might be able to "instinctively" catch a fly with its tongue, without however having "subjectively" experienced it. A frog—like other creatures—needs to build up its phylogenetically preprogrammed instinct hierarchy during biological ontogenesis. The same is true for the biological (physical) ontogenesis of the physical systems involved in visual perception.

According to the ETVG, after the biological ontogenesis, humans and higher vertebrates begin a nonbiological, that is, psychical, ontogenesis. It consists of a learning process through which the contents of visual memory arise. Just as the genetical equipment (e.g., in the case of instincts) transpires during a process of adaptation to environment, the same may be said for the psychical equipment. The biological (genetical) adaptation process takes place during phylogenesis, and individual biological (physical) ontogenesis can be understood to be a recapitulation of phylogenesis which is termed "biogenetic law" (Haeckel, 1866). The psychical adaptation process, however, takes place during individual ontogenesis as shown in the ETVG. Actual genesis can be understood to

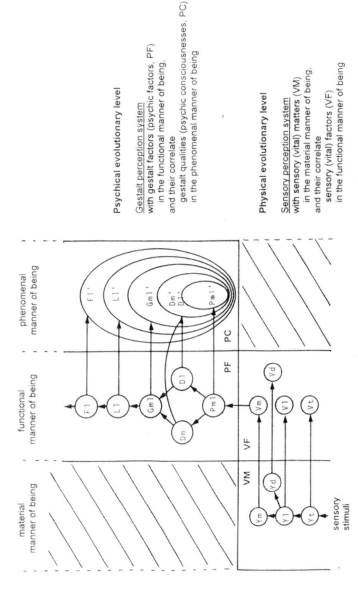

Psychical evolutionary level

Gestalt perception system
with gestalt factors (psychic factors, PF)
in the functional manner of being,
and their correlate
gestalt qualities (psychic consciousnesses, PC)
in the phenomenal manner of being

Physical evolutionary level

Sensory perception system
with sensory (vital) matters (VM)
in the material manner of being,
and their correlate
sensory (vital) factors (VF)
in the functional manner of being

Figure 1.7.   The system of the physical and psychical factors conditioning the formless and static, two-dimensional "figure in its outfield" experience (Kleine-Horst, 2001, Figure 1.4).

be a recapitulation of this ontogenesis, which can be termed "psychogenetic law."

What is the course of the adaptation to environment in the case of visual perception according to ETVG? The objects of the three-dimensional environment are optically projected onto the eye's retina as a two-dimensional image. These many simultaneous excitations from those photoreceptors that are lying closely to each other, associate with each other in an implicit (unconscious) memorization process and produce a first memory content: the gestalt factor Pml. This gestalt factor leads, if superthreshold actualized, to the experience of "brightness (m) at a location (l)" (see Figure 1.7). A second step of adaptation now follows: many simultaneously actualized Pml factors associate with each other and produce—on a higher hierarchical level—two further memory contents. One of them is the factor Dm, which allows for the experiencing differences in brightness. The other gestalt factor on this second psychic evolutionary level is Dl, allowing for the experiencing of location differences. The totality of the gestalt factors (memory contents) is the content of the "world" of "psychic functions" (PF), whereas the visual experiences are the content of the world of "psychic consciousnesses" (PC). Although produced by "single" gestalt factors, each single content of consciousness is from the beginning on a *Ganzheit*, which is symbolized by interlocking ellipses in Figure 1.7. Here they represent only some aspects of the totality of visual experience, which are, according to the suggestion of Christian v. Ehrenfels (1890), designated "gestalt qualities."

How does the adaptation process continue? The next gestalt factor is formed on the third level and is designated "modal-local gradient" (Gml); it is the quantitative ratio of Dm to Dl, according to the illumination relationships at both the "sharp" border of the moon-image, where two very different brightnesses lie near together, and the inner field of the moon-image (and the sky) where same, or similar, brightnesses are spread out over a larger area.

These often occurring relationships between the optical projections of objects are memorized as memory content Gml, the actualization of which leading to the experience of "inhomogeneity" or "homogeneity." As inhomogeneities are arranged in a row, and homogeneities are arranged in two clusters beside the row, a new gestalt factor is formed on the fourth level, which allows for the experiencing of "lines" and "fields" (Ll). As the lines enclose the smaller field, the memory content and gestalt factor "closure" (Fl) is formed on the fifth level which allows for the experiencing of both "closedness" of this smaller field (the moon-field, for example) and "openness" of the larger surrounding field (the sky-field, for example).

The forming of the six five-level factors up to and including Fl takes place during the first weeks of life. Now the infant has finished the first step of adaptation to its optical environment. The baby is now able to visually perceive (experience) an "object in its surroundings" as a "figure in its outfield."

Development of Figure/Outfield Perception in Early Infancy

I found a nice investigation from Salapatek (1969) that might corroborate this empiristic hypothesis to a certain degree. The author published a comparative study of 1- and 2-month-old infants. These "subjects" were exposed to figures and, with the aid of photographic methods, it could be determined which parts of the figure they preferred to look at. When presented with a finely textured homogeneous field, the gaze was not directed at a particular spot in the field, but instead strayed widely. With the introduction of a geometric figure into the central visual field, the gaze was quickly fixed on the figure and held for some time.

Characteristic differences in the gaze behavior of two age groups (4 to 6 weeks and 8 to 10 weeks old) were revealed. The infants' gaze behavior took the course as shown in Figure 1.8, targets A-C, according to the infants' advancing in age. According to the ETVG: A = P-D-Gml-stage, B = Ll-stage, C = Fl-stage, D = Q-stage. Salapatek's findings correspond to the theory. At first, the infant will gaze steadily at any spot on the edge of the triangle or at one of the corners, where there is brightness (Pml), brightness and location difference (Dm, Dl), and even a large Dm/Dl-gradient (P-D-Gml-stage in Figure 1.8 target A). When slightly older, and after the line/field gestalt factor Ll has been formed, the infant's gaze will range along one or more sides of the triangle (Ll-stage in Figure 1.8 target B), and finally, with the help of the closure factor, will focus directly on the figure as a whole (Fl-stage in Figure 1.8 target C). The gaze will

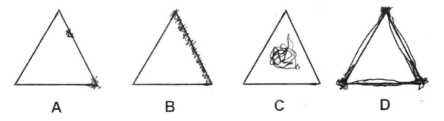

Figure 1.8.   A series of four, or five, initial developmental stages of looking at a figure of infants. Sketches according to both experiments of Salapatek (1969) and the empiristic theory according to Kleine-Horst (2001, Figure 4.2).

remain within the borders, but whisk back and forth across the infield, as there is no visually perceivable fixation point.

The Ontogenesis of the Quantity, Orientation, and Form Factors

The more the factors of the levels 1 to 5 are memorized, the more the baby is in a position to experience 2 and then 3 and 4 "figures in their outfield" simultaneously. The gaze jumps from figure to figure and back. Whereas relationships and relation-relationships between the excitations of the photoreceptors have been memorized for the forming of factors 1-5, the relationships and relation-relationships between the eye-muscle innervations necessary for these saccadic eye movements, are memorized. Thus the quantity factor Q with at least 4 subfactors (Q1, Q2, Q3, and Q4, see Figure 1.9) is formed, with which 1 to 4 objects simultaneously as a definite number of objects can be perceived, however, in the form of a holistic experience each time: as oneness, twoness, threeness, and fourness of figures.

Figure 1.8 target D shows incidentally a continuation of the sequence of Salapatek's (1969) observations with the following expectation according

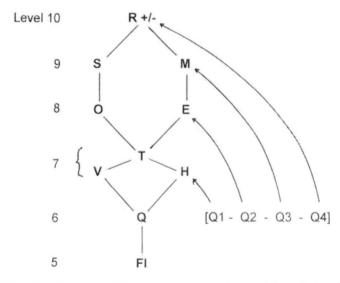

Figure 1.9.   The hierarchy of the quantity, orientation, and form factors in world PF built up on the fifth-level figure/outfield factor Fl (Kleine-Horst, 2004, Figure 2.4).

to the ETVG: the babies' gazes can jump from corner to corner of the triangle with the help of the subfactor Q3. In the ETVG it will be exactly shown, that after a new Q subfactor (up to Q4) has been formed, new relationships between the eye-muscle innervations are developed, which can however not be shown individually here. If the baby can perceive one single, but peripheral to the retina, projected object from its random fixation point, three memory contents (gestalt factors) are built on the next level which allows for the experiencing of "vertical" (V), "horizontal" (H), and (as their combination allows) "tilted" (T) directions. Two further factors result through the memorizing of the innervation relationships conditioned by the gaze's jumping to and fro between two (Q2, twoness) objects. The one factor allows for the perception of *two polar directions* ("orientedness," "orientation," O), and the other factor allows for the perception of the *equality of the spatial distance* from object A to object B, on the one hand, and from B to A, on the other ("extendedness," "elongatedness"/ "length," E).

While perceiving a threeness of objects, other innervation relationships are established: After having memorized these relationships, the quantitative ratio of two extensions following each other can be experienced as "measurement equality," or "inequality" (M), and the memorized quantitative ratio of two orientations following each other leads to the experience of "straightness" or "non-straightness" (S).

The last new innervation relationships result from a repeated perception of a fourness of objects with the help of the subfactor Q4. The resulting gestalt factors allow for the experience of "rectangularity" (R+) und "parallelity" (R-). The gestalt factors V, H, and T (7th level) constitute the "egocentric coordinate system," with which the spatial location of an object can be perceived in relation to its position to the perceiver's head, whereas the factors of the 8th to the 10th level allow for the experience of objects with relation to their position to each other: they make up the "geometric coordinate system."

Confirmation of the Theory

The ETVG demonstrates with the help of many different examples, how known visual phenomena might be accounted for by the EVTG. Here only two examples related to actual genesis, or ontogenesis, will be mentioned. If the Empiristic theory of the ontogenesis of visual factors is true, the development of the infants' visual capabilities must follow also the predictions from the factors of levels 5 to 10.

Whereas Salapatek's subjects were 4 to 10 week old infants, Graefe (1963) performed experiments on visual form perception of 10- to 13-

week-old infants. It is to be expected, that in this time further and higher-level factors are formed. Graefe's results correspond to these expectations. The author concluded that the perceptual structures in early infancy are acquired in the following biographical sequence: first, a pure figure-ground segregation, second, the severalty and dividedness of standing-out configurations, and third, the elongatedness and nonelongatedness, that is, compactness, of these configurations. The ETVG predicts this sequence of visual qualities as produced by the factors Fl, Q, and E. Moreover, Graefe reported that his subjects were also able to perceive horizontal (H), vertical (V), and tilted (T) orientations. Exactly this is to be predicted in the case of being able to perceive elongatedness, as the actualization of the V/H/T-factors is a precondition for the actualization of E and O.

Of the same importance as these positive results by Graefe (1963) are his negative results, according to which the 10- to 13-week-old babies showed no reaction toward differences in both the length and the parallelism of sides. This means, in respect to the ETVG form factor hierarchy, that up to the 13th week of life, the gestalt factors up to and including the eighth level have been formed but not yet the factors at the 9th and 10th levels. Only with actualization of the 9th-level factor M, difference and sameness of lengths are to be perceived, and only with the 10th-level factor R are parallelism and rectangularity of lines perceivable, of a figure's "sides," for example.

Graham, Berman, and Ernhardt (1960) reported experiments on the development of the capability of 3- to 5-year-old children in copying given forms. It could be shown (Kleine-Horst, 2001, Figures 5.43–5.47) that the ETVG hierarchy can be discovered even in this case, as the different form aspects which could be copied exactly correspond to both the increasing life-span and the form factor hierarchy, that is, the older the children, the higher leveled the gestalt qualities were that the children were able to exactly copy. Despite an annually increasing number of neurobiological papers on the topic "visual perception," a neurobiological theory of sight is not expected in the near future. The neurobiologists Hubel and Wiesel received the Nobel Prize for their pioneering examination of the humanlike visual system of cats and monkeys. Hubel (1988), however, summarized the results of neurobiologists' research into sight, up to 1987, as follows:

We are far from understanding the perception of objects, even such comparatively simple ones as a circle, a triangle, or the letter A—indeed, we are far from even being able to come up with plausible hypotheses. (p. 222)

Eight years later the situation had still not improved, so that Hubel (1995, p. 228) only needed to replace "1987" with "1995."

Of course, neurobiologists are as far from having plausible hypotheses on visual perception as psychologists are; all perceptual scientists want to account for perceptual phenomena, but they refuse to investigate these phenomena. How should they then be able to explain them? Scientists think, for example, if there is an "A" on a sheet of paper, they have to explain our experience gained under everyday inspection: two tilted lines connected to each other "above" and being connected by a smaller horizontal line below (or in the middle)—or how the experience of the object "A" may be described. They have, instead, much more to explain, namely all the percepts that can occur under noneveryday inspection, as there are the actual-genetic and/or actual-lytic lower-level percepts. Figure 1.10 shows only few: negative afterimages from the percept that emerged after I had focused on the tiny cross in stimulus "a" for about 10 seconds. Everybody can produce further negative afterimages from the letter "A." The single cell research of the neurobiologists established a number of findings that correspond to the predictions of the ETVG (Kleine-Horst, 2001, Part 3): (a) a neuron possesses the same general properties, and shows the same general behavior, as a gestalt factor; (b) cells found in the visual brain that are considered to have certain special visual functions correspond to predicted gestalt factors that have the same, or similar, visual functions; (c) the lowest (five- or six-level) parts of the hierarchies, in which the functionally corresponding cells and gestalt factors are ordered, also correspond to one another; (d) the shape of a cell's receptive field is the same as, or does not contradict, the predicted shape of the receptive field of the ETVG factor that corresponds to the cell.

TOWARD A QUADRIALISTIC THEORY OF MAN

After having developed the ETVG, I became aware of both a world below VM, different from VM and containing matter without life functions (VF) and a world above PC, which contains entities differing from those found

Figure 1.10.   Five different negative afterimages from the letter "A" that emerged after focusing on the tiny cross in Stimulus "a" for about 10 seconds (Kleine-Horst, 2004, Figure 1.7).

in PC—a kind of a higher leveled consciousness. I thus conceived a weltbild of four evolutionary levels. Knowing that natural scientists in particular love symmetries, I conceived a very symmetrical "theory of everything." Certainly, physicists are also searching for a theory of everything, however, the first point is that they have not yet found it, and the second point is that I do not expect them ever to find it, as they understand "everything" to be "every material thing," whereas I have already found two other "things," that is, functional and phenomenal entities. So I have conceived quite a new weltbild as shown in Figure 1.11, consisting of four evolutionary levels and four manners of being.

Four levels, or layers, of reality were already conceived by Aristotle, Thomas Aquinas, and Nicolai Hartmann (1964), and were interpreted as evolutionary levels by Konrad Lorenz (1981). My own contribution to ontology is to view the evolution as taking place in four "manners of being" and due to this, this weltbild is designated "quadrialistic" (Kleine-Horst, 2004).

Figure 1.11 schematically shows the hierarchical structure of the *four-level evolution* that exhibits four different, and definable, *manners of being*. Even if the ETVG assumes the visual process to take place in a frame of three manners of being, this *trialistic* view would already be in opposition to all other theories of sight that are either (materialistic) monistic or (matter/consciousness) dualistic, but the deviation of the *quadrialistic* (4-manner) concept from those concepts and theories is even greater.

I developed the new model by assuming reality to be very symmetrical, so that, for example, all four evolutionary levels possess the same structure, and all manners of being also possess the same structure (although different from that of the evolutionary levels). Each evolutionary level expresses itself in two manners of being, and each manner of being expresses itself in two evolutionary levels. The "left-hand" manner of each level contains an independent "primary hierarchy," which is, so to speak, a direct result of the evolutionary process. The "right-hand" hierarchy is only a "secondary hierarchy" that depends on the "left-hand" primary hierarchy insofar as it consists of the same entities, albeit in a different manner. In Figure 1.11, the right pointing arrows indicate that the secondary entities are dependent correlates of the primary entities. The upwardly pointing arrows indicate the direction of the evolution of being. The reflexive arrows indicate the reflexivity of the respective entities, that is, their capability of reproduction, of producing replicas, producing themselves, so to speak. Each primary entity possesses this capability, but only one secondary entity possesses this capability: the uppermost, as this is at the same time the lowest entity of a new primary hierarchy, running through the next-

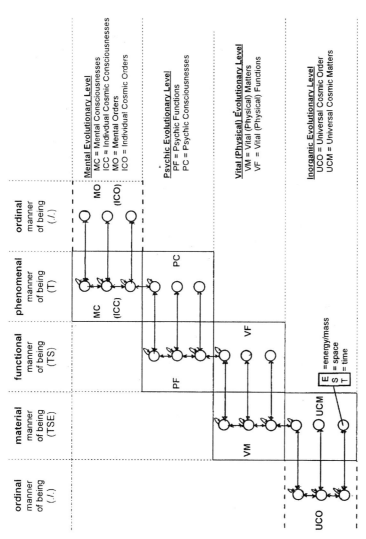

Figure 1.11. The 4-level 4-"manner of being" model. Vertical axes indicate the quadrialism of ordinal-material-functional-phenomenal manner of being and horizontal axes indicate the quadrialism of inorganic-physical-psychical-mental evolutionary level. The interfaces of the two groups of entities form eight "worlds," the hierarchies of which are symbolized only by three circles (Revised version according to Kleine-Horst 2004, Figure 3.2).

higher evolutionary level. The arrows pointing downwards show the backward influence from the higher-level to the lower-level entities.

Since the uppermost secondary entity also influences the uppermost primary entity (left pointing arrow), information is processed from the bottom up as well as from the top down through all four evolutionary levels of being.

Let us outline the entire evolution, with its four levels, and two manners at each level. At the lowest level, there is the "universal cosmic order" (UCO), the actualization of which led to the "Big Bang," through which inorganic matter (universal cosmic matter, UCM) came into existence. When inorganic matter occurs, the ordinal manner of being, that is, the UCO entities, has changed only into the material manner of being. The same can be expressed in different words: at the lowest evolutionary level, the universal-cosmic entities of being express themselves in two different manners, that is, in the ordinal manner and in the material manner. The same entities are at every level—they only "look" different. Later I shall demonstrate what the difference between these two manners of identical entities is.

The material entities of the uppermost UCM level reproduce themselves (shown by the reflexive arrow) according to M. Eigen's "hypercycle" (Eigen & Schuster, 1979), and cause material entities to exist at a higher level: vital matter (VM). The actualization of vital matter causes the creation of a third manner of being: the functional manner, with its vital functions (VF). At this second level, too, it is the same entities that express themselves twice, in this case, however, once as matter and once as function. With this physical (or bio) evolutionary level of being, "life" was created and represented by a phylogenetic hierarchy of life forms. The uppermost vital matter is the neuron—its function is excitation. This function reproduces itself so that functional circuits, that is, neuronal circuits, are formed.

The self-reproduction of neuronal functions is the condition for the development of a new, third, evolutionary level. This level is, as Figures 1.7 and 1.9 shown in greater detail for the domain of visual perception, also hierarchically structured as there is a hierarchy of psychic functions (PF) that is based on the hierarchy of physical (vital) functions (VF). The psychic functions' actualization causes psychical (perceptual) consciousnesses (PC) to exist. This means that the psychic entities change their manner from function to phenomenon. In the ETVG, it was assumed that the actualization of the psychic functions, the "gestalt functions (factors)," create a new manner of being, containing gestalt qualities. Now we can also say: the actualization of the third level entities, expressed in functional manner, creates a new manner of the same entities, the phenomenal manner.

By means of the self-reproduction of the uppermost entity of the PC (i.e., "self-consciousness" in the lowest sense), another sort of consciousness at a new evolutionary level, the mental level, is developed, designated "mental consciousnesses" (MC), or "individual cosmic consciousnesses" (ICC). When actualized, it expresses itself in a second manner: "mental orders" (MO), or "individual cosmic orders" (ICO). The train of thought will become clearer in the following.

In this respect, it is very significant that the secondary manner at the fourth level is the same as the primary manner at the first level: the ordinal manner. Thus reality in its entirety is "circular": reality "starts" in ordinal manner of being with a primary hierarchy (UCO), and "ends" in ordinal manner of being with a secondary hierarchy. This individual cosmic order (ICO) is to be thought of as "part" of the universal cosmic order (UCO). In other words: the ICO (MO) is an individuation of the UCO.

This is a more formal description of the new model of reality, which still contains much speculation. Sometimes, however, a suggestion has been given on how to interpret the model in detail. When I tried to analyze the structure of the first evolutionary level, I had to assume that matter (UCM) is hierarchically ordered. I conceived inorganic matter as a hierarchy of the entities "time," "space," and "energy/mass"—in this order from the bottom up. According to the four-manner model, these right-hand entities (UCM) are only material manner expressions of the same entities on the left (UCO), which are considered to be in the ordinal manner. Thus, as ordinal manner entities are not material manner entities, nonmatter is the condition of matter, a concept that agrees with the modern speculations of quantum theorists. After this four-manner four-level model (or *"eight world model"*) of being has been published. Rainer Diriwächter asked a critical question (personal communication), and I was prompted to improve my concept of the beginning of the evolution. Matter began to exist with the "Big Bang" some billions of years ago. This happened when the lowest entity of the UCO transformed into matter and thus became the lowest entity of a new, the *material*, manner of being (*"Seinsweise"*). My mistake has been (see Kleine-Horst, 2001, 2004) to believe that time, space, and energy/mass are "entities" like those hierarchically ordered entities symbolized by circles in Figure 1.11 which, furthermore, constiture the material world of UCM only. However, first of all, T, S, and E, are not three entities in this sense, they are "aspects" or "contents" of matter and E "refers" to S, and S refers to T; only the hierarchy of T, S, and E as a whole behaves as such a kind of "entity" of a world. Second, not only the entities of UCM are TSE-hierarchically structured, but also the entities of VM and thus all entities of the material manner of being. Every entity of the material manner of being "contains" the "fixed" hierarchy of T, S, and E from its beginning on, that is, since the lowest entity, or sublevel, of UCM was—in the Big Bang—created by actualization of the lowest UCO entity which contains the fixed hierarchy of TSE conditions. In other words, in the entities of the material manner of being, there is not any energy, or mass, without space to which E refers, and there is not any space without time to which S refers. Moreover, in contrast to all other evolutionary hierarchies in which every lower hierarchical level can exist without its next higher level, in the fixed TSE-hierarchy of any entity of the material manner of being it can not. As we will see and is already indicated in the topmost line in Figure 1.11, the entities of the next—the functional—manner of being contain T and S, but not E, and those of the phenomenal manner contain T, but neither S not E. Moreover, those of the world ICO of the ordinal manner of being contain neither E, nor S, not T. This also applies to the other entities of the ordinal manner of being, belonging to UCO.

If this concept is true, then the four-manner four-level evolution can be interpreted as the *"progressive" deactualization of the hierarchy of TSE-conditions*, the actualization of which happened with the "Big Bang." The deactualization of a "normal" evolutionary primary hierarchy as that PF, or part of it, can be designated "regressive," that is, it causes a gradual cessation of the hierarchically ordered entities "from the top down" through which every further step contains less content than the previous one. A *progressive* deactualization means, in contrast, that with cessation of the hierarchically ordered entities (time-space-energy/mass) from the top down, new entities are created, that is, every further step contains more content than the previous one. This is the case in the evolution of reality as a whole, in which with every step of deactualization a new, and higher, evolutionary level emerges, in which process one of the three crucial entities is always dismissed, step by step, first, the energy/mass, second, the space, and third, the time.

At the lowest evolutionary level, matter (UCM) was created, that is, the hierarchy of time, space, and energy/mass, in this order from the bottom up. This happened through the actualization of the hierarchy of the conditions of matter, that is, the condition of time, the condition of space, and the condition of energy/mass, in the universal cosmic order (UCO).

At the second evolutionary level, vital matters (the time-space-energy/mass hierarchy) create functions. The functional manner, however, differs from the material manner in that it is lacking in the highest-level material content: energy/mass. Function is bound on matter, also on its energy/mass, but is not itself energetic, and does not possess mass. It still contains, however, space and time. This is the first stage in the progressive deactualization of matter-conditions.

At the third (psychic) level, the entities change their functional manner into phenomenal manner, when actualized. Phenomena are lacking not only in energy/mass, as are the functions, they are also lacking in space. Perceptual consciousness (PC), that is, visual experience, for example, is not located in space, it is not spatial itself—only its contents are often spatially organized, as for example, when we visually perceive any spatial "configuration." The phenomena themselves, psychic consciousnesses, are not spatially three-, two- or one-dimensional. Yet they remain temporally organized—they occur in time and need a certain time to exist. This is the second stage in the progressive deactualization of the three-level matter-condition.

At the fourth level, the third and last stage of deactualization is attained. We find, on the left, time consuming entities, that is, mental consciousnesses. On the right, however, there are the same entities, without however temporal aspect, or temporal locations—and so they are indeed not only lacking energy, mass and space, but also time. For example: thinking is an important entity of the world MC and consumes time, but its products, the thoughts, belong to the world MO because they are in the true sense of the words "time-less" entities; they are, so to speak, pure order.

Now, after three steps, from the first to the fourth level, the progressive deactualization of the three-level conditions of the time-space-energy/mass hierarchy has come to an end, and the three contents of matter: energy/mass, space, and time, have been withdrawn in this sequence in three steps. On the other side, with each further step of deactualization, the "freedom" of reality increased. At the first level, reality was limited through time, space, and energy/mass. At the second level, the limitations caused by the necessity of a certain amount of energy/mass for matter to exist, ceased. At the third level, the spatial, and at the fourth level, the temporal limitations ceased.

Some readers may still not be following the train of thought. This system looks for them like an interesting speculation, but without any importance for progress in science. Only when taken as pure speculation, however, is it without importance; when taken as a "theory of everything," its scientific implications become apparent, as a theory is capable of being tested. One cannot expect this four-manner four-level super-theory to be tested by confronting it immediately with facts. But one can expect to derive subtheories from it, or to find subtheories that have already been proposed, that can immediately, or again via deriving further subtheories, be tested with facts. The ETVG is a subtheory that can be considered to have been derived from the four-manner four-level model of being, although it was developed historically "individually," and then directed to the theory of everything as its super-theory.

Since UCO and UCM contains only three ontologically relevant contents, T, S, and E in a hierarchical order, evolution can exhibit only three further evolutionary levels above the universal-cosmic (inorganic) level and can exhibit only three further manners of being after the material manner—the last of them being again the ordinal manner. This means, that evolution can exhibit neither a fifth evolutionary level nor a fifth manner of being. In this way, the structure of the four-level four-manner evolution of being is "completed," and ontologically "explained." If the being (*Sein* or *Wirklichkeit*) is actually organized into four evolutionary levels and four manners of being, then the ordinal manner is a whole (*Ganzes, Ganzheit*) that does not actually "occur" twice—as UCO and ICO. Instead, the ordinal manner of being must be that from which "everything else" starts, and the ordinal manner itself belongs to this "everything" as its basis. Thus the material, the functional, and the phenomenal manner of being are *embedded* in the ordinal manner of being (see Figure 1.12). In the new diagram of the 4-level- "manner of being" model in Figure 1.11, there is one relationship which has been not referred to until now, although it is a most important one. Not only from the uppermost secondary entity of a world an arrow to the left starts, it starts from all other secondary entities beneath it as well. What does this mean? It means that at every sublevel of every evolutionary level, the secondary entity influences "its" primary entity to which it is correlated; in other words, the secondary entity sends a "feedback" to that primary entity from which it has been created. Since secondary entities belong to a manner of being that has less content than its primary entity (they lack in E, or in E and S, or even in E, S and T), they are more "free" in doing something, so to speak. Thus, together with their uppermost secondary entity of the same world, they can cause the less free primary entities to do something which is not just against the capability and the possibilities of the primary entities, but which does not belong to their "normal" activities (i.e., what they do not do of their own accord). By following this thread of thought of continuous backward causation, that is, following the arrows pointing to the left from ICO to UCO, we have to realize that an influence of mind over matter is quite a "normal" thing. Thus, for example, my nonenergetic "will" (at the mental evolutionary level) can "actualize" the energy of vital matter (at the physical evolutionary level) to move my hand

With this, a theory of everything has been established. Since the personality of man is considered but a derivation of the evolution of being, a theory of man has also been established. In order to transform the statements on a quadrialistic theory of being—a theory of everything—into statements on a quadrialistic theory of personality—a

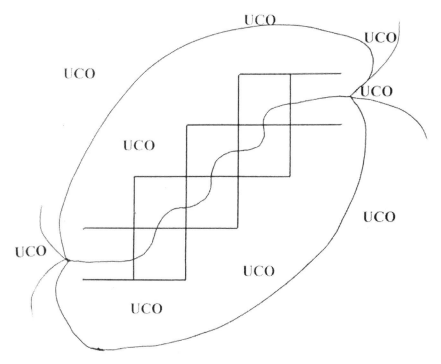

Figure 1.12.   The holistic "round" being, the individual cosmic order (i.e., the human mental order, MO) of which merges in the being's ground: the universal cosmic order (UCO) according to Kleine-Horst, 2004, Figure 3.3).

theory of man—one does not need to do more than to substitute "evolutionary level" with "personality layer."

PAST, PRESENT, AND FUTURE

Past

If until now only the "positive" side to the history in the field of actual genesis has been reported on, here its "negative" side will also be mentioned, a history characterized by momentous errors and falsifications.

1. The *Ganzheits*—and gestalt psychologists of the time accorded primary importance to phenomenology.

> Krueger ... believed that before we can look at an organization of any
> kind (e.g., experiences or personality) we must first thoroughly
> describe (in their entirety) the given qualities of the conscious
> experience. (Diriwächter 2004, p. 7)

(a) However, no psychologist has ever described the visual experience
of so simple a form as for instance, the square, a description
through which the gestalt qualities of this form would arise
"automatically." So far as the visual gestalt qualities are concerned,
everything has remained at the talking stage instead of going over
at last to active research. Only the ETVG systematically describes
visual gestalt qualities.

(b) When a problem of definition arose, the phenomenon was
perverted in its meaning in order to save the definition, rather than
adopting the definition to suit the phenomenon. Thus the Leipzig
gestalt psychologist Sander defines the phenomenon "gestalt" as a
unity segregated from its surroundings by a border, the border itself
containing a number of differentiations (form, gestalt, articulation,
Gliederung). But Sander himself referred to two exceptions: neither
a circle nor a straight line contains any articulation. In order to
make the phenomenon fit to a wrong definition, Sander explains
away the lack of articulation by accepting that articulation exists but
claims that it is "flowing" (Sander, 1962a, p. 77), and another
Leipzig gestaltist, Hans Volkelt, called it *gliedverschliffen* (smoothed
articulation). These statements were accepted even by the Leipzig
theorist Albert Wellek. One cannot, however, experience any flow or
trails when one views a circle or a straight line. So Sander and his
colleagues effortlessly violated the highest principle of all gestalt
psychologies: the priority of phenomenology, that is, description of
(subjective) experiences, over explanation, or "definition."

Furthermore, there is a note from the Berlin gestalt psychologist
Wolfgang Metzger, according to which Metzger and even the phi-
losopher Christian von Ehrenfels, to whose article of 1890 all
gestalt psychologies refer, had been aware, *"dass Gestalt bzw. Form
eine Sekundärkategorie ist, der als Primärkategorie die Zusammengefass-
theit bzw- die Ausgrenzung vorausgeht"* [that what might be called
gestalt or form is a second category following what might be called
unity or segregation as its primary category] (Metzger, 1966, p.
697). This means that a segregated unity and the form of this unity
are in a hierarchical relationship to each other, the form being situated one level above the unity, but nobody appropriated this idea of
a hierarchy to explain or at least to describe the "gestalt" phenomena. According to the ETVG, (formless) unity and its form refer to

two absolutely different evolutionary sublevels of the visual system. The unity itself (figure) develops by memorizing the relationships and relation-relationships between the excitations of photoreceptors (sublevels 1-5), and the form of the unity develops by memorizing the relationships and relation-relationships between eye-muscle innervations (sublevels 6/7-10).

2. According to F. Krueger, the (phenomenal) experiences are conditioned by entities in the "transphenomenal psychic being," also designated "structure" (Diriwächter, 2004, p. 7). But owing to a lack of knowledge about gestalt qualities and their possible interrelationships, Krueger's idea came to nothing. It did not occur to Krueger and Sander, nor indeed to any other psychologist, to research the transphenomenal structure of the actual-genetic visual phenomena. It was only with the first version of the ETVG (Kleine-Horst, 2007), that Krueger's idea of such a structure began to assume concrete features: in the world PF. This is conceived as the transphenomenal psychic being of visual perception, as in this the gestalt factors are to be found which are the conditions of "their" (phenomenal) gestalt qualities. Krueger did not go so far, however, as to conceptualize a third manner of being lying between matter and consciousness.

3. Who reads anything at all by or on Friedrich Sander, should certainly bear in mind that Sander was a forger. There is no point in listing here all the tricks which he used to try to obtain recognition for himself as the founder of actual-genesis in place of Wohlfahrt, or to draw a veil over the absurdity of his actual-genesis theory, nor is it worth listing the falsifications of history, made by his coworker Carl Friedrich Graumann, in order to support Sander's claim to be the founder of actual-genesis research (see Kleine-Horst, 1992). The one thing which is important is very clearly to show the damage which Sander has caused science both directly and indirectly, so as to fully grasp what facts and theoretical insights over the last 80 years have passed international perceptual psychology by.

4. According to Diriwächter (2004), feelings (*Gefühle*) are among the most important objects of research of genetic *Ganzheitspsychologie*. Indeed the feelings which were elicited in the course of Wohfahrt's actual-genetic experiments were unwelcome to Sander, so he handed Wohlfahrt a protocol in which the feelings he wished to encounter were described, feelings which he had thought up himself at his own desk.

5. Sander had also thought up a little theory to explain actual-genesis. Not only can his theory upon closer examination be seen to be utterly nonsensical, it also contradicts the actual-genetic facts (Kleine-Horst, 1992).

(a) In order to prevent the nonsensical nature of the theory from becoming public knowledge and after Dun (1939), Butzmann (1940), and Mörschner (1940) within a short period of time had countered Sander's theory with their own evidence, Sander simply terminated the actual-genesis experiments. He saved his skin but the experimental and theoretical fruits also of these investigators remained unknown to the present day, if we do not include Butzmann's summary, the summary which Sander's student, Udo Undeutsch, plagiarized and with the help of which he became internationally known.

(b) Sander compelled Voigt (1944), in his postdoctoral thesis on the actual-genesis of thought, to delete the theoretical part before he would accept it.

(c) Sander had secretly submitted the Hausmann doctoral thesis (1935) to the faculty as a torso devoid of theory, as a result of which he lost his chair on the board of the German Society of Psychology (*Deutsche Gesellschaft für Psychologie*). He was, however, immediately reinstated in 1938 after having asserted in the previous year that "the extinction of parasitically rampant Jewry is profoundly, ethically justified" (*Die Ausschaltung des parasitisch wuchernden Judentums hat ihre tiefe ethische Berechtigung*). After 1945, this man, vulnerable to blackmail by his colleagues because of his racism and his scientific fraud, was elected president of the German Society of Psychology three times in succession.

(d) What in fact had the actual-genesis investigators uncovered, that Sander was so anxious to destroy? All their experiments point to the fact that not only did the "tendency to *Gestaltetheit*" depend on endogenous process (which had been known for a long time), but so also did the "development to adequacy," which represented what was fundamentally new about actual genesis. But Sander wanted to go on passing this off without comment as exogenous. Sander was fully aware of the strict regularity of the actual-genetic evolution (without having researched the laws individually or even showing any desire to do so); in his U.S. article we read: "whereby the evolution of configurations is exhibited in logical order" (Sander, 1930, p. 193). He altered this article in several relevant places so as to present a version less dangerous to German ears, which he brought out in 1932 as a "reprint," in which the "logical order" turns into a harmless "becoming of gestalts" (*Werden von Gestalten*) (Sander, 1962b, p. 245).

According to ETVG, actual geneses and actual lyses are endogenous developments; however, "development to adequacy" and the "tendency to *Gestaltetheit*" do not refer to two different processes but to just one, which is controlled from one and the same gestalt factor hierarchy.

Present

1. The appearance of the three parts of the report on the fraud (Kleine-Horst, 1992) in 1984/85 has not prompted anyone to turn to the suppressed facts of actual genesis. Too many German university lecturers were and are involved in this criminal case and thus today an entire academic discipline stands behind their forgers.(Kleine-Horst, 1998).

2. International vision science has been aware of the fraud for 7 years now and the prevention of organic further development of research in perception (Kleine-Horst, 2001, pp. 0.50 & 51), for which it is responsible, but this does not bother a soul.

3. The actual-genetic/actual-lytic facts have not been forgotten, they are simply ignored and are subject today to the refusal on a massive scale to carry out research. What significance they could have for the progress of science was known not only to Friedrich Sander, but also to Wolfgang Prinz (1983, p. 43, footnote), whose judgment of actual-genetic methods was: "They pose more questions than they answer." Quite. This tends to be the case when new facts are discovered that do not fit in with dominant modes of thought. We should be grateful to Prinz for this nod in the direction of the research potential of actual genesis, even if he prefers in his capacity as director of the Max-Plank Institute for Psychological Research in Munich not to get involved with objects of research of this kind, objects which challenge the dominant fundamental perspective of the mainstream.

4. In 1998 the then President of the German Society for Psychology, Prof. M. Amelang, received my two books on fraud and deception (Kleine-Horst, 1992, 1998) and wrote to me: "The accusations contained therein are so far-reaching, that the board has decided to request that a hearing of the disciplinary court be convened." On later enquiring as to the outcome I received a letter from his successor, Prof. R. Kluwe, with the reply that, after careful study of the contents by the chairman of the disciplinary court (Prof. Dr. A.

Eser, Freiburg), "there was no concrete evidence for the truth of your accusations. The chairman of the disciplinary court came to the conclusion that there was no reason to continue with the procedure." As a result the board ceased to deal with the case. In the Psychologische Rundschau, the "organ" of the German Society for Psychology, I then read in the January 2007 edition, on page 47, that up to present day no procedure of the disciplinary court had ever taken place.

5. On March 16, 2007 I sent my complete collection of 10 scientific books together with a 20-page résumé on the contents to the head of the German Federal Ministry for Education and Research (BMBF), minister Dr. Annette Schavan, and asked her to have the relevance of my scientific findings appraised. Five months later, still having received no reply, I made enquiries and assured her of my understanding for the long period of waiting, which was quite justified in the case of a thorough examination, as a rejection due to lack of competence on the part of the Ministry or to technical humbug in the matter of the books themselves would have been obvious. After waiting a further 6 months, on February 11, 2008 I received the books back with a short note "Please understand that the Federal Ministry is not in a position to advance a qualified opinion." Thus the research sabotage of the German psychologists mafia, in which a large number of internationally active perception, and cognition, scientists are taking an interest, has now reached the offices of the German Federal Research Ministry. (Details on http://www.enane.de/m5.htm)

Future

So far as visual actual genesis is concerned, nobody should imagine that for the foreseeable future a perceptual psychologist will be found who is prepared to behave like a scientist, that is to say, who will accept facts as facts and who will examine theories relating to those facts, instead of ignoring both facts and theories, which has been the case up till now. There is too much at stake for them. But even philosophers get the chance to change their views.

*   Philosophers should consider that for the last 350 years the fact that they know two groups of entities at the most (body/matter on the one side and soul/consciousness on the other—see their monism/dualism discussions) may be because human beings have direct access to them. However, this does not exclude the existence

of other groups of entities, those which can only be found through reflection.

- Philosophers must also accept that they should not regard body and matter as the same, nor soul and consciousness as the same; such identifications contradict reality, a fact which had already been pointed out to Descartes.

- Neurobiologists must recognize that they are conducting a great deal of superfluous research, since it would be more economical to look for precisely those classes of visual neurons whose precise functions have already been anticipated by the ETVG (starting as far back as 1961. See Kleine-Horst, 2007).

- Researchers into perceptual psychology throughout the world must internalize the simplest of principles, namely that the phenomena which they are seeking to explain should be first of all described. A science which "explains" phenomena which it does not know and which it does not want to know, is, not to put too fine a point on it, ridiculous. There again, who among them would run the risk, by quoting directly and without comment from ETVG, of making ETVG become known and consequently having to throw out their own theories into the dustbin of history?

- And what is one to say about researchers into perceptual psychology who flatly refuse to include ESP in their research program?

I only know two conceptions of reality from mainstream philosophy (and science) whose adherents need have nothing to fear from ETVG and the quadrialistic model of reality, for they do not challenge their fundamental principles.

1. The four layer "Structure of Real World" by Nicolai Hartmann (1964). The writer refers to Aristotle's doctrine of layers (*Schichten*), a theory which was also taken over by Thomas Aquinas and has gone into current and official Catholic (neo-Thomist) philosophy. Hartmann's concept of reality that is "vertically" organized into four layers was taken over by the quadrialistic model of being (*Sein*) (Kleine-Horst, 2001, 2004) according to which, however, the four evolutionary levels/layers are also "horizontally" subdivided in four "manners of being" (*Seinsweisen*) to which alone the label "quadrialistic" relates.

2. The genetic *Ganzheitspsychologie*. The idea from Krueger of "structure" as a "transphenomenal psychic being" (Wellek, 1941) is aimed at breaking out of the traditional rigid conceptions of the

"direct contact" of matter and consciousness. In this respect it points to a similarity with the "world" of "psychic functions" (PF) formed for visual perception in ETVG.

But both conceptions of reality, ignored by the mainstream, are only represented by a small group of adherents today. The time depends upon them when psychology, following physics and biology, develops at last into a mature science.

REFERENCES

Bender, H. (1935). Zum Problem der außersinnlichen Wahrnehmung. Ein Beitrag zur Untersuchung des "Hellsehens" mit Laboratoriumsmethoden [On the problem of extrasensory perception. A contribution to the examination of "clairvoyance" with laboratory methods]. *Zeitschrift für Psychologie, 135*, 20-130.

Butzmann, K. (1940). Aktualgenese im indirekten Sehen [Actual genesis in peripheral vision] *Archiv für die gesamte Psychologie, 106*,137-193.

Diriwächter, R. (2004). Ganzheitspsychologie: The doctrine. *From Past to Future, 5(1)*, 3-16.

Dun, F. T. (1939). Aktualgenetische Untersuchungen des Auffassungsvorgangs chinesischer Schriftzeichen [Actual-genetic examinations of the perception of Chinese characters]. *Archiv für die gesamte Psychologie, 104*, 131-174.

Ehrenfels, Ch.von (1890). Über Gestaltqualitäten [On gestalt qualities]. *Vierteljahresschrift für wissenschaftliche Philosophie, 14*, 249-292.

Eigen, M., Schuster, P. (1979). *The hypercycle. A principle of natural self-organization*. Heidelberg, Germany: Springer.

Evans, C. R., & Piggins, D. J. (1963). A comparison of the behaviour of geometric shapes when viewed under conditions of steady fixation, and with apparatus for producing a stabilized retinal image. *British Journal of Physiological Optics, 20*, 261-274.

Graefe, O. (1963). Versuche über visuelle Formwahrnehmung im Säuglingsalter [Experiments on visual form perception during infancy]. *Psychologische Forschung 27*, 177-224.

Graham, F. K. Berman, P. W., & Ernhardt, C. B., (1960). Development in pre-school children of the ability to copy forms. *Child Development, 31*, 339-359.

Hartmann, N. (1964). *Der Aufbau der realen Welt. Grundriß der allgemeinen Kategorienlehre* [The structure of the real world. Outline of the general theory of categories]. Berlin, Germany: de Gruyter.

Hausmann, G. (1935). Zur Aktualgenese räumlicher Gestalten [On actual genesis of spatial gestalts]. *Archiv für die gesamte Psychologie, 93*, 289-334.

Haeckel, E. (1866). *Generelle Morphologie. I: Allgemeine Anatomie der Organismen. II: Allgemeine Entwickelungsgeschichte der Organismen* [General morphology. I: General anatomy of the organisms. II: General history of the organisms' development]. Berlin, Germany: G. Reimer.

Hubel, D. (1988). *Eye, brain, and vision.* New York: Scientific American Library.

Hubel, D. (1995). *Auge und Gehirn. Neurobiologie des Sehens* [Eye and brain. Neurobiology of vision]. Heidelberg, Germany: Spektrum der Wissenschaft.

Kleine-Horst, L. (1989). *Visuelle Sinnes- und Außersinneswahrnehmung des gleichen Objekts. Die Versuchsobjekte "Kreis mit Kreuz," "Ellipse" und "Stern"* [Visual sensory and extrasensory perception of the same object. The targets "Circle with cross," "Ellipse," and "Star"]. Köln, Germany: Enane.

Kleine-Horst, L. (1992). *Die verhinderte Wissenschaft. Ein Gaunerstück aus der deutschen Psychologie* [The prevented science. A swindle in German psychology]. Köln, Germany: Enane. Retrieved March 10, 2008, from http://www.enane.de/betr.htm

Kleine-Horst, L. (1994). *Die außersinnliche Wahrnehmung der Schwarz-Weiß-Figuren "Kreis mit Kreuz," "Ellipse" und "Stern." Eine quantitative wahrnehmungspsychologische Untersuchung* [The extrasensory perception of the black-white figures "Circle with cross," "Ellipse," and "Star." A quantitative perception-psychological investigation]. Köln, Germany: Enane.

Kleine-Horst, L. (1998). *60 Jahre deutsche Psychologenmafia (1938-1998)* [60 years of German psychologists mafia]. Köln, Germany: Enane. Retrieved March 10, 2008, from http://www.enane.de/betr.htm

Kleine-Horst, L. (2001). *Empiristic theory of visual gestalt perception. Hierarchy and interactions of visual functions.* Köln, Germany: Enane. (Retrieved March 10, 2008, from http://www.enane.de/cont.htm

Kleine-Horst, L. (2004). *Der Anfang des nach-naturwissenschaftlichen Zeitalters. Gedanken und Experimente jenseits der Lehrmeinungen* [The beginning of the post-natural-scientific era. Ideas and experiments beyond the schools of thought]. Köln, Germany: Enane. Retrieved March 10, 2008, from http://www.neues-weltbild.de/inhverz.htm

Kleine-Horst, L. (2007). *Theorie der optischen Gestaltwahrnehmung. Das Studentenmanuskript von 1961* [Theory of optical gestalt perception. The student's manuscript of 1961]. Köln, Germany. Enane.

Kotik N, 1908. *Die Emanation der psychischen Energie* [The emanation of psychic energy]. Wiesbaden, Germany: J. F. Bergmann

Kragh, U. (1955). *The actual-genetic model of perception-personality.* Lund, Sweden: CWK Gleerup.

Lorenz, K. (1981). *Die Rückseite des Spiegels. Versuch einer Naturgeschichte des menschlichen Erkennens* [The reverse of the mirror. An attempt at a natural history of human cognition]. München, Germany: dtv.

Metzger, W. (1966). Figuralwahrnehmung [Figural perception]. In W. Metzger (Ed.), *Handbuch der Psychologie I,1* [Handbook of psychology, I,1] (pp. 693-744). Göttingen, Germany: Hogrefe.

Mörschner, W. (1940). Zur Aktualgenese des Gegenstanderlebens [On the actual genesis of object experience]. *Archiv für die gesamte Psychologie, 104,* 125-149.

Piggins, D. J. (1970). Fragmentation of a geometric figure viewed under intermittend illumination. *Nature, 227,* 730-731.

Prinz, W. (1983). *Wahrnehmung und Tätigkeitssteuerung* [Perception and activity steering]. Berlin, Heidelberg, New York: Springer.

Pritchard, R. M., Heron, W., & Hebb, D. D. (1960). Visual perception approached by the method of stabilized images. *Canadian Journal of Psychology, 14*, 76-77.

Rothschild, H. (1923). Über den Einfluß der Gestalt auf das negative Nachbild ruhender visueller Figuren [On the influence of the gestalt on the negative afterimage of static visual figures]. *Graefes Archiv für Ophthalmologie, 112*, 1-18.

Ryzl, M. (1982). *Hellsehen und andere parapsychische Phänomene in Hypnose* [Clairvoyance and other parapsychic phenomena under hypnosis]. Genf, Switzerland: Ariston

Salapatek, P. (1969, December). *The visual investigation of geometric pattern by the one- and two-month-old infant.* Paper presented at meetings of the American Association for the Advancement of Science, Boston.

Sander, F. (1930). Structure, totality of experience, and gestalt. In C. Murchinson (Ed.), *Psychologies of 1930* (pp. 188-204). Worcester, MA: Clark University Press.

Sander, F. (1962a). Experimentelle Ergebnisse der Gestaltpsychologie [Experimental results of gestalt psychology] (pp. 73-112). (Reprinted from *Bericht über den 10. Kongreß der Deutschen Gesellschaft für Psychologie in Bonn, 1927.* Jena, Germany, 1928)

Sander, F. (1962b). Funktionale Struktur, Erlebnisganzheit und Gestalt [Functional structure, totality of experience, and gestalt]. In F. Sander & H. Volkelt (Eds.), *Ganzheitspsychologie* (pp. 303-320). München, Germany: C. H. Beck'sche Verlagsbuchhandlung. (Reprinted from *Archiv für die gesamte Psychologie, 85*, 1932)

Sinclair, U. (1930). *Mental Radio.* Monrovia, CA: Upton Sinclair.

Tischner, R. (1920). *Über Telepathie und Hellsehen* [On telepathy and clairvoyance]. München, Germany: J. F. Bergmann.

Voigt, J. (1944) *Das Denken als aktualgenetischer Prozess und seine typischen Erscheinungsweisen* [Thinking as an actual-genetic process, and its typical phenomena]. Unpublished postdoctoral thesis, University of Jena, Germany.

Wellek. A. (1941). Das Problem des psychischen Seins. Die Strukturtheorie Felix Kruegers: Deutung und Kritik [The problem of the psychic being. The theory of structure of Felix Krueger. Interpretation and criticism]. *Zeitschrift für angewandte Psychologie und Charakterkunde, 16*, 129-238.

Werner, H. (1956) Microgenesis and aphasia. *Journal of Abnormal Social Psychology, 52*, 347-353.

Wohlfahrt, E. (1932). Der Auffassungsvorgang an kleinen Gestalten. Ein Beitrag zur Psychologie des Vorgestalterlebnisses [The perception of small gestalts. A contribution to the psychology of the pregestalt experience]. [Doctoral thesis, Jena, Germany, 1925] *Neue Psychologische Studien, 4*, 347-414.

CHAPTER 2

DEVELOPING "DEVELOPMENT" IN THEORY AND METHOD

A Commentary on Kleine-Horst (2007)

Brady Wagoner

Developmental thinking begins when we stop looking for the *things* of the world and start focusing on *unfolding events*. I will refer to the "things" orientation as an **objects approach** and its alternative as a **process approach**. An objects approach is concerned with classing and comparing static things. In contradistinction, by process I mean to imply an interest in movement, transformation, and synthesis. From this orientation we ask questions about the mechanisms and constraints of movement, how processes come into being and fade away. Abstractly we can distinguish the two by saying that an objects approach (nondevelopmental) is concerned with "being," while a process approach (developmental) is concerned with "becoming" (Valsiner, 2003). Table 2.1 represents the logical form.

Innovating Genesis: Microgenesis and the Constructive Mind in Action, pp. 41–63

Table 2.1.   A Contrast Between Objects and Process Approaches

Objects Approach	Process Approach
X = [is] = X	X — [remains] $\rightarrow$ X
or	or
X $\neq$ [is not] $\neq$ Y	X — [becomes] $\rightarrow$ Y

Source: Modified from Valsiner (2003).

In this essay I will explore ways of developing the process (or developmental) approach in both method and theory. Psychology has largely forgotten how to study and think about processes. Even if they use the language of change—such as "feed-back loops," "interactions," "dynamics"—rarely is this vocabulary reflected in their methods. Secondly, few psychological studies attempt to develop a theory to comprehend interactions between findings at different levels of organization. Instead, studies remain local.

Kleine-Horst (this volume) gives us an alternative. His methods and theorizing are attempts to understand the form of **X — [becomes] $\rightarrow$ Y** within the field of visual perception. Yet his insights have relevance in the context of developmental thinking more broadly. I will consider Kleine-Horst's method and theory both in the context of perception and as a possible framework for any developmental investigation. This essay will be structured in two parts. The first will explore developmental methods, while the second will explore the structure of developmental theorizing.

PART I

Skeleton of a Developmental Method

I will first consider the essential steps or elements of Kleine-Horst's developmental method in abstract and after flesh them out with empirical examples. The basic steps presented here are meant to be guides in understanding developmental research coming out of this tradition *not* orthodoxies of method. I have broken down the method into five essential steps. Each will be treated in turn.

Step 1

The researcher delineates the process in which they would like to investigate. The process may occur on the time scale of a fraction of a second, a minute, days, weeks, decades, etc. For example, perception is an instantaneous process, whereas the change of word meaning in a society might take place over several decades. Part of this method's value is its ability to access processes at many different levels.

Step 2

The researcher must then find a way to simulate the process. Conditions to trigger the particular process under study are required. But also the researcher must find a way to regulate the *speed* of the simulation to create a time frame in which the researcher can work with the process. Perceptual processes happen so quickly that we miss the process unless we find a way of *decelerating* them, whereas other processes must be *accelerated* such as those occurring over decades. There will also be processes in which the speed they occur in is amiable to experimental study, such as afterimages in Kleine-Horst's essay. Here the question is one of finding a way of foregrounding the process over other more salient processes (normal perception). This is done by viewing the afterimage against a white background.

Yet simulation on its own is not enough. The researcher must also find a way of abstracting data from a series of moments within the process. This will often require slicing the process or stopping it at various points in its evolution, which can also be an effective strategy in *decelerating* a process. The selection of moments in the process can be dictated by increasing a stimulus magnitude (e.g., from a vary small image to a normal sized one), by how much time has elapsed (e.g., 5 minutes, 10 minutes, 20 minutes), or by task demands (e.g., Kleine-Horst's ESP [extrasensory perception] experiments, where the subject must *stop* to draw their image before they continue to imagine).

Step 3

Selecting moments in the process is for the purpose of creating a *genetic series*. At each one of these moments the subject must *externalize* or *objectify* something. For example, Wohlfahrt required subjects to articulate their perception in a drawing at each progressive increase in stimulus size. Having done this he was left with a series of forms to analyze (see Figure 2.1). It is important to emphasize that the series is not composed of random forms but rather the forms are related to each other as a single movement. They are either moving toward something or away from something; each one is a step in this holistic movement.

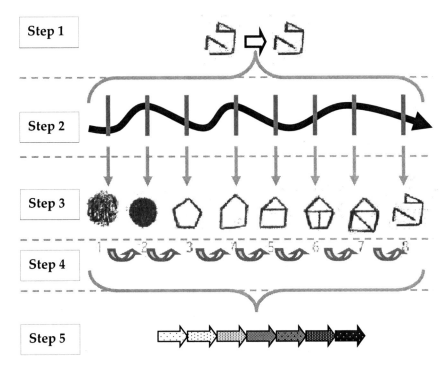

Figure 2.1.   Steps involved in a developmental method: the researcher must first break up a process and then piece it back together.

Externalization of experience is a capturing of it within a medium of expression, for example, speech or a drawing. The method requires subjects to reflect on the stimulus presented to them and in doing so form it within the medium designated by the researcher. Imagine looking at an inkblot and reporting your associations and how they relate to the picture. You are giving form to a formless (or incomplete form) image in your speech and at the same time you elaborate that form in the image. The medium of articulation does in fact transform the experience. The research must designate the most fitting medium of articulation for his or her particular interests. Capturing the total unmediated experience is impossible and unnecessary.

Step 4

Many researchers go this far but fail to analyze the genetic series as a totality. In order for the method to remain developmental a distinctive kind of analysis is required whereby the researcher reads the series as a single movement. Rather than isolating forms from each other the researcher reads *between* the forms by looking for *qualitative transformations* in the movement from one form to the next. The aim here is to *reconstruct* the slices of process into a unified process once again.

Step 5

Through the analysis of transformations from one form to the next the researcher pieces the process back together again and in so doing develops a *general model* of the process under investigation. *All* individual cases in all experiments should then conform to the model (Valsiner, 2003). If there are deviations the general model must be amended to accommodate them. Kleine-Horst's model of successive actualization of different gestalt factors should be confirmed through both microgenetic and ontogenetic findings. If one factor seems to be actualized *before* an earlier one, within the hierarchy, his model would have to be revised.

Figure 2.1 summaries the five steps. In step 1 a process is identified, in this case it is perception. In step 2 the researcher intervenes by simulating the process and stopping it at various points in its evolution. Step 3 subjects articulate (or complete) a form at each stop, which serves as the basis of analysis in step 4. Here, the slices in the processes are analyzed as a series, that is, a holistic movement. This is accomplished by attending to what is transformed *between* two slices (represented by the curved arrows). Finally, in step 5 the researcher compares the results with those of other experiments and develops a general model of the process being investigated. The skeleton of a developmental method will be fleshed out in what follows. I will first use it to analyze methods in Kleine-Horst's essay and then consider methods from further a field. My aim will be to explain the research orientation with examples, as well as show its power and versatility. For this reason I have selected diverse examples of methods that utilize the skeleton just described.

KLEINE-HORST'S METHODS

Perception: Actual Genesis

Visual perception is experienced under normal conditions as an immediate phenomenon. If a table is in front of me my perceptual awareness of it will seem to come into focus all at once, without delay. Developmental theorizing begins with the assumption that even within seemingly instantaneous processes a series of intermediate forms exist. Processes like perception simply proceed rapidly through the sequence, such that they appear to be immaculately conceived by the object on the sense organs. If the immediacy is merely an illusion the question becomes, "how can we study the intermediate forms absent to our awareness?"

The researcher must invent ways of slowing down the process by stopping it at various points in its evolution (step 2). In Kleine-Horst's essay he speaks of several ways to do this: (1) one could gradually increase the size of an extremely small stimulus (e.g., Wolfahrt's strategy); (2) begin by presenting the subject with an extremely fuzzy stimulus image which is then progressively put in focus; (3) locate the stimulus at the very periphery of the subject's visual field and progressively move it toward the center of the field; and (4) the "tachistoscopic procedure," flash a stimulus on a screen for increasingly longer intervals. All four strategies involve a stepwise articulation of a stimulus toward a full actualization.

At each new exposure the subject produces a form in graphic depiction (step 3). This is obviously not the only possible medium of expression but it produces data most relevant to visual perception. The intermediate forms are read in light of the whole series and its realized form product (step 4). In the movement from one form, in the sequence, to the next the researcher must assess what features are more fully articulated and which are less articulated. For example, Kleine-Horst (2007) analyzes the movement from 3 to 4 (in Wohlfahrt's series on p. 5 and Figure 1.1 in this volume) as a change from a "regular contour" to an irregular contour more closely resembling the "actual" stimulus contours. However, this trend is reversed in the movement from 4 to 5 as attention is directed toward the infield of the figure, where an inner line is articulated. This analysis requires attending to the movement *between* forms rather than each form in isolation from the others. Development can only be understood holistically, that is, the whole series as a single movement.

On the foundation of these results, Kleine-Horst builds a theory of progressive actualization of different hierarchically organized gestalt factors (represented in Figure 2.1 by the stage by stage darkening of the arrows). His model should be confirmed through both actual genetic and ontogenetic findings. If one factor seems to be actualized *before* an earlier one, within the hierarchy, his model would have to be revised, or at least further explanation would be required. He could not merely apply a statistical test to make the incongruent finding disappear. Such thinking would be inconsistent with single case analysis and developmental theorizing more generally.

Extrasensory Perception

Though at the fringes of scientific acceptability ESP is a potentially productive place to look for actual genesis. As in perception, the percepts of ESP should come into being through a series of intermediate forms. The problem here, as in the above experiments, is to stop the process at various points in its evolution to create a series of forms. However, in this case there is a danger of extinguishing the process by manipulating it. For this reason the act of slicing up the process must be controlled by the subject. In these experiments subjects were asked "to close their eyes, receive images that appeared, and then copy precisely what they had seen onto a sheet of paper, with their eyes open" (Kleine-Horst, this volume, p. 13). This procedure divides the subject's activity into two phases, an *actualizing process* phase, with closed eyes receiving images, and the *subject's construction phase*, with open eyes (see Figure 2.2). The two phases correspond to steps 2 and 3 respectively. The movement between the two phases is decided by the subject, yet the task requires such a movement. This procedure has the potential of creating a series of forms moving toward the actualization of a given form, in this case a "ring with a cross." Yet this is only possible if the subject "decides" to work on the same image when they re-enter the actualizing process phase. If this does not occur only

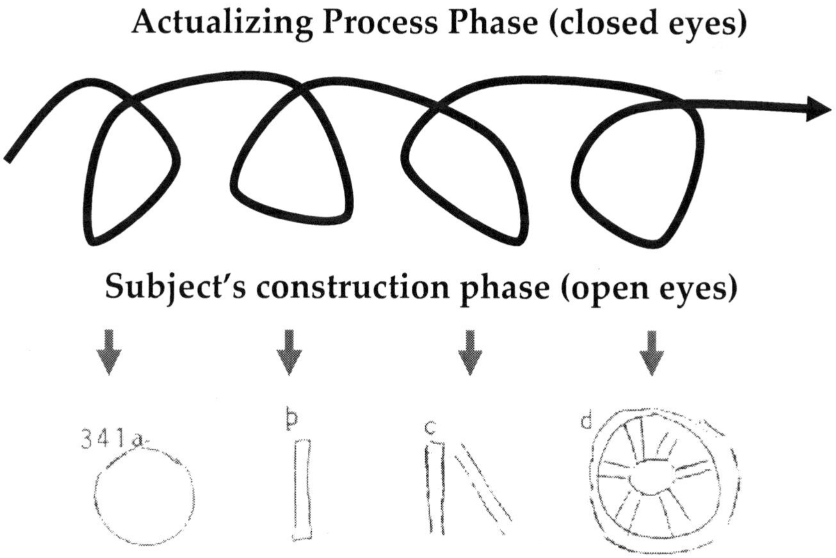

Actualizing Process Phase (closed eyes)

Subject's construction phase (open eyes)

Figure 2.2.   A schematization of ESP procedure and the possibility of creating a genetic series.

isolated forms will be constructed by the subject. It is therefore unsurprising that only four genetic series were produced using this method, and without the series it is impossible to read between forms to reconstruct the process. His other findings of *isolated* intermediate forms (e.g., glasses, a knife, a key, etc., on p. 14) can contribute very little to a developmental analysis. Instead, they seem to be arguments for ESP within his larger theory of hierarchical actualization of gestalt factors.

Perception: Actual Lysis

Kleine-Horst is absolutely right to look for the counter-process to actual genesis, that is, actual lysis. Just as systematic changes occur in actualization, we would expect similar systematic changes occurring in the opposite direction for actual lysis. One powerful way of developing the theory is to show the symmetry and/or asymmetry of the two processes. His method for studying actual lysis is equally convincing. A major virtue of the method is its simplicity: anyone with a pen, paper and two usable eyes can run this experiment and test Kleine-Horst's results for themselves. Having tested myself several times, I did find some of the same decomposition trails Kleine-Horst outlines (this volume, p. 9), mainly $X \rightarrow C \rightarrow A$, $X \rightarrow D \rightarrow E \rightarrow F$, $X \rightarrow D \rightarrow C$, $X \rightarrow D \rightarrow E \rightarrow F$. I encourage readers to do the experiment themselves and decide whether your findings fit Kleine-Horst's hierarchical model in your series of de-actualizing forms. As mentioned above *every* new experiment should confirm to the model he has outlined. If you find a slightly different process this is enough to warrant adjusting the model.

BEYOND PERCEPTION: CAPTURING OTHER DEVELOPMENTAL PROCESSES

The above developmental methods were created for perception research but are not limited to it. The goal of this section will be to show some possibilities of extending the skeleton method, how it can be utilized to understand processes on all levels of organization. The following studies differ from the above in their widening of focus to include processes that *model* psychological dynamics of a more complex process but *not* the whole process. Analogously, a model train does simulate some real train functions, such as the switching tracks, but obviously does not capture the whole complexity of the real phenomena.

Aphasic Speech

Heinz Werner has been acknowledged as a key figure in the advancement of *Ganzheitspsychologie* (Catán, 1986; Diriwächter, 2005; Valsiner & van der Veer, 2000). Like the *Ganzheit* psychologists he was interested in perception but he went further and applied their developmental methods to other phenomena. Here, we will consider his study of aphasic speech with the use of "normal" subjects. In terms of the method this study is quite close to the above research strategies. He gradually articulates verbal phrases in stepwise fashion (step 2) asking for subject's verbal interpretations at each partial articulation (step 3). From analyses of individual cases he is able to show the "inner experience of the semantic sphere of the linguistic forms" (Werner, 1956, p. 348) to be a developmentally earlier to the linguistically discrete form: we get a feeling of the stimulus before we can fully articulate what it is. Consider the following example of a subject who read the tachistoscopically articulated phrase *sanfter Wind* (gentle wind):

1. "—? Wind." What stood before "wind" feels like an adjective specifying something similar. Definitely not a word defining direction.
2. "—ter Wind." Know now that the word is "heavier" than "warm" … somehow more abstract.
3. "—cher Wind." Now it looks more like an adjective-of-direction.
4. "—ter Wind." Now again somehow more concrete, it faces me and looks somewhat like *weicher Wind* (soft Wind), but *ter* is in my way.
5. Now very clearly: "sanfter Wind." Not at all surprised. I had this actually before in the characteristic feel of the word and the looks of it (p. 348).

As in the perception experiments above, there is the gradual articulation of a stimulus (step 2) and the reconstructions of meaning taking place at each exposure to the phrase (step 3). However, Werner goes further by using this data to make inferences about aphasic speech. He assumes "the functions underlying abnormal behavior are in their essence not different from those underlying normal behavior" (p. 347). Speech aphasics simply do not reach the end of the process (discrete articulation of precise words) that we do. Normal and abnormal linguistically functioning individuals go through the same process but for aphasics that process is cut short. This model of the process would fit into step 5 of the above scheme. In short, Werner *slowed down* the process of perception in normal subjects to show intermediate forms in an attempt to model processes of aphasics.

His innovation was to use the method comparatively to study the similarities between aphasic and normal individuals, which is done by *modeling* aphasic processes in normally behaving individuals.

Ethnogenesis of Music Notation

Following Werner's (1956) elaboration of the developmental method Catán (1989) set out to model "conditions surrounding the emergence of modal notations." As communication between monasteries improved, sending musical text over long distances became possible; the roles of composer and performer separated and the need grew for a notational system to communicate between the composer and the performer. A *miniaturized* simulation of the ethnogenesis of music notation was created by pairing children as "scribes" and "performers." The scribes notated a micromelody (e.g., baa baa black sheep in drum beats) in order to communicate the rhythm to the performer, who was to reproduce the song from the notation. In both the real sociogenetic process and the modeled process, notation developed toward a discrete hierarchically organized system of marks that were capable of recording the complexity of the communicated music.

Though this method does not capture the total complexity of the sociological processes of transmission and transformation of the notation system, it does aptly foreground the psychological dynamics involved in this process. The notation is itself both an expression of the child's experience of the music and a means by which the child experiences the music; as the medium becomes increasingly sophisticated so do the child's ear for the music and vice versa. A two-way process is at work. The researcher does not have to vary the stimulus (i.e., the drum beats) toward a fully articulated form of music (step 2). The child subjectively experiences greater complexities in the music with the help of notation after more and more trails, though the objective complexity of the music will not have changed. The series of forms to be analyzed is the child's developing system of notation, which is an objectification of the child's experience. Consider the series (Figure 2.3) of stages in notational development found by Catán (1989) (see Figure 2.3). Unfortunately, Catán only analyzed general trends of development and not individual cases. Step 4 of her method was undertaken by clustering children's similar notations together and then considering them as a genetic series. This strategy is problematic from a developmental orientation in two respects: (1) in reading between forms for any particular form we are unable to compare exactly what changes the particular child created in his last trail. The stages of development

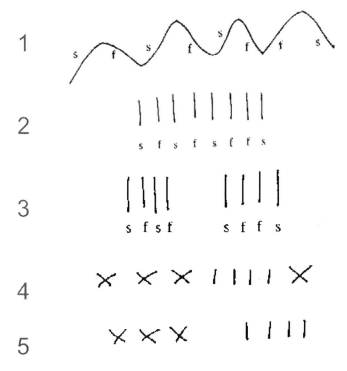

Figure 2.3.   Development of sophistication in child's musical notations of drum beats.

in effect become isolated from one another. And (2) in creating a general model (step 5) deviations from the "norm" are ignored. It is only through attending to no-standard cases that we can further develop the general model; the movement of innovation spirals between particular cases and general models.

   In spite of these critiques, we can still use examples she gives us of each stage to piece together a possible individual sequence, which is what I have done in Figure 2.3. At first children used an embodied notational system. Children mimic on paper the rhythm felt in their body, for example, like the tapping of their leg or finger which the music induces. Second, children learn to represent each drumbeat as a discrete mark. Here, children get the number of drumbeats right but fail to differentiate their temporal duration. Third, they further exploit the medium in clustering marks together to achieve a more accurate rendering of the temporal duration between drumbeats: the greater spacing between drumbeats the longer the period when "nothing happens." Fourth, children differentiate between "relatively shorter or longer" drumbeats with different marks. Finally, "when children wished to differentiate a third duration in addition to simply making a distinction between longer and shorter drumbeats, they resorted to the earlier spatial grouping procedure [in stage 3 above]" (Catan, 1989, p. 161).

Thus, Catán (1989) captured progressive stages of psychological organization and the movement between them for a sociological process. Here the developing medium of experience and expression (i.e., the notation system) is also the series of intermediate forms that the researcher must analysis. The researcher does not control the direction in which the notation system develops. In several cases children would even "progress" one stage forward and in the next instance "regress" to an earlier form. A possibility for advancing Catán's method would be to systematically intervene within children's development, for example, show children other notational systems without explaining them or have the child notate the beats performed by the second child using the first child's notations. By intervening in the process the research could further explore the dynamics of development, regression or stasis of notational sophistication.

Transmission of Culture Between two Groups

F. C. Bartlett (1932) is the only psychologist I consider that did not directly build from *Ganzheitspsychologie*. In fact, he started his experiments on remembering in the 1910s before actual genesis had been discovered in Germany.[1] Yet I feel Bartlett's methods share many of the same assumptions, for example, individual case analysis, interest in subject's experience, developmental analysis, and so forth. I also think that Bartlett adds a greater social psychological dimension to the group. In what follows I will analyze perhaps his best known method, the method of serial reproduction, which he used to simulate what happens to cultural material (such as folk-stories) when it enters a group from outside.

University of Cambridge students were presented with an image or a story from a foreign group. One of his most famous stimuli was a Native American folktale titled *War of the Ghosts*. The strategy of using this unfamiliar material ensures significant transformations will take place when subjects reproduce it. The material is then taken away and a short delay ensues. After 15 minutes or so the subject is asked to reproduce the material from memory. His or her reproduction is then given to another subject who reproduces the first subject's reproduction after a delay. This process is continued until each progressive reproduction is no longer substantially different from the one it preceded. At this point a long *genetic series* will have been created. Consider the series of reproductions for the Egyptian hieroglyph (of an owl) in Figure 2.4. In this experiment the process of transmission between people is accelerated in comparison to the delays which would occur between reproductions in the social situation it is meant to simulate. Waiting a week between exposure to the stimulus and its first reproduction would already have significantly distorted the original. By using shorter delays in the simulation of the process we capture more intermediate forms; the 15 minute delay creates just the right amount of distortion between subject's reproductions. Finding the proper delay is a negotiation between where you slice up the process (step 2) and the kinds of forms produced by the subject (step 3). The movement toward some form (in this case a cat) is the product of pre-existing conventional group forms and not an end established by the psychologist as in the other experiments, for example, a fully articulated

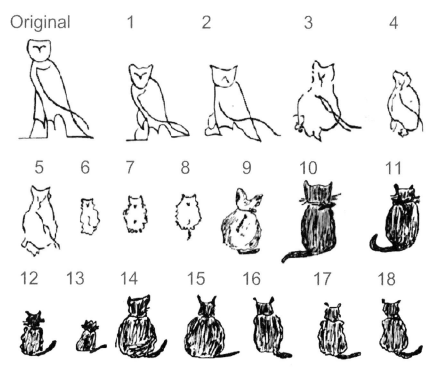

Figure 2.4.   A series of forms produced through Bartlett's (1932, pp. 180-181) method of serial reproduction.

image, a given word meaning or an advanced notational system relative to less advanced.

Bartlett (1932) analyzes the series by attending to what is *added*, *deleted*, and *transformed* from one reproduction to the next (step 4). It is worthwhile to quote Bartlett's own interpretation of the above series here:

> The elaboration in this series is obvious. The reversal of the direction of the wing curve by subject 3, and its doubling, at once suggested a tail, and thereafter the tail drops lower and lower until it assumes its proper tail position, and is greatly emphasized, in which process it is reversed twice more. The apparently disconnected lines in the original drawing are all worked into the figure, and the original beak mark is elaborated into a ribbon with a bow. Whiskers are introduced in due course, and the small lines of the back are multiplied and become shading.... A rather unusual figure, carrying a fairly strong suggestion of a realistic representation, becomes greatly elaborated into a familiar whole. (p. 181)

Through this analysis Bartlett tracks holistic changes through the series of forms toward a conventional form of the cat, which many subjects reproduce accurately, suggesting that the process has reached a stable form. But the analysis does not end there. From this Bartlett derives a general model of social transmission and transformation (step 5), that specifies the psychological mechanisms that move and shape this process. Most importantly he recognizes that remembering (within a group or individually) is mediated by the group's conventions, which can be distilled out at the end of a genetic series using the method of serial reproduction. He calls this mechanism *conventionalization*, whereby any unfamiliar material is shaped in the direction of what is already familiar in the group. Similarities can be draw to *Ganzheitspsychologie*'s observation that unactualized forms leave subjects in a state of tension, which causes them to impose order on the stimulus in the direction of conventions, which "feel right."

Second, there is the supporting process of *rationalization*. In Bartlett's (1932) own words "[**rationalization**] is to render material acceptable, understandable, comfortable, straightforward; to rob it of all puzzling elements" (p. 89). For example, once reproduction 9 is recognized as a cat by subject 10 whiskers are introduced: "it is a cat; it must have had whiskers!"

These two mechanisms go below the surface of the process to explain what drives and constrains it; they are *explanations* of the process. The general model once developed then applies to all particular cases. We can even expect to find the same mechanisms at work within a written medium as opposed to a graphic one.[2] With this in mind consider the following series of reproductions for Bartlett's most well known stimulus, the Native American story *The War of the Ghosts*. The last line of the original text reads:

> When the sun rose he fell down. **Something black came out** of his mouth. His face became contorted.

In succession this becomes:

> When the sun rose he fell down. And he gave a cry, and as he opened his mouth **a black thing rushed** from it.
> When the sun rose he suddenly felt faint, and when he would have risen he fell down, and **a black thing rushed out** of his mouth.
> He felt no pain until sunrise the next day, when, on trying to rise, **a great black thing flew** from his mouth.
> He lived that night, and the next day, but at sunset **his soul fled black** from his mouth.
> He lived through the night and the following day, but died at sunset, and **his soul passed** through his mouth.
> Before the boat got clear of the conflict the Indian died, and **his spirit fled**.
> Before he could be carried back to the boat, **his spirit had left** this world.
> **His spirit left** this world.
> ("Nonsense," said one of the others, "you will not die.") But **he did**. (Bartlett, 1932, p. 127, emphasis added)

We can clearly see, in this series, the two mechanisms mentioned above. Let us analyze this text more closely in the same method as the above, attending especially to the transformations occurring to the vague but vivid "something black," which becomes an increasingly more concrete entity and finally completely disappears. To understand this transformation we must read it as an unfolding process toward a stable conventional form. Something black becomes the slightly more tangible "black thing." This image is eventually linked with "flew" from his mouth, transformed from the original "came out of his mouth," which facilitates the transformation from the ambiguous "thing" to "soul" that in turn gives way to the slightly more concrete "spirit." At this point the story is still supernatural but in a familiar form. However, the group mind strives for concreteness to the point that in the end no supernatural elements remain: there is no mention of spirit or even the "ghosts," which were left at the heading of the story, by Bartlett, in an attempt to keep these supernatural elements.

Summary

The presentation and interpretation of several *genetic series*, produced by way of diverse but unified methods, should give the reader an appreciation for the power and versatility of the strategic method. Further, I hope that the reader will be able to play with these strategies to construct a method to address the processes they themselves are interested in. Having advanced a strategy for pursuing method we must now link it to theory, which both supports method and is transformed through the implementation of method.

PART II

In a discipline that has forsaken theory for a proliferation of local empirical findings Kleine-Horst's embedding of research within a highly developed theoretical apparatus is welcomed. Psychologists too often narrow their focus to the very concrete phenomena they are investigating without looking for interrelations with surrounding areas of research. An integration of diverse fields of research requires theoretical development, and thus time for thinking rather than simply the mindless accumulation of facts. Kleine-Horst has thought through a sophisticated theory which touches on the phenomena of physics, biology, neurology, psychology, sociology, and so forth—in fact, he considers it to be a proper "theory of everything." Grand theories of this sort have fallen out of favor in philosophy but are still passionately pursued in physics. In what follows I will explore (1) the theory and its foundational assumptions, (2) how this theory answers long standing philosophical paradoxes, and (3) ask what research questions we can derive from it.

The Theory and its Assumptions

Kleine-Horst's theory is grounded within a philosophical and psychological tradition, whose assumptions will be unfamiliar to most contemporary readers. For example, we tend not to think of reality as hierarchically organized nor as developing. In this section I will unpack and contextualize some key philosophical ideas that hold the theory together, namely *development, holism,* and *hierarchical order.* I will treat each idea in turn but at the same time I hope to communicate their interrelation:

1. **Development**. We have already surveyed various developmental methods, which access phenomena in change by slicing up a process and then piecing it back together holistically. A developmental theory dictates that this must be done, for from its standpoint, *reality itself is developing*: All things are in movement. We cannot therefore classify or categorize the world; instead, we must try to identify the mechanisms and constraints of movement. In philosophy, for example, Hegel attempts to understand the movement of history, thought and reality as a *dialectical process*, whereby tensions in an existing system are resolved in a synthesis producing a higher stage of thought. Kleine-Horst's theory is developmental in that it does not stop at creating a taxonomy of reality; it goes further to say how one aspect arises out of another and how they interpenetrate each other in their operation. In sum, reality is a process moving through multiple levels of organization and in so doing transforming itself. Psychologists and philosophers cannot be content with merely enumerating the kinds of reality in existence but must show how they are developmentally related.

2. **Holism**. What are these "multiple levels of reality?" How should we understand them? Here we come to the problem of *emergence*: Each higher level is dependent on the one below it but cannot be understood completely by reference to the subordinate level alone. Take the classic example of H_2O: if there is a fire either hydrogen or oxygen applied separately will cause the fire to burn all the more furiously. However, when put together in the molecule H_2O they can help extinguish the fire. There are emergent properties at higher levels of organization; therefore explanations must fit the level of the phenomena. There is a common misconception in the public and much thinking in the sciences that all questions are reducible down to physical explanations. Therefore, psychology is believed to be explainable by reference to brain processes and likewise biology can then be explained by chemistry, and chemistry by physics, which will give us a theory of everything. Built into Kliene-Horst's theory of reality is the recognition of multiple levels and their nonreducibility: Processes of nonvital matter are important in situating vital matter (VM) but we must realize that vital matter has properties not found in nonvital matter, such as its *active* response to the world. More importantly for his own research, consciousness is not reducible to the processes of VM (i.e., neuroscience). This is not to say that understanding VM cannot be helpful in the study of consciousness—it can be; the point is merely that the final explanation must be at the proper level.

3. **Hierarchical order.** These levels are related both *genetically*, that is, by which came into being first, and *holistically*, that is, emergent properties are found at higher levels. Thus, without the two above assumptions the notion of hierarchical order would require a different grounding. In Plato the ideal mode of being is privileged over the material because the eternal is given priority over the flux. However, Plato—as in most theorists who posit multiple modes of being—fails to adequately connect the modes (the Socratic paradox is precisely how the eternal can be expressed in the transitory). The advantage of Kleine-Horst's criteria of demarcation is that in making a distinction it also connects the levels to one another. We will pursue this further in the section on resolving philosophical paradoxes. For now suffice it to say that development and holism are connected in and through the notion of hierarchical order.

Having reviewed philosophical underpinnings of the theory we can now explore more precisely how they relate to Kleine-Horst's theory of reality. Kleine-Horst makes a distinction between "spheres or manners of being" (represented in the vertical columns in Figure 2.5) and "evolutionary levels" (represented in the horizontal rows). By making this distinction he is able to connect up the different levels to each other: a manner of being, such as VM *produces*, another manner, in this case functional manner simply by existing. This is what Kleine-Horst means when he says "the same entities express themselves twice"—in this case, in the mode of matter *and* function. One may explain the workings of the heart purely in terms of a mechanistic universe, but we could also give a teleological explanation. Neither is wrong: they are *two* approaches to the same object. VM does serve functions, for example, the heart pumps blood, the eyes see, the stomach digests, and so forth. Even at the cellular level we find that different components of the cell serve various purposes for its overall functioning. These *functional* properties of VM are not found in nonvital matter; thus we can say it is a subordinate level. At the highest level of VM we have the neuron, whose vital function (VF) is to stimulate the organism. Here VFs of the neuron is transformed into a psychical reality, where the action of the world on the sense organs is expressed in holistic configurations, that is, gestalts. Groups of neurons form associative bonds which when excited produce another manner of reality, phenomenal reality or consciousness. To reiterate, neuron's function (now in the primary hierarchy of psychic functions) is precisely to produce different gestalts in the consciousness of the organism (secondary hierarchy psychic consciousness or PC) when the requisite stimulation is present from the world on the sense organs. We see again that psychic functions (PF) have properties not found in VFs, mainly that they give rise to consciousness and

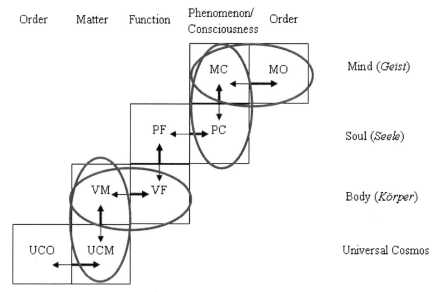

Figure 2.5.   Kleine-Horst's "spheres or manners of being" (vertical columns) and "evolutionary levels" (horizontal rows).

Sources: Modified from Kleine-Horst (this volume) and Diriwächter (2008).

are configured in such a way to enable certain kinds of conscious experiences.

In summary, the *development* of reality takes place in stepwise fashion, whereby higher levels are dependent on the lower yet go beyond them in creating emergent properties. Kleine-Horst's theory does much more than elaborate a taxonomy of manners and levels: they are related to each other by way of a developmental movement through this hierarchical order. The stepwise movement involves both a primary hierarchy producing a secondary hierarchy for every evolutionary level (e.g., the heart pumps blood) and the highest level of the secondary hierarchy realizing a new evolutionary level (e.g., a neuron's function enables consciousness). The horizontal and vertical movements create new spheres and levels of reality.

Two is Less Than Three

Descartes has become a whipping boy for much of contemporary philosophy and psychology, yet we must appreciate his insight that consciousness is not the same kind of reality as matter, that it cannot be reduced to matter. Where he failed was in theorizing the link between the two, which was said to occur at the pituitary glad but this only specifies a location not a mode of interaction. To solve this paradox of interaction many have settled on the unimaginative solution of *monism*, that is, considering only matter as real. This strategy has major problems attached to it: (1) it does not recognize emergent properties, (2) it denies something very real to all of us, our own experience, and (3) it renders the work of social sciences and humanities theoretically pointless, while ending in physics worship.

Rather than elaborating an argument against monism I will take a more positive approach and show how productive the opposite move can be. Instead of denying the existence of consciousness Kleine-Horst recognizes another sphere of being between it and matter, function. Thus, Descartes' problem becomes one of not including enough spheres of being into his conception of reality. Likewise, by considering mind and consciousness, and body and matter to be synonymous Descartes has remained blind to the subtle distinctions that might help bridge the two spheres of being. In Kleine-Horst these terms differ in that one (e.g., matter) is a sphere of being, while the other (e.g., body) is an evolutionary level (see the circles in Figure 2.5). We can see from Figure 2.5 that even here these terms do not touch each other—for interaction they need the PF, which produces PC.

It becomes imperative at this point to understand VM as being *both* mechanistic and teleological. Thus, we can explain the working of heart by showing what triggers what or we can point to the way it functions to serve the purpose of sending blood through the body as if it was designed for the role. When it comes to PF the purpose or function is to produce a certain quality of consciousness, or gestalt configuration, which itself is not material. In Kantian language, PF become a necessary condition for any experience to occur, that is, for phenomena. Likewise, PF are bound to VM but their configurations cannot be deduced from VM alone.

In short, by attending to the intermediate link between matter and consciousness Kleine-Horst was able to bridge the gap. It is clear that VM does have properties not found in nonvital matter, mainly *functions*—the fact that it is active in responding to its environment for a particular end. Reality is then an interpenetration of matter, function and consciousness.

Deriving Questions for the Future

Given the interaction between the three spheres of reality charted out above we might expect to find certain neuron configurations and teleological brain processes. One way to begin the search would be to use an actual genetic sequence with a patient having a MRI (magnetic resonance imaging). We might find progressive areas of the brain lighting up as gestalt configurations are actualized. Though this may seem too simple a correspondence I do not know that anyone has yet even tried it, and if this were the case we would have found the physical substance that supports higher levels of reality. Likewise, we might look "upward" from the experiments on perception and ask how they support the next level in the hierarchy, that is, mind. For example, we might ask, "How does imagination rely on and go beyond perceptual processes?"

It also needs to be stressed here that the relationship between different spheres and manners of reality is bi-directional. The addition of mental consciousness (MC), for example, alters processes at lower levels, as in the case of the placebo effect. Reality is on the move constantly actualizing itself in higher forms and de-actualizing itself back down to lower levels of organization. In charting out MC we would simultaneously keep an eye to how this addition transforms PC. Vygotsky and Luria (1996), for instance, showed how when language began to be used lower psychological processes, such as perception, attention, memory, and so forth, were as a result transformed. Also, the studies mentioned above in the method section (i.e., "Beyond Perception") all deal with MC. Due to the similarity of presentation, that is, through the development of intermediate forms, insights should abound.

CONCLUSION: FINAL WORDS ON DEVELOPMENT IN PSYCHOLOGY

In this paper we have explored a variety of developmental methods, including those discussed by Kleine-Horst, as well as taken a close look at Kleine-Horst's theoretical framework in an attempt to draw out insightful ideas for *developing "development."* In Part I argued for the need to analyze individual cases and look for qualitative transformations. This could only be fulfilled by analyzing a sliced up process as a single movement; in all the genetic series we analyzed the emphasis was on reading *between* intermediate forms in order to develop a general model of the processes involved. The diversity of processes that were studied using the method showed its versatility in dealing with a wide range of *processes.* In Part II we stepped back to the frame, which made the developmental method interesting and insightful. Too often psychologists think too small, too locally. Kleine-Horst's paper shows us the virtues of thinking BIG. Theories that present the big picture can be helpful in integrating research, forging links between research programs, pointing to areas in need of research, and can modify aspects of big picture from individual studies (have conversation across research programs). The trilogistic theory helps us do this by conceptualizing different levels, what phenomena belong to each, and by working out how they interrelate.

Looking to the future of developmental thinking in psychology we must reassert that development means a study of *process*, *movement*, and *qualitative transformation*, which can only be adequately accessed through the analysis of single cases seen through the lens of complex theory. When developmental psychology has devised adequate methods for accessing *process* and advances by way of analysis of single cases to theory that integrates diverse findings it will have earned its title.

NOTES

1. Bartlett first published research on remembering in 1920, although this research had been submitted earlier, in 1916, for his fellowship dissertation, St. John's College, Cambridge. Also, in 1916, Bartlett published "An Experimental Study of Some Problems of Perceiving and Imagining," which used seemingly Ganzeits methods.
2. Bartlett (1932) actually considers graphic reproduction after written reproduction. Yet, this need not worry us in showing how the method functions; either way the outcome should be the same.

REFERENCES

Bartlett, F. (1916). An experimental study of some problems of perceiving and imagining. *British Journal of Psychology, 8,* 222-266.

Bartlett, F. (1920). Some experiments on the reproduction of fold stories. *Folk Love, 31,* 30-47.

Bartlett, F. (1932). *Remembering: A study in experimental and social psychology.* Cambridge, MA: Cambridge University Press.

Catán, L. (1986). The dynamic display of process: Historical development and contemporary uses of microgenetic method. *Human Development, 29,* 252-263.

Catán, L. (1989). Musical literacy and the development of rhythm representation: cognitive change and material media. In A. Gellaty, D. Rogers, & J. Sloboda (Eds.), *Cognition and social worlds.* Oxford, England: Clarendon Press.

Diriwächter, R. (2005). Ganzheitpsychologie: The doctrine. *From Past to Future, 5*(1), 3-17.

Diriwächter, R. (2008). Genetic Ganzheitspsychologie. In R. Diriwächter & J. Valsiner (Eds.), *Striving for the whole: Creating theoretical syntheses.* Somerset, NJ: Transaction.

Valsiner, J. (2003). Culture and its transfer: Ways of creating general knowledge through the study of cultural particulars. In W. J. Lonner, D. L. Dinnel, S. A. Hayes, & D. N. Sattler (Eds.), *Online readings in psychology and culture* (Unit 2, chapter 12). Bellingham, WA: Center for Cross-Cultural Research, Western Washington University. Retrieved October 10, 2004, from http://www.wwu.edu/~culture/

Valsiner, J., & Van der Veer, R. (2000). *The social mind: Construction of the idea*. Cambridge, MA: Cambridge University Press.

Vygotksy, L., & Luria, A. (1996). Tool and symbol in child development. In J. Valsiner & R. van der Veer (Eds.), *The Vygotsky Reader*. Cambridge, England: Blackwell.

Werner, H. (1956). Microgenesis and aphasia. *Journal of abnormal Social Psychology, 52*, 347-353.

PART II

MEANING MAKING ABOUT VIOLENCE

CHAPTER 3

THE MAKING OF NONVIOLENCE

Affective Self-Regulation in a Shooting Game

Nicole M. Capezza and Jaan Valsiner

*Willis came abreast of him, his M-16 pointing at the man's chest. They stood not
five feet apart. The soldier's AK 47 was pointed straight at Willis. The captain
vigorously shook his head. The NVA soldier shook his head just as vigorously. It was
a true cease-fire, gentlemen's agreement or a deal…. The soldier sank back into
the darkness and Willis stumbled on.*

(Grossmann, 1996, pp. 118-119)

This chance encounter of an American commander (Willis) and a North
Vietnamese soldier in an unexpected moment illustrates the cultural
framing of all homicidal activity. Even in such general contexts as wars,
where it is considered to be socially legitimate to kill the enemy—this
need not happen. Under some circumstances the soldiers do not shoot
one another. Likewise, in our peacetime environment, the use of shotguns
for homicide is remarkably rare given their public availability.[1] Most

Innovating Genesis: Microgenesis and the Constructive Mind in Action, pp. 67–91
Copyright © 2008 by Information Age Publishing

67

human-made tools are made to be used purposefully, for context-dependent actions rather than indiscriminately.

UNCERTAINTY OF WAR AND PEACE

Most human relevant actions are generated under uncertainty. The actor does not have access to all necessary information, and cannot fully anticipate the different consequences of one or another way of acting. Some actions can lead to dramatic consequences that cannot be reversed. All creativity in biological evolution has been dependent on the uncertainty of the current setting and of possible outcomes of actions. A previously unknown fruit may be a potent nutrient—or a killing poison—for an inquisitive animal. Invention of how to make fire can lead to a new culture of nutrition (cooked food) but it can also lead to the burning down of one's living quarters. The cultural invention of hunting tools may lead to improved of the nutrition for a group—as well as a means to be eradicated by a rival group.

Firearms are a quintessential cultural invention that set up new conditions for the uncertainty of being. The decision to shoot a target may take a small amount of time yet may lead to fatal outcomes, for the target or for the shooter. Within these few milliseconds or seconds, the person's meaning construction system either enables the act of shooting, or blocks it. Examples of quick action based on fear combined with the meaning of *self-defense* are numerous in military settings. Less known are examples where in an otherwise certain homicidal situation that outcome is blocked. In war-time situations filled with fear and fatigue it is not surprising to find sudden reversals between the opposites of human action tendencies—ranging from indiscriminate shooting to no shooting, or from irrational frontal attacks to panic-driven retreats (Sen'yavskaya, 1999, pp. 126-141). The survival of the person under conditions of enduring danger entails the mobilization of the whole personality in its efforts to survive the current situation (Green, 2002). It involves here-and-now decision making—to act or not to act—which has irreversible consequences all of which are unpredictable.

Decision process analysis. In contemporary cognitive psychology, acting under uncertainty has been analyzed within the framework of decision making—mostly along the lines of "cognitive heuristics" that violate basic principles of inductive (statistically based) reasoning. Most of the problems utilized in the decision research are either artificial tasks based on verbal evidence (Tversky & Kahnemann, 1982), or decisions about business content materials. Rarely are these decisions studied on the basis of issues crucial for human survival—such as in medicine (Hoffrage,

Kurzenhaeuser, & Gigerenzer, 2005), accident analysis, or in the case of war. While psychology's basic theory has undoubtedly appropriated wartime phenomena, and built on social needs created by wars, the decision processes involved in crucial, life-or-death matters, have not been critically examined.

The decision processes we analyze here—deciding whether to initiate a violent act or not, under pressure of time—come closest to the *fast and frugal heuristics* (FFH) that have been offered as solutions to human evolutionary adaptation to immediate needs to act. The introduction of the FFH concept into psychological theorizing constitutes a major step towards conceptualizing the approximate nature of human mental functioning. Thus,

> Fast and frugal heuristics employ a minimum of time, knowledge, and computation to make adaptive choices in real environments. They can be used to solve problems of sequential search through objects or options, as in satisficing. They can also be used to make choices between simultaneously available objects, where the search for information (in the form of cues, features, consequences, etc.) about the possible options must be limited, rather than the search for the options themselves. FFH limit their search of objects or information using easily computable stopping rules, and they may make their choices with easily computable decision rules. (Gigerenzer, Todd, & ABC Group, 1999, p. 14)

Gigerenzer's (1999) perspective opens the door for basic analysis of the mental processes—yet the term FFH remains merely a label unless it leads to actual analysis of the satisficing process. It needs also to specify the stopping rules—conditions under which the decision is considered finished. Of course any such arrival in a satisficing state is but a moment in a flow of decision tasks. The human world is inherently ambiguous; what is a sufficient solution now can change at any moment to create a new problem.

Semiotically mediated decision processes. It is here where Gigerenzer's (1999) "fast and frugal heuristics" need complementation through a look at semiotic mediation. The latter reflects the conditionality of the states of the world—different fast and frugal decisions are made under the influence of enabling signs that promote the mental process to move in some expected directions (Valsiner, 2001a). The semiotically mediated world creates the tools for human use of the FFHs. This personal world is a "cautious world"—in it, different possible scenarios for what *might* happen with a person under different conditions flash through one's mind, linking with meanings that might be applicable to the given situation. Thus, cultural heroes, mothers, tricksters are employed in myth stories and discourse in general to reflect the possible (conditional) changes of their conduct from one extreme to another.

Cultural guidance of acting, feeling, and thinking. Social institutions guide developing children towards the establishment of semiotic regulatory mechanisms that can be guided—when socially needed—to make the same person act in opposite ways under different circumstances. The same person who is expected to excel in killing enemies in a war is not expected to shoot his neighbor in a trivial dispute, and may even be expected to fight against violence in general. How can such—double— socialization goals be achieved? Our premise in this paper is that these opposite outcomes (readiness for violence and nonviolence) are socially guided in ontogeny by differentiating the contexts within which such acts are allowed ("zone of freedom of movement," or ZFM), promoted ("zone of promoted actions," or ZPA) and made ready to be activated at the next moment in time ("zone of proximal development," or ZPD—see Valsiner, 1997, on this terminology). Each ongoing activity is guided by a "zone system" where some parts of the event become highlighted, some others—demanded, and still others ruled out, in the course of the ongoing activity. Yet there can be multiple trajectories of action that lead to similar (equifinal) outcomes. Different general meaning complexes— or social representations (Valsiner, 2003)—act as catalysts in the move into one or another trajectory.

Self-regulation through signs. The narrow question posed here—to shoot or not to shoot—is embedded in the system of meanings of the personal culture (Valsiner, 2000, pp. 55-57). It entails all of a person's hyper-generalized semiotic fields of self-regulation (Valsiner, 2001b, 2005), based on which the specific meanings of the setting become constructed "online," which in their turn either enable or block the shooting decision. The externalization of such personal cultural constructions (the here-and-now microlevel phenomena) into the interpersonal world—collective culture (meso-level semiotic phenomenon)—sets the stage for the ways in which actions with guns become socially organized in a given society (macrolevel of the "phenomena of shooting").

When a human constructs meaning to relate with their world, the field of opposites is automatically implied at every moment (Josephs, Valsiner, & Surgan, 1999). Meaning arises in the form of complexes of united opposites. A sign that is constructed immediately coconstructs its opposite—a countersign. This idea can be traced back to the thinking of Alexius Meinong (1983) in the late nineteenth century. He claimed,

> as I am apprehending an A, I also apprehend a non-A in some sense. So we have to do with a difference regarding what is apprehended ... a difference regarding what stands opposite [gegenübersteht] each intellectual experi-

ence as its object [Gegenstand].... In the non-A, then, there is a further objective factor, the "non," as it were, supervening on the A. (pp. 14-15)

Meinong (1983) understood the basic asymmetry between the two components of each sign. Following Meinong's tradition one can conceptualize signs as systems of duality of meanings—a system that entails two (or more) opposites. This focus on internal dialogicality of human meaning construction processes has been maintained by both dialectically (Marková, 1990) and dialogically (Hermans, 2001, 2002; Salgado & Hermans, 2005) oriented thinkers. Thus, within each notion of X (e.g., "love," "justice") is embedded its nonmanifest opposite ("non-love," "non-justice") which may exist in a nondifferentiated or quasi-differentiated state (e.g., duality in myths: Gupta & Valsiner, 2003). These opposite fields may become differentiated, such that, "non-love" turns into hate, and "non-justice" into revenge. As we all know, people have been killing one another in the name of hatred and fighting injustice throughout our recorded human history. Socially legitimate (and illegitimate) violence is thus defined through the oppositional system of meanings.

VARIETIES OF VIOLENCE

The phenomena of violence—purposeful interference into the nature of being of places or persons—are natural events that occur in any society. The forms of actions vary, of course. We are violent towards nature (by cutting down trees), towards children (by punishing them for their wrong-doings), and one another. Perhaps the most violent acts are conducted by the social institutions that force ordinary citizens to pay taxes and so on. Yet most of these acts do not end up being our targets of investigation of "violence in contemporary society." Some acts of annihilation of fellow human beings—in wars, in execution squads, or police chases, are not included in "violence". Others are—a criminal shooting at a policeman is involved in violence, while the policeman who injures a criminal is doing his duty. An adult hitting a child may be "disciplining him"; while a child hitting the adult is "being violent." What is considered "violent" and what not is a result of cultural meaning construction. Being stoned to death legally—based on Shariah law—is violent, its counterpart by lethal injection is not, at least as its meaning may be construed. Violence is an act against some object in which illegal methods are used (Klausner, 1987), while the very same methods utilized within the legal meaning system of a society does not get such designation.

Thus, we can look at the notion of violence as a dual sign complex that can have different affective valuations linked with it:

		VIOLENCE <> non-VIOLENCE	
Socially Added Value (SAV)	"peacetime"	negative	positive
Social canalizing actions		restricting	promoting
	"wartime"	positive	negative
		promoting	restricting

The combination of the dual nature of the meaning complex with different kinds of metalevel contexts (peace/war) indicates the flexibility of the human cultural regulatory system. Dependent on the metacontext, allowable and preferred sets of actions take on reverse character. This was already noted by Kurt Lewin (1917) during his experiences of moving to the frontlines in World War I and served as a phenomenological basis for his adoption of a field-theoretic stance in his version of the Gestalt theory of human action. It furthermore corroborates Georg Simmel's (1904) observations on the unity of war and peace.

Such differentiated construction of the meaning of the violence <> nonviolence complex guides the actions of human beings who internalize these meanings by way of filling them in with their personalized sense. Children grow up in the social world filled with half-ready general meaning schemes to explain actions of others, of their own, and to lead them in new actions. Their experience includes play and imagination where means of homicide (toy guns, tanks, military airplanes, GI Joes, etc.) are either pregiven, or self-made (e.g., using tree branches as toy guns in war games). At the same time they may be kept away from other experiences—seeing corpses in morgues, agony of death, and realities of economics. Some of them grow out of the interest in war-games, others—look for the glory and misery of violent encounters all their lives. At the same time, their growth is guided by the social institutions who frame the same kind of violent acts by different meaning systems.

It is by the difference between countries—in our case, the United States and Estonia—where such cross-societal comparisons become important. The United States has had no direct wartime activity on its continental territory over the past century—but has been involved in most overseas military conflicts of the twentieth century. For two centuries the United States has emphasized its independence and exceptionality. In contrast, Estonia has been the battleground of two World Wars, long period of colonization (by Russia and former Soviet Union), and complicated struggle for independence. Estonia has had no social representation of exceptional status in the world, nor has it been militarily involved in conflicts outside of its own small territory.

Acting With a Gun: Contrasts Between United States and Estonia

Violent acts that are recognized socially occur in a variety of forms. It is often the young—adolescents and young adults—who become both agents and targets of gun-based violence. A major distinction to be made is that of self- or other-centeredness of these acts. Hence general societal comparisons of suicide and homicide rates provide some background for the two societies from which our research participants came. In the United States in 2001, of all the 29,573 people who died from gunfire, about 57% were from suicide, 38% from homicide (the rest being of varied causes) (Arias, Anderson, Kung, Murphy, & Kochanek, 2004). If we look at it from a worldwide perspective, the United States has the most gun-related deaths than any of the 36 richest countries in the world. The United States accounted for 45% of all gun deaths reported by the 36 countries. In 1994, the United States had 14.24 deaths by guns per 100,000 people who died that year. The lowest death by gun rate was found in Japan only 5 deaths by guns per 10,000,000 people who died that year (Krug, Powell, & Dahlberg, 1998).

Estonia has a different history relating to death in general and to shooting death in particular. Throughout the early 1990s, Estonia had one of the highest rates of both homicide and suicide throughout the world, with suicides relatively more frequent than homicides. In 1994 the homicide rate was 25.12 per 100,000 and the suicide rate was 34.05 per 100,000. These rates have been declining during the past several years (Estonian Human Development Report, 2000). The use of firearms is not as prominent in Estonia as in the United States, especially for suicide—with only 2.86 per 100,000 suicide deaths by firearms in Estonia compared to 7.35 per 100,000 in the United States (Krug et al., 1998). Of course these data are predicated upon the accessibility of guns being different in the two societies. In the United States today there are about 44 million gun owners. This is equivalent to 25% of the population, with at least one gun in 40% of U.S. households. This includes 65 million handguns, which have proven to be the most dangerous type of gun. The number of gun sales continues to rise; approximately 37,500 guns are sold each day (Office of Juvenile Justice and Delinquency Prevention, 1998).

There are interesting differences in the age cohorts of gun users. In the United States, gun violence has decreased for adults age 25 and older, and increased for juveniles and adults under age 25. Handguns are used as the weapon of choice for the majority of all homicides regardless of age (Office of Juvenile Justice and Delinquency Prevention, 1998). However, the increase in young adults preference for using guns is quite concerning for society at large. This age-linked tendency may be viewed in the context of socialization of people for war in general. It is the juveniles and young adults in any society who are prepared for socially legitimate homicidal acts—in the context of military conflicts where all parties claim to be defending themselves from outside intruders. Or likewise in the contexts of "crime of passion"—a jealous lover first kills the object of love, and then may kill oneself. This kind of act can be understood as the killing of a *relationship* rather than merely exterminating the other (Simmel, 1904, pp. 524-525). The shooter and the target may be in—or establish instantly—some kind of interpersonal relation that may be preserved, or terminated. In the latter case both the shooter and the one shot may perish—homicide and suicide become united.

How, then, is gun use made possible at the psychological level? How is it possible that a person aims a gun towards another person (including oneself), and decides to pull the trigger? Where are the presumed values of humanism, concern for others, human rights, respect, and so forth, at the moment of actual decision towards whom to orient the weapon, and whether to pull the trigger?

Microgenesis of Actions: A Look Into Shooting

Microgenesis is a basic process that entails constant construction of intermediate forms within the process of developing to some outcome state (Valsiner & van der Veer, 2000, pp. 303-320). These intermediate forms are the means through which the new percepts and action schemes are created. The presence of such intermediate forms testifies to the constructive nature of the given process.[2] While taking a gun into one's hand certainly is constructed to afford pulling the trigger, the demand character of such an affordance is usually resisted. Human beings are not automata who act along every available affordance. In fact our ordinary conduct probably overlooks the vast variety of immediately available affordances in any setting, and blocks some of them through affectively organized semiotic over-control (Valsiner, 2001b).

Semiotic regulatory construction. Microgenesis of meaning construction entails the creation of regulatory hierarchies of signs. In a most general sense, exemplified by the act of shooting, this begins from the recognition of the affordance:

(1) PERSON   ("I can pull the trigger")
(who has taken
gun into hand)

This representation of the affordance does not lead to actual shooting. Only when it becomes regulated by a presentation, this may happen:

(2A) PERSON ("I can pull the trigger") ("I must do it") {shoots}
(who has taken
gun into hand)

(2B) PERSON ("I can pull the trigger") ("I may not do it") {does not shoot}
(who has taken
gun into hand)

In terms of semiotic regulation, 2A and 2B are of the same basic structure (but of clearly opposite outcomes):

PRESENTATION (REPRESENTATION of [ACTION POSSIBILITY])

Presentation ("I must..."; "I may not...") is a higher-level semiotic regulator that operates upon the suggestion entailed in representation of the action possibility ("I can..."). We here have thus a 2-level semiotic regulatory hierarchy, to organize the actual use of the affordance of the hand <> gun system.

But what differentiates 2A from 2B? A general semiotic presentation field (that of constructed hyper-generalized statement "I am...") regulates the meaning-making about the presentations:

(3) PERSON   Self-definition: "I am a ..."
(who has   "I **can**   ...**PACIFIST**" ("I **may not** do it") {does not shoot}
taken gun →   pull the
into hand)   trigger"   "...**PATRIOT**" ("I **must do** it") {shoots}

From here (3) suggests that a generalized self-identity—built upon values as semiotic affective fields—has a crucial role in any socialization system. The role of such identity meanings enables or blocks specific actions at relevant moments—in specific contexts. As we will see in the empirical part of this paper, as well as in other results of our projects (Capezza, 2003), the semiotic regulatory hierarchy construction can take much more complex forms than this abstract 3-level (generalized field> presentation > representation) entails. A case of such complex form is the embeddedness of the act in a context—a semiotic field that is generated by the person as she comes into contact with the particular setting in the first place.

Centrality of the feeling of "aboutness." Given the inevitable uncertainty of moving towards the future, the feeling orientation is of the general kind "SOMETHING is ABOUT to happen", or—"I DESIRE that the SOMETHING that is ABOUT to happen be X," is the central feature of human psychological worlds. What that "something" is, is not yet known—it is only anticipated. Yet the person constructs a personal-cultural frame for that anticipated event. To continue the general depiction from above, this scenario is given by the hierarchical semiotic order:

"ABOUTNESS" ORIENTATION	"we are about to go to war"
IDENTITY SIGN	"I am a patriot" / "I am a pacifist"
PRESENTATION	"I must..." / "I may not..."
REPRESENTATION of	
ACTION POSSIBILITY	"I can..."

The hierarchy here is not a linear one—it can flexibly change its structure (Poddiakov & Valsiner, 2008). Here of course it does not matter whether the feeling orientation leads to the "patriot" or "pacifist" meaning activation—in either case the setting allows for staging a personal action precisely to fit the person's set goals. Yet from the perspective of our present goals as researchers, the "truth" about the outcome (shoot or not shoot) is immaterial for our interest in the actual process of constructing the semiotic regulatory system to regulate the act. What it indicates, however, is that our experimental procedure captures only a small portion of the real-world situations where acts of destruction of something—plates, houses, ethnic groups, or forests—are being practiced.

The unified opposition of construction and destruction. The whole history of humankind—and the evolutionary process in nature—are organized around this opposition. The act of construction necessarily entails its opposite (nonconstruction), or in some cases. The very act of inventing cultural tools entails destruction of the previous state of nature—yet is fully dependent upon that nature. Most of psychology has been oriented to the study of human constructive efforts—ranging from studies of children's play to social group formation and to conflict resolution in social relations. The counterpart of construction—explicit efforts at destruction such as children's (or jealous adults') breaking of household things, nations purposefully throwing bombs on cities of other nations, and so forth—have been largely out of the focus of psychologists. The rare exceptions in classic social psychology (e.g., Milgram, 1974) have been both revered and denigrated.

However, the real socialization of human beings in any society prepares young people for tasks of both constructive and destructive kinds. The major cultural-psychological issue in these tasks is their unity—the same cultural tool (gun, knife, drugs, mass media campaigns, jealousy bouts, etc.) can, under different circumstances, be used for both functions. How is this distinction of the circumstances created?

The socialization system for constructive forms of aggression needs to be socialized at the general feeling orientations level while each destructive act by a human being is particular, context specific. Yet, each socialization context for the sake of establishing the general feeling orientation is itself a particular context! Human societies set up particular tasks for persons to direct them towards generalized orientations that can be translated into new specific acts of other kinds. The issue is the transfer of constructed meaning systems from particular contexts, through generalization, to be further re-contextualized in new contexts. This is similar to many general future-oriented and indeterminate task settings—wartime and peacetime (Simmel, 1904), preventing accidents from happening to children (Gärling & Valsiner, 1985), prevention/coping with partner violence (Arriaga & Capezza, 2005), adherence to moral norms (Menon & Shweder, 1994), and so on. Human psychological system works under constant uncertainty, and our theoretical models necessarily need to account for that (Fogel, Lyra, & Valsiner, 1997). Play and imagination are the forms of human activity that are oriented towards coping with such permanently uncertain personal worlds.

Play and Reality: From Video Games to War

Video games are everywhere these days—and so are opinions about them. Parents who worry about their adolescents "going wrong" (meaning: being different) point to the dangers or futility of these commercially provided entertainment devices. The proponents of these gadgets point to the skills they provide.

Of course video games become easy targets for attributing causality for dramatic events. In the United States we have surpassed most other countries in the frequency of high school students shooting one another and teachers on school premises, and causality for these acts clearly needs a convenient scapegoat. The media have suggested that the students involved in these shootings may have been influenced by violent video games. Yet a federal judge has dismissed a lawsuit filed by the victims of the Columbine shooting against the software companies that produce video games. The families that sued alleged that these companies influenced the actions of the two shooters (Varanini, 2002).

How central are video games in the social ecology of current childhoods? Children, ages 8-18, spend over 40 hours per week using some form of media entertainment. Boys, ages 8-13, play video games (both computer and console) over 7.5 hours per week. Adolescent and college aged individuals also frequently play video games, about 15% of college students reported playing 6 or more hours of video games a week A review of existing literature on the relationship between video games and violence shows that short-term exposure to violent video games temporarily increases aggression (Anderson & Bushman, 2001). Yet not all video games—like other toys—are the same. Many types of games, such as fantasy and adventure games, allow children to be creative and improve their problem-solving abilities (Greenfield, 1984).

What role do video games have on a long-term basis? Anderson and Dill (2000) suggest that playing violent games can have long-term negative effects, such that playing more violent video games can cause a person to become desensitized and more aggressive in outlook. In a correlational study, a positive relationship between violent video game exposure, aggressive personality, and aggressive behavior was found. Although their interpretation is tentative due to their correlational data, their claim about long-term *de*sensitization can be viewed also as one for the establishment of a metameaningful frame *for* enabling the kind of action that is being overtrained in the game context (such as shooting). Our empirical data on the microgenesis of shooting provide evidence for this viewpoint.

MEANING CONSTRUCTION IN A SHOOTING SITUATION: EMPIRICAL DATA

In our study (for full exposition, see Capezza, 2003), young adults—university students in the United States (*n* = 30) and Estonia (*n* = 40)—were asked to aim a toy gun at a screen, onto which different images of objects were projected (sequence of 18). They were told to describe each appearing image and any feelings or thoughts that they had about the image, and to make a decision to shoot or not to shoot at the image. Whether they decided to shoot or not, they were instructed to explain immediately how they reached their decision. The selection of images included those of different recognizable symbolic value. Some were neutral for shooting (e.g., regular "bull's eye" target for shooting), others were expected to work against shooting (e.g., photograph of a young girl, or an old man) as it was assumed that the socialization background of all persons includes exclusion of the act of aiming a gun towards human beings, or play-shooting them. There were still other stimuli (e.g., Hitler, member of KKK) that were supposed to trigger a conflict between the general value-laden interpretation of these images, and the prohibition against aiming and shooting.

Three stimuli—which represented three recognizable linkages with the living world are of interest in the present paper—a duck image from a video game (Duck Hunt) (see Figure 3.1a), a photo of a bronze duck sculpture (see Figure 3.1b), and that of living ducks (see Figure 3.1c).

In addition, the image of a cartoon soldier (see Figure 3.2) was utilized to further explore the influence that collective culture has on interpretations and decision-making strategies. This image depicts a cartoon U.S. soldier (wearing army fatigues) that is carrying a large gun. While the caricature is holding a large gun, he is not pointing the gun at the subject. The following examples are selected from the empirical records, for illustration of how the semiotic regulators operate within the shooting situation—with added emphases.

The symbolic nature of the Duck Hunt duck enables the following subjects to shoot at this duck; however, the subjects did not shoot at the other two nonsymbolic duck images:

U.S. #3 FEMALE

Duck Hunt: It's Duck Hunt! Ok, yeah that I have to shoot at, because I use to play this when I was little (shoots at image) ... that's a video game where you are suppose to shoot an imaginary gun at the duck and I use to play it so that comes naturally.

Bronze Duck: It looks like a make believe duckling. A statue, but it is not ... umm ... it's a statue of a duck, I'm not going to shoot because it is a statue and it's a duck ... I'm not going to deface public property.

Living Ducks: Those are real ducks. And I certainly wouldn't shoot those. They never did anything umm ... to hurt any-one and they're just swimming in a pond.

U.S. #4 FEMALE

Duck Hunt: Umm ... I see a bird on a video game and it makes me feel like playing a video game so I'd have fun and since you're suppose, the object of the game is to shoot the duck, I probably would. So, I'm going to shoot the duck. (Shoots at image)

Bronze Duck: Umm ... it's a statue of a duck. And it makes me feel like (pause 2 sec) I'm in a park so I'm having fun and

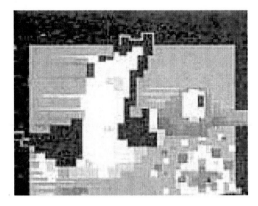

Figure 3.1a. Duck Hunt (video game) stimuli used in the study.

Figure 3.1b. Bronze Duck stimuli used in the study.

Figure 3.1c. Living Ducks stimuli used in the study.

Figure 3.2.   The soldier image
used in the study.

	I'm not gonna shoot at it because you're not suppose to shoot at ducks at the park so I don't
Living Ducks:	I see a real duck in a pond and it makes me feel happy and like I'm having fun seeing ducks. And I wouldn't shoot at it because I'd probably end up killing it and I don't want to do that.

U.S. #14 MALE

Duck Hunt:	Ha ha, it's the Duck Hunt duck. And uh, I'd be lying if I said I wouldn't shoot at it cuz I played this game like hours and hours on end so yeah I'd probably (shoots at image) have to shoot the little video game duck.
Bronze Duck:	(Pause 2 sec) No, I like that it's like a little bronze duck statue thing. I probably keep that or uh I definitely wouldn't shoot at it, it looks nice.
Living Ducks:	Oh, it's real ducks. I wouldn't shoot at them, no.

The subjects only chose to shoot at the video game duck because they had experience shooting this duck in the past (73% of the subjects that had experience playing this game shot at the image). That experience established for them the arena for action within which shooting is enabled ("videogame-ness" of the setting, created by recognition of the origin of the stimulus). Using toy guns while playing a video game is an acceptable action, however, no such norms are available for the bronze duck or the living ducks, and thus the subjects did not shoot at these images.

Differently from most of the U.S. subjects, in Estonia the same norms for shooting at the Duck Hunt duck were not as readily available. None of the subjects from Estonia who shot at the video game duck knew the specific game that the duck was from—they did not mention the game Duck Hunt or mention having played the game in the past. Some of them recognized that the image was from some video game:

ESTONIA # 5 FEMALE

Duck Hunt: It is a computer-game and I think that umm … the meaning of this computer-game is to shoot ducks. Umm.... If I am playing this game right now then I should shoot. So, I'm gonna shoot (shoots at image). I think that I missed and I am happy that I missed.

Bronze Duck: This is some mmm, … that is not real duck so I think that there is no point in shooting it. I am not gonna shoot. I don't know why, but I don't feel like shooting.

Living Ducks: Ohh, these are real ducks. I am sure that I am not gonna shoot. I like ducks, so I'm not gonna shoot.

ESTONIA #7 FEMALE

Duck Hunt: A bird, seems like sad duck who is flying away. Don't want to shoot, I love animals.

Bronze Duck: Although the bird have been drawn by computer, I can imagine the bird in its natural environment. Don't want to shoot, don't want to kill birds.

Living Ducks: Birds again! 2 ducks who want to get babies. Don't shoot, crime to kill animals.

ESTONIA #15 FEMALE

Duck Hunt: So this is a flying bird and since I don't very much eat meat and I'm against hunting so <u>I would never shoot a bird.</u>

Bronze Duck: The same thing. <u>I could never shoot at an animal.</u>

Living Ducks: This is also a bird, so… I bet if I was a hunter I would shoot them, they are so easy targets, but <u>I would not. No, I'd probably feed them.</u>

ESTONIA #31 FEMALE

Duck Hunt: Well, it is quite a confusing picture again. Oh, it is a duck. <u>I don't want to shoot at it. I think it is a beautiful little bird.</u>

Bronze Duck: A duck again. <u>It is also a very nice duck. I like it and I don't want to shoot.</u>

Living Ducks: Again birds. I like water and I like birds. <u>It is beautiful and I don't want to shoot.</u>

All of the duck images were viewed similarly, animals that could not be shot at. The theme of never hurting an animal was seen for each of the duck images. Even subject 5, who did shoot at the video game image, said that she hoped she missed. These subjects did not have the same experience of shooting at the video game duck that was shown above by the subjects from the United States.

The cartoon soldier image further shows the differences among persons from the two societies. Two examples from the U.S. are shown below:

U.S. Subject 3 (female): It's a cartoon. An army type person, a U.S. army, kind of like a Bailey type thing. <u>Umm it looks like an army person, so I think **more of a protective type than** an aggressive type. So, I'm **not** gonna shoot him. He's from the US so **he is on my side.**</u>

U.S. Subject 27 (female): Hahaha, it is a guy with his belly hanging out in an army fatigue with a shotgun. <u>He's got a thing on his hat that maybe makes me think he is part of the</u>

<u>US and he's also got a little thing on his</u> <u>belt that says US, so I don't think I</u> <u>would shoot at him because **he's proba-**</u> **bly on our side** but someone should tell him to button his coat up (laugh).

These two examples demonstrate how this image was interpreted as being a "***protective type***" and being "***on our side***." Again, like in the Duck Hunt example, specific meaning-triggering perceptual cues lead to the construction of a situation in the personal culture of the shooter, creating the action arena for not shooting. The same image can be interpreted much differently however, as we shall see:

Estonia Subject 6 (female): That's very aggressive. This man is<u> aggressive </u>and also his big gun<u> symbol-</u> <u>izes aggressiveness</u>…. And his pose how he's standing there…. I feel it makes me aggressive and I want to shoot (shoots at image).

Estonia Subject 22 (female): Give me shoot (shoots at image) … because <u>it seems too bad and mean.</u>

Estonia Subject 34 (female): The picture<u> associates with shooting, so</u> I shoot at this (shoots at image).

Estonia Subject 1 (female): <u>It is a very unpleasant man with a</u> <u>machine gun. I still don't want to shoot</u> <u>him because violence gives birth to vio-</u> <u>lence and so on</u>, it's a never ending cycle, so if there would be any problems with him I would try to talk them out. (did not shoot)

These subjects' reports illustrate how the same image can be viewed differently depending on each person's background and personal culture. The two subjects from the United States thought the soldier was positive and protecting "us" while the subjects from Estonia saw the image as negative and "aggressive." Some of them chose to shoot at the image, others did not. Using the microgenetic method allowed us to assess how a person develops their own meaning constructions—from initial impression to shooting decision to reassessing or justifying the decision.

Each society has their own norms associated with what is and what is not acceptable to be shot. Children from the United States have grown accustom to "shooting" certain images in the course of playing a video game. We have shown above how this simple cartoon duck can be seen as both a target to be shot and as a beautiful animal that should never be harmed. Similarly, the cartoon soldier was viewed as a protective force and also as an aggressive violent image. In some instances shooting is accepted and in others it is forbidden. Yet the decision about which instance is which is made by individual persons-in-contexts.

CONCLUSION: CULTURAL ARENAS FOR ACTION

Socialization *for* potential violence takes place in a disguise of the primacy of social discourse *condemning* violence. Condemning aggression easily becomes an act of aggression itself—a fierce fight for the cause of peace is an act of war (even if a symbolic one). In a paradoxical way, trying to promote peace may actually prepare human beings for its opposite (Simmel, 1904). The introduction of peace-keeping military troops in warring areas is not an act of peace, but one of (meta)war that may suppress the present conflict by military threats.

From a perspective that is based on contemporary cultural psychology, the unity of violence and nonviolence is not a paradox, but a regular feature of human cultural self-organization. In the human dialogical minds (Hermans, 2001; Marková, 1990) the opposite sides of meanings are closely linked. Creating one of the opposites (A) sets the stage for the other—a field consisting of a range of various counterpart (non-A, see Josephs, Valsiner, & Surgan, 1999). Thus, by setting up a violence-free environment for developing children we may inadvertently create the basis for the construction of violent acts by some of the developing children. The overly "sanitized" environment of no aggression allowed, suggested, or even hinted may lead to the construction of bouts of violence at unexpected moments, by adolescents who have always been seen by others as epitomes of peacefulness. Yet they may—even at an instance of thrill-seeking (Lightfoot, 1997)—create a new feeling for themselves through an unexpected act of violence.

An analogy with the immune system may be useful—if children were to grow up in a totally germless environment and never become infected, the success of such "purity of environments" may be actually a failure. Their immune systems would not be ready to cope with new infections. In a similar vein, if children are kept away from observing the horrors of violence (and see it on TV screens or video games) their semiotic regulatory system may be unprepared to block their own move into violence. In countries where most people own guns (e.g., Israel) violent uses of those are rare, as compared to other countries where guns are kept far away from children. It is the contextualization—cultural regulation—of when to use (or not use) these instruments that leads to one or another outcome. Socialization processes work on making distinction between different catalysts—meanings that create the situation—which then block or enable the action sequences.

Creating arenas for action. In general we can describe socialization as a process for creating for the developing person an interconnected system of *arenas for action*. These arenas are organized by semiotic catalysts that "carry" the person to a particular arena, rather than another. These arenas operate by modulating the psychological distance (see Cupchik, 2002; Sigel, 2002) between the actor and the act. Before the act has actually been accomplished—in the beginning phase of it—its consequences are not clear. It is thus possible to consider the ongoing reality *as if it were* a game. Furthermore, it is possible to prepare the actors in the distanced "as-if-a-game" domain for actions that can be made to lose the distance from reality when need be. Hence the possibility that video games—more than violent movies because the latter are void of immediate participation by the persons—constitute an arena where the act of aiming a gun and pulling the trigger is being socialized on materials that are not in and by themselves leading to increased immediate violence. Rather, such "as-if-a-game" is just one of the parts of the causal system that—when constituted as a system—guarantees the participation of the person in violence. Furthermore, video game playing need not even be a necessary part of such a system—wars existed for centuries before video games ever came into existence. It may be a facilitating part of the system, which has the social representations of *hunting* and *nonhumanizing the opponent* in its core. Hunting has been part of human activities in the phylogenetic history of the species, and making ingroup/outgroup distinctions with down-valuation of the latter is a basic state of social group dynamics. Under circumstances of peace, these obligatory components (as well as facilitative ones) may be organized in a loose form (quasi-differentiated state). Once there is the move from peace-time towards war-time, or in personal cultural world—the constructed need to eliminate the opponent—it is only then that the parts of the psychological system become hierarchically integrated into a functional system that makes violence possible. Not so long ago, Georg Simmel (1904) had a similar idea:

> the state of peace within the group permits antagonistic elements to live side by side in a somewhat undecided situation, because each may go his own way and may avoid collisions. The state of conflict, however, draws the elements so closely together that they either tolerate each other with perfect reciprocity, or they must completely repel each other. On this account foreign war, in the case of a state split by internal antitheses, is often the ultimate means of overcoming the same. It also happens that the foreign war may, however, give occasion for fatal development of these antipathies. (p. 676)

Systemic transformational causality. There is a general principle observable here—that of conditional temporary causal systems (see Figure 3.3) Causal systems can be temporarily assembled—hence we can talk of *systemic transformational causality*. When the parts of a causal system are prepared separately, but their synthesis left to the time of need for its full function, we get the picture not only of systemic causality in operation, but of the contextually assembled causal system. When not needed, none of its differentiated parts is effective separately.

How would the notion of systemic transformational causality explain the examples from our data? Young people may play video games or watch violent movies, but no direct outcome of that to their acting violently is empirically demonstrable. Likewise, people may develop prejudices against some outgroup but, again, these prejudices by themselves do not lead to violence against the group. Guns may be available in a society, together with internalized social norms against aiming them at fellow human beings and pulling the trigger. Unless these norms break down in

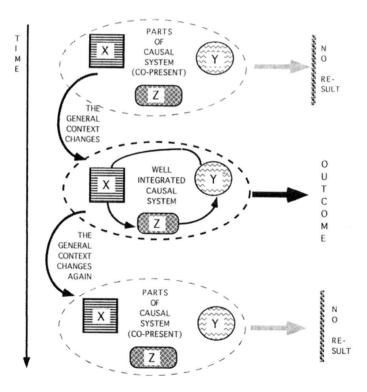

Figure 3.3.   Systemic transformational causality.

some individual cases the guns remain unused. At the same time—again in a separate vein—hunting is an accepted, socially legitimate pastime for some of the population, some of the time. Yet hunting is directed to animals of the kind that are socially accepted as "huntable" and not towards one's next-door neighbor. As long as all these elements coexist in a society in parallel, there will be no empirically demonstrable "effects" of each of those on the potential or actual violent actions of the people involved in all of them: playing video games, watching horror or action movies, going hunting, keeping a gun at home, or gossiping maliciously about neighbors or—publicly—about some foreigners.

All this changes when—under the catalytic role of a general change of social atmosphere—these elements become constituted as a causal system. Then the video-game player, as well as hunters, and gossipers, may all line up to join an army, rebel force, or an "ethnic cleansing" squad, and genocide is in the making. The move from ordinary life to violence is prepared by most ordinary everyday ways of living and takes place in concrete everyday life settings. Yet its microgenesis entails the semiotic setup of the arena for violent actions.

We thus can place the role of contemporary action constraining devices—such as video games—into a wider perspective. We look at them in the historical participation in basic human lives. Like any other device of its kind, video games can be made to be a part in the system that sets up the arena for violent action. Yet in and by itself—isolated from the texture of coordination of acting, feeling, and thinking—playing video games has no sufficient power to be the arena for violence, nor evoke a violent act itself. It is also not a necessary part of the arena-generating system. Since video games have been invented as consumer products, they can be turned into parts of that system, but if they are not available something else takes (and has taken, all over history) that role. The recurrence of violence in its many disguises all over human history remains a basic—even if undesirable—feature of human psychology. It is built on the basic CONSTRUCTION <> non-CONSTRUCTION oppositional meaning of which the violence <> nonviolence complex is one small part.

Cultural psychology thus can explain both the making and nonmaking of violence in our human lives. Yet it cannot prevent it—as the mechanisms for violent action can be assembled in different conditions, and are well prepared by the needs of different social forces. As shown above, useful insights about these mechanisms and conditions can be ascertained through the microgenetic method. Such studies are essential components to gaining a better understanding of the process behind why a person may or may not act violently.

ACKNOWLEDGEMENTS

We would like to thank everyone in Estonia, especially Kersti Jakobi and Liina Kadari, and Kadi Liik at the psychology department of Tallinn University for all of their assistance in this work. Part of the work was supported by the Colin Creativity Award of the first author, and to Clark University faculty travel fund and the Hiatt Fund to the second author. The authors were also awarded the Lee Gurel Prize of Clark University for this work in 2002. A preliminary version of this chapter was presented at the 5th International Baltic Psychology Conference, Tartu, August, 23, 2002.

NOTES

1. Around 40% of U.S. households have guns, but the percent of intrahousehold gun use violence is not at a comparable level.
2. In cases where constructivity is denied—such as James Gibson's ecological psychology—the actions studied are indeed of the kind where the organism needs to relate with the environment through immediate mutuality. These are actions that require speedy coordination of the agent and the environment. Undoubtedly such tasks exist, yet it would not be adequate to reduce all of human action to full complementarity with the environment. It is precisely through semiotic means that the person can transcend the here-and-now action demands and refuse to act, or create a goal for action that goes beyond the immediate fit to the environmental demands.

REFERENCES

Anderson, C. A., & Bushman, B. J. (2001). Effects of violent video games on aggressive behavior, aggressive cognition, aggressive affect, physiological arousal, and prosocial behavior: A meta-analytic review of the scientific literature. *Psychological Science, 12*, 353-359.

Anderson, C., & Dill, K. (2000). Video games and aggressive thoughts, feelings, and behavior in the laboratory and in life. *Journal of Personality and Social Psychology, 78*, 772-790.

Arias, E., Anderson, R. N., Kung, H., Murphy, S. L., & Kochanek, K. D. (2004). Deaths: Final data for 2001. *National Vital Statistics Reports, 50*(15). Retrieved June 16, 2005, from http://www.cdc.gov/nchs/data/nvsr/nvsr52/nvsr52_03.pdf

Arriaga, X. B., & Capezza, N. M. (2005). Targets of partner violence: The importance of understanding coping trajectories. *Journal of Interpersonal Violence, 20*, 89-99.

Capezza, N. M. (2003). The cultural-psychological foundations for violence and nonviolence: An empirical study. *Forum: Qualitative Social Research* [Online

Journal], 4(2). Retrieved July 13, 2005, from http://www.qualitative-research.net/fqs-texte/2-03/2-03capezza-e.htm

Cupchik, G. C. (2002). The evolution of psychical distance as an aesthetic concept. *Culture & Psychology, 8*, 155-187.

Estonian Human Development Report. (2000). Society and culture: Homicide rates in Estonia and Europe. Tallinn, Estonia: Author.

Fogel, A., Lyra, M. C. D. P., & Valsiner, J. (Eds.). (1997). *Dynamics and indeterminism in developmental and social processes*. Mahwah, NJ: Erlbaum.

Gärling, T., & Valsiner, J. (Eds.). (1985). *Children within environments: Towards a psychology of accident prevention*. New York: Plenum.

Gigerenzer, G., Todd, P., & ABC Group. (1999). *Simple heuristics that make us smart*. New York: Oxford University Press.

Green, L. (2002). Fear as a way of life. In A. L. Hinton (Ed.), *Genocide: An anthropological reader* (pp. 307-333). Oxford, England: Blackwell.

Greenfield, P. M. (1984). *Mind and media: The effects of television, video games, and computers*. Cambridge, MA: Harvard University Press.

Grossmann, D. (1996). *On killing*. Boston: Little Brown.

Gupta, S., & Valsiner, J. (2003). Myths and minds: implicit guidance for human conduct. In I. E. Josephs (Ed.), *Dialogicality in development* (pp. 179-195). Westport, CT: Praeger.

Hermans, H. (2001). The dialogical self: Toward a theory of personal and cultural positioning. *Culture & Psychology, 7*, 243-281.

Hermans, H. J. (Ed.). (2002). Special Issue on dialogical self. *Theory & Psychology, 12*(2), 147-280.

Hoffrage, U., Kurzenhaeuser, S., & Gigerenzer, G. (2005). Results of medical testings: Why the representation of statistical information matters. In R. Bibace, J. Laird, K. Noller, & J. Valsiner (Eds.), *Science and medicine indialogue: Particulars and universals* (pp. 83-98). Stamford, CT: Greenwood.

Josephs, I. E., Valsiner, J., & Surgan, S. E. (1999). The process of meaning construction. In J. Brandtstädter and R. M. Lerner (Eds.), *Action & self development* (pp. 257-282). Thousand Oaks, CA: Sage.

Klausner, S. Z. (1987). Violence. In M. Eliade (Ed.), *The encyclopedia of religion*. (Vol. 15, pp. 268-272). New York: MacMillan.

Krug, E. G., Powell, K. E., & Dahlberg, L. L. (1998). Firearm-related deaths in the United States and 35 other high- and upper-middle-income countries. *International Journal of Epidemiology, 27*, 214-221.

Lewin, K. (1917). Kriegeslandschaft. *Zeitschrift für angewandte Psychologie, 12*, 440-447.

Lightfoot, C. L. (1997). *The culture of adolescent risk-taking*. New York: Guilford.

Marková, I. (1990). A three-step process as a unit of analysis in dialogue. In I. Markova & K. Foppa (Eds.), *The dynamics of dialogue* (pp. 129-146). Hemel Hampstead: Harvester.

Meinong, A. (1983). *On assumptions*. Berkeley, CA: University of California Press.

Menon, U., & Shweder, R. A. (1994). Kali's tongue: Cultural psychology and the power of "shame" in Orissa. In S. Kitayama & H. Markus (Eds.), *Emotion and culture* (pp 237-280). Washington, DC: American Psychological Association.

Milgram, S. (1974). *Obedience to authority*. New York: Holt.

Office of Juvenile Justice and Delinquency Prevention. (1998). *Gun violence in the United States: Promising strategies to reduce gun violence.* Retrieved June 28, 2005, from http://www.ojjdp.ncjrs.org/pubs/gun_violence/sect01.html

Poddiakov, A. N., & Valsiner, J. (2008). Intransitivity cycles and their transformations: How dynamically adapting systems function? In L. Rudolph & J. Valsiner (Eds.), *Qualitative mathematics for the social sciences.* London: Routledge.

Salgado, J., & Hermans, H. J. M. (2005). The return of subjectivity: from a multiplicity of selves to the dialogical self. *E-Journal of Applied Psychology: Clinical Section, 1*(1), 3-13. Retrieved from http://www.swin.edu.au/lib/ir/onlinejournals/ejap

Sen'yavskaya, E. S. (1999). *Psikhologia voiny v 20om veke.* [Psychology of war in the 20th century] Moscow: ROSSPEN.

Sigel, I. E. (2002). The psychological distancing model: A study of the socialization of cognition. *Culture & Psychology, 8,* 189-214.

Simmel, G. (1904). The sociology of conflict. *American Journal of Sociology, 9,* 490-525; 672-689; 798-811.

Tversky, A., & Kahnemann, D. (1982). Evidential impact of base rates. In D. Kahneman, P. Slovic, & A. Tversky (Eds.), *Judgment under uncertainty* (pp. 153-160). Cambridge, London: Cambridge University Press.

Valsiner, J. (1997). *Culture and the development of children's action* (2nd ed.). New York: Wiley.

Valsiner, J. (2000). *Culture and human development.* London: Sage.

Valsiner, J. (2001a). Process structure of semiotic mediation in human development. *Human Development, 44,* 84-97.

Valsiner, J. (2001b, September 5). *Cultural developmental psychology of affective processes.* Invited Lecture at the 15. Tagung der Fachgruppe Entwicklungspsychologie der Deutschen Gesellschaft für Psychologie, Potsdam.

Valsiner, J. (2003). Enabling theories of enablement: In search for a theory-method link. *Papers on Social representations, 12,* 7.1-7.16 [http://www.psr.jku.at]

Valsiner, J. (2005) Affektive Entwicklung im kulturellen Kontext [Affective develoopment in cultural context]. In J. Asendorpf (Ed.), *Enzyklopädie der Psychologie* (Vol. 3, pp. 677-728). *Soziale, emotionale und Persönlichkeitsentwicklung.* Göttingen: Hogrefe.

Valsiner, J., & van der Veer, R. (2000). *The social mind: Construction of the idea.* New York: Cambridge University Press.

Varanini, G. (2002). Judge dismisses Columbine lawsuit. *GameSpot VG.* Retrieved April 20, 2002, from http://www.gamespot.com/news/2852842.html

CHAPTER 4

THE NEED FOR MICROGENETIC ANALYSIS OF SEMIOTIC FIELDS IN SOCIAL PSYCHOLOGY

Gyuseog Han

No other age than the current has seen so much violence, extending into every facet of life. Graphical images of violence, such as those from 9/11, are as extreme as they are real. Maybe people are over saturated with such violence and become immune. In spite of many models proposed by psychologists, psychological explanations of violent acts, from fist fighting to suicide bombing, have not been satisfactory. Experimental social psychologists have long been dealing with the frustration-aggression theory and social learning theory. These theories are based on a stimulus-response framework. When a person is situated in the "right" context, he or she engages in violent acts. Perhaps, the most puzzling yet intriguing phenomenon is that people engage in violent acts very selectively even in seemingly identical situations. This difference is usually treated as inviting further investigation of situational characteristics prompting violence (such as stress, provocative events) or is simply treated as individual precariousness or unpredictability and thus, left unaccounted for.

Innovating Genesis: Microgenesis and the Constructive Mind in Action, pp. 93–105
Copyright © 2008 by Information Age Publishing
All rights of reproduction in any form reserved.

It is this theoretical vacuum that Capezza and Valsiner's (this volume) work addresses. Not only filling this vacuum, the authors move beyond to present a scheme of understanding societal violence. The approach the authors present here is very distinctive, contrasting sharply with a more traditional approach. As a commentator, being trained in the discipline of social psychology, I will compare the approach taken here with the more traditional approach in social psychology to the topic of violence and aggression. By doing so, I hope to make the value of Capezza and Valsiner's current approach clear, and to point out possibilities for future work.

ISSUES IN THE TRADITIONAL SOCIAL PSYCHOLOGICAL APPROACH TO VIOLENCE AND AGGRESSION

Since social violence and aggressive acts are everyday occurrences, the topic has never failed to attract research attention. Many models and theories have been proposed, such as the frustration-aggression theory, social learning theory (Bandura, 1973), the cognitive neoassociation model (Berkowitz, 1984), the social information processing model (Dodge & Crick, 1990), the affective aggression models (Anderson, Deuser, & DeNeve, 1995; Geen, 1990), and the excitation transfer model (Zillman, 1983). These traditions are not all alike; for example, the frustration-aggression theory is linked to a psychoanalytic approach and many others are linked to the learning and information processing approaches. Despite this diversity of intellectual heritage, all approaches do share some common features.

First, all view aggression and violence as seen as a distinctive and problematic social behavior which is very much responsible for causing societal problems and malaise. It is a behavior in the human repertoire needing special treatment. This view postulates that special circumstances, bad learning, or bad character can predispose one to violence. Research efforts have tried to establish the specific relationship among those determinants and aggression.

Second, all view human beings as mechanistic information processors (cf. Pepper, 1942/1961). The notion of information processing is not used in the frustration-aggression model. But this view is much taken by the theory: input of a frustrating event leads to output of an aggressive act. The main feature of this view posits that behaviors are outputs of information processing of various inputs (situational properties & perception) and intermediaries (i.e., schema & scripts). To state it more extremely: aggression is almost an automatic outcome given aggression eliciting stimuli which cue aggression schema or scripts. "Whether an aggressive behavior is emitted depends on what behavioral scripts have been activated by the various input variables and the appraisal processes. Well-learned scripts come to mind relatively easily and quickly and can be emitted fairly automatically" (Anderson & Dill, 2000, p. 774).

The dominant concern is what situational characteristics (frustrating events, high temperature, stress, provocation, etc.) invite aggressive thinking and behaviors, and how the information process can be mapped out. Once it is mapped out, the solution follows to prevent those situational cues and to block and/or rechannel the cognitive flow.

All these common threads contain some basic thorny problems which are hard to deal with from the perspective of the traditional approach. First is the problem of human agency. Human beings are agentive beings; they are not merely responding passively to situational properties with a repertoire of cognition, scripts, and behaviors. They are intentional beings. This intention is backed up by their own meaning system which is created uniquely across individuals and over time (Bruner, 1990). To defend against this criticism, recent social psychological models posit an important role of cognition. They insert evaluation or appraisal of situational cues operating in the process. But then again, this evaluation is linked to some established schema or scripts which may or may not lead to aggression depending upon the evoked schema. This concept deals with some part of the criticism. However, two main theses are barely touched:

First, an agentive mind allows for a totally different unfolding of new behavior and thinking, for better or worse. For example, hijacking an airplane in order to collide into the World Trade Center was beyond anybody's imagination. This kind of unprecedented act is the basic faculty of human minds for survival in uncertain environments. Uncertainty in the environment poses ever new tasks for survival (Valsiner, 1987). Humans do not merely react but also proact to uncertainty. Positing cognition to explain agency does not adequately deal with this proactivity problem as long as the cognition is treated as part of a reaction system.

Second is the issue of individual differences. Individual differences have been a favorite dish on the menu for psychologists. To account for aggressive behavioral difference among individuals, personality models have been proposed, such as authoritarianism (Rokeach, 1984), type A (Strube, 1989), and narcissistic personality (David & Kistner, 2000) However, such personality traits have at best weak correlation with behavior. This weak relationship is mainly because even those individuals who score high for such personalities are not consistently aggressive. Aggression can serve at times as an adaptive behavior on a contextual basis. When the social context changes, a new meaning complex is constructed, resulting in different behaviors. Aggressive personality, if exist, fails to be adaptive and thus, has to be linked weakly to aggressive behavior.

Another thorny problem lies in the constructional nature of violence in society. That is, there is no inherently aggressive behavior distinguishable from nonviolence. Aggression and violence are socially constructed phenomena. As Capezza and Valsiner note, the same act of shooting a gun at another individual is violent if done by a criminal but nonviolent if done by a policeman. Shooting a gun at the target is acceptable in a shooting range or in a video game but is prohibited in the schoolyard and home. Despite this contextual change, the same shooting behavior may come out. But then the behavior is the result of totally different meaning systems. Capezza and Valsiner showed that even in the seemingly identical setting of holding a gun, the different stimuli on the screen elicit different general meaning complexes or social representations, which elicit a different action (shooting or not shooting). This representation works as a catalyst in guiding the gun-holder into one or another trajectory (that is, shooting or not-shooting).

Due to the social construction of violence, living in the reality of a violent environment does not necessarily influence people to act violently. As the authors contend, Capezza (2003) showed that the Estonian participants tend to refrain from shooting the target more than the U.S. participants did. The same shooting behavior is conceived differently in the two countries. In the laboratory, even repeated exposure to violent media does not make people aggressive (see Anderson & Dill, 2000 for summary). The same behavior is violent in one context and nonviolent in another context.

CONTRIBUTION AND ISSUE OF
THE CAPEZZA AND VALSINER APPROACH

Capezza and Valsiner's approach to violence throws a new light on the problem of social violence as it has been dealt with by traditional social psychology. Two features are most distinctive in their approach: semiotic regulators and microgenetic analysis.

Semiotic Regulators (SR)

Capezza and Valsiner's most prominent distinction from traditional social psychology is their view of the human being. Instead of positing the human being as a computer like information processor, they posit humans as meaning makers (Bruner, 1990; Gergen, 1999). Personal acts are governed by the meaning system they derive under a given context. Between the moment of facing a situation and the moment of acting humans are going through a semiotic world in which they construct and even create meaning systems by using and manipulating various symbols and signs. Unlike the cognitive world which is filled up with various schemas and scripts, the semiotic world is a mediated world where symbols and signs are used to create meaning complexes whose characteristics are fundamentally dynamic, uncertain, and unpredictable.

Taking this perspective, pulling a trigger is not an automatic (learned) response even at certain situations. Persons do (or do not) pull the trigger not because of some automated reaction pattern or some situation-provoked-cognition. The decision is primarily dependent upon what SR is provoked and how it operates in each individual. So, a cartoon duck can be seen as both a target to be shot and as a beautiful animal to be protected. This meaning construction either enables the act of shooting or blocks it. The decision to shoot or not to shoot is made by the individual person-in-context, depending upon the meaning constructed.

SR is a very useful theoretical concept. Its function is multiple. First, it can fill the theoretical gap between the situational determinants and behavior. SR allows common aggression-triggering situational characteristics; this represents typical research questions in social psychology. It does not obliterate the previous approach but allows for significant leaps beyond the existing theoretical deadlock. Second, it also allows individual variations, as under the same situation one's personal culture (which is broader than the concept of personality) interacts with the situation, creating different meaning systems; this has been treated as unpredictability or error variance in social psychology. Finally, the use of SR allows for individual inconsistency across similar situations (Molenaar, 2003); this is not due to some precariousness of the individual but due to the variation of SR constructed at different times while facing the same situation.

SR is a very general, abstract, flexible, and encompassing theoretical concept. These features are both its strength and weakness. It serves very fittingly to develop a grand scheme of analysis for human behavior, as partly shown in the authors' analysis. Although the scheme can be nicely organized, it is not without problems. The foremost problem is that SR is not specific enough to provide a realistic understanding of behavior. Because of the unpredictable nature of SR, we can not predict what semiotic regulator is to be constructed at the given situation, what it characteristics are, and how it operates in influencing behavior. Capezza and Valsiner (p. 74, this volume) state that "the 'truth' about the outcome (shoot or not shoot) is immaterial for our interest in the actual process of constructing the semiotic regulatory system to regulate the act." If the outcome is concerned, however, the outcome can not be predicted, for the SR can vary unpredictably. We can speculate the type of SR from the resulting behavior or thinking. This can be regarded as tautological. A similar problem has been raised against the concept of social representation by Bertacco (2003). Semiotic regulator is a more encompassing concept than social representation. The former seems to place more emphasis on the procedural quality while the latter seems to posses more of an entity quality. But Valsiner (2003a, 2003b) notes an important property of those concepts. According to him, both SR and social representations work as a node-like or field-like constructs; a semiotic regulator will "emerge for the moment in which it functions (and then disappear) or become fixed as a collective-cultural meaning complex" (Valsiner, 2003b, p. 12.3). In this case, it may be impossible to prove its existence or operation via traditional experimental methodology. It is precisely here that microgenetic analysis is needed to see the operation of SR.

Microgenetic Approach

Capezza and Valsiner took a microgenetic approach which is rarely employed in social psychological research. A microgenetic approach is the sequential analysis of events which are assumed to occur in the temporal period between the presentation of a stimulus and the formation of a single, relatively stable cognitive response (percept or thought) to this stimulus (Flavell & Dragus, 1957, p. 197). This method, underutilized in psychology, and is a promising method for disclosing causal and genetic relationships.

In a typical experiment, the researchers preselect independent variables which are expected to exert influences on dependent variables. For example, the kind of video games may be taken as an independent variable to see whether viewing them differentially influences aggressive thoughts and behaviors. The results may validate the researcher's hypothesis or may not. Because of the time sequence, a causal relationship is established in case of expected results. This does not mean the postulated causal relationship is the only relationship possible. A reverse relationship can be postulated and experimentally validated in the same manner. Of course, the causal relationship between an independent variable and a dependent variable may not be direct but mediated through unknown variables. Nevertheless, the relationship is treated as a direct relationship. Later studies, however, may show the mediated relationship, disproving the direct relationship. The emergence of the cognitive revolution in psychology to replace behavioral psychology is a case of illustrating the importance of such mediatory roles.

Another point regarding the experiment is that it shows frozen slices of working relationships among the variables. Then the explanation tries to sketch out the field where those variables are taken. Experimentation deals with variables taken from the field where only those variables picked up for investigation are allowed to vary, and only in predetermined ways. Thus, we do not know how those variables are working in reality where the field is never frozen (cf. Lewin, 1936). Unlike the traditional experimental approach, microgenetic analysis tries to approach the field without "freezing" it. It allows the existing variables, expected ones and unexpected ones, to exert influences in many possible ways. It allows generation of new variables and thus, new microgenetic development becomes revealed. Several types of different microgenetic analysis have been reported (see the other chapters in this volume). It is best when used with data sequentially obtained as in developmental studies; such cases show how the changes are generated.

Issues Concerning the Analysis

Capezza and Valsiner ask what makes people pull the trigger discerningly and what specific process underlying any particular decision making. They start from the scene where a participant is holding a gun in his/her hand and faces a target on a screen in a game-like setting. Starting there to the moment of pulling the trigger or lowering the gun, each individual goes through the semiotic field where individuals construct the semiotic regulatory system to regulate the act of pulling or not-pulling the trigger.

The verbal protocol presented in the preceding chapter showed the types of SR emerging upon seeing the target on the screen; they were games, hunting, animal protection, and so forth. Capezza and Valsiner conclude that videogame experience has established for the participants (especially for U.S. participants) an arena for action within which shooting is enabled. Admitting this conclusion seems hardly arguable. But, there is one concern. A full report of the data (Capezza, 2003) showed that the majority of U.S. participants (56.7%) shoot the duck's computerized image but only small number of Estonian participants (17.5%) shoot it. Both groups alike did not shoot the other images (bronze duck & real duck). Apparently, only the game or game-like SR led to the shooting. It is somewhat odd, though, that the shooting of images other than the "duck-hunting" computer game was so rare for participants from both countries. It is because in the semiotic field many types of SR compete or one semiotic regulator can easily replace the other. For example, "live" ducks in the experiment/study are just images, not the real duck. In many computer games, the images portrayed to represent animals are computer graphics which often are hard to distinguish from the real ones. Therefore, the real duck image in the game-like setting as employed in the current experiment should easily invite shooting as well. Then we may question "why is shooting such a rare occurrence in the experiment?" Considering the many possibilities of shooting, the rareness of shooting may be an outcome of experimental artifacts. Maybe the participants were more concerned with how they appear to others (i.e., the researcher); apparently the verbal reports did not show this at explicit level. Most of the verbal reports at facing the real-duck image portray the participants as nice animal lovers, environmentalists, or/and violence haters. It appears that the participants chose behavior that was allowed by social norms; the game ducks were shot and art-pieces/real ducks were not shot. Capezza and Valsiner state that "using toy guns while playing a videogame is an acceptable action. No such norms are available for the bronze duck or the living ducks, and thus the participants did not shoot at these images." It may be more likely that instead of absence of norms, other norms or concerns become more salient when faced with the living ducks. Yet people's concern regarding violence involves the opposite; shooting a "target" against the norms. Therefore, we are left with the question "what about shooting at inappropriate targets?" This question was not raised in Capezza and Valsiner's experiment because no such shooting occurred.

Regarding this concern, two issues can be raised. One is that "is the semiotic regulator really called upon?" Answering "yes" is not fully warranted due to the methodology they used in this work. The participants were asked to *think aloud* while they are coming up with the decision of shooting or not. This procedure may not reflect solely what is being processed sequentially in their mind. The narration is a process of thinking and expressing themselves publicly. A host of psychological concerns come into play here: rationalizing their preference, guarding against negative evaluation from social audiences (e.g., the experimenter), seeking positive evaluation, weighing different norms. The narration in one situation is more of association than of genesis. What is not known furthermore is that the reported thinking process may be somewhat removed from the actual psychological process. It is entirely plausible that some rudimentary affective reaction determines the decision, and verbalization serves to merely rationalize it. Treating the verbal report as the psychological process may not lead to the right picture of the genetic process (cf. Nisbett & Wilson, 1977).

The second question is closely related to the first but more to the method issue. Is the use of microgenetic analysis appropriate for this kind of verbal data? Verbal data is *sine qua non* to see the psychological process. But the current data is not showing the sequence of the thinking process. The data is the products of narrated associational thinking, but that narration does not necessarily reveal sequence. Therefore, it is not proper to treat the data in a genetic sense. Capezza and Valsiner managed to get away from this criticism by taking the microgenetic analysis only to get a picture of SR operation; however, the emergence of SR remains obscure.

Societal Violence: A Scheme of Systemic Transformational Causality

Moving beyond their analysis of data, Capezza and Valsiner propose a theoretical scheme, analyzing destruction and construction at the societal level. According to the scheme, all those violence-prone elements (e.g., violent games, horror movies, hunting, negative stereotypes, etc.) coexist in a society without effects on violence. It argues that a causal system, however, gets constituted where all those elements become causal factors, affecting violence when the social atmosphere changes to play the role of catalyst. When a new social atmosphere takes place, replacing the old one, the symbolic unity (such as in-group/out-group distinction) and the activity constraints (such as taking the in-group identity) set the cultural arena for communal violence (see also Kakar, 1996). Different general meaning complexes, or social representations, act as catalysts in the move into another trajectory. This scheme can serve as a working model for further work.

It is a very interesting scheme to explain genocide. Previously, moral disengagement, dehumanization, routinization, and obedience were proposed as the psychological mechanisms which enable people to commit behavior leading to mass destruction (Bandura, 1999; Kelman & Hamilton, 1988; Milgram, 1974). These mechanisms are probably the constructs working under the atmosphere of genocide. The change or forming of such an atmosphere is left to other disciplines, such as politics, history, and so forth. It will be an important task to understand how the catalysts shape up and generate the change for an integrated causal system. Many such cases, including *jihad* (the holy war) hitherto unaccounted for, become targets for this type of analysis from a psychological perspective.

CONCLUSION

The influence of violent media on society has been widely speculated upon, especially since the infamous Columbine shooting in 1999, resulting in 13 deaths. Since the two killers were high school boys playing addictively a violent computer game, violent video games become an easy culprit for such tragic events, due to the similarities of the shooting in reality and in game situations. However, simple transfer of the game scene into reality does not seem to be a sensible answer.

Capezza and Valsiner took a creative approach, noting that the move from ordinary life to violence is prepared by mundane ways of daily living. Employing the semiotic framework, they postulated that violent acts are a transfer of constructed meaning systems from a particular context to a new context which may not be similar to the former. They chose a video game and showed that playing a violent video game can serve as a setting for creating arenas for violent action.

The important difference between experimental social psychological approaches to aggression and the current approach is that the situational constraints and personal characteristics are emphasized in the former. On the other hand, semiotic constraints are emphasized in the latter. It is important to point out that aggression is not a guaranteed response to certain situational contexts, but its expression is dependent upon the meaning system operating under the context. Therefore, the curious finding that violent media exposure does not necessarily increase violent behavior (Anderson & Dill, 2000) can be explained. Although Capezza and Valsiner approach is different from the traditional social psychological approach to aggression, some reconciliation is also possible. As Capezza and Valsiner note, the desensitization effect caused by the long-term exposure to violent media (Anderson & Dill, 2000) can be viewed as the establishment of a metameaningful frame for enabling the kind of action that is being overtrained in the game context (such as shooting).

Although there are issues not adequately dealt with in the present work, they can not decrease the value of their effort and of the potential contribution to social psychology. I find the discipline of social psychology has much to gain by incorporating Capezza and Valsiner's approach to various social phenomena. First, the theoretical frame of semiotic mediation can serve to reconcile many contradictory findings in social psychology. The results of empirical investigations show often inconsistencies, brewing controversies, including the relationship between self-esteem and aggression (Bushman & Baumeister, 1998), the universality of the self-enhancing tendency across cultures (Heine, 2005; Heine, Lehman, Markus, & Kitayama, 1999), the cathartic effect of watching violent movie (Bushman, Baumeister, & Phillips, 2001), the nature of the groupthink phenomenon (McCauley, 1989), and so on. Most of these controversies originate from the view of human beings as a mechanistic information processor. As Capezza and Valsiner's paper clearly shows, a slight variation of the context can construct different meaning complexes, leading to different behavior. Therefore, theoretical incorporation of the notion of a meaning maker (Bruner, 1990) can contribute greatly in resolving the contradiction and inconsistencies in social psychology. This can also help to resolve the theoretical fragmentation attack mounting against social psychology (Bertacco, 2003; Valsiner, 2003a, 2005). Second, incorporation of the microgenetic approach can help move the discipline to take a field theoretic approach (Lewin, 1936). Such an approach was originally proposed by Lewin, the forefather of the discipline, but later almost entirely forgotten in social psychology. Third, the microgenetic approach can enrich the array of methods in social psychology. It is no exaggeration that currently there are mainly two methods available; experimentation and survey research. Consequently, the discipline has been filled with method-bound research. Research interest has been guided by the methods not by the questions (see Branco & Valsiner, 1997; Diriwächter & Valsiner, 2005). It is not the phenomena but the method which is directing the research effort. This practice alienates the discipline from the phenomena.

REFERENCES

Anderson, C., & Dill, K. (2000). Video games and aggressive thoughts, feelings, and behavior in the laboratory and in life. *Journal of Personality and Social Psychology, 78,* 772-790.

Anderson, C. A., Deuser, W. E., & DeNeve, K. M. (1995). Hot temperatures, hostile affect, hostile cognition, and arousal: Tests of a general model of affective aggression. *Personality and Social Psychology Bulletin, 21,* 434-448.

Bandura, A. (1973). *Aggression: A social learning analysis.* Englewood Cliffs, NJ: Prentice-Hall.

Bandura, A. (1999). Moral disengagement in the perpetration of inhumanities. *Personality and Social Psychology Bulletin, 3*(3), 193-209.

Berkowitz, L. (1984). Some effects of thoughts on anti- and prosocial influence of media events: A cognitive neoassociationist analysis. *Psychological Bulletin, 95,* 410-427.

Bertacco, M. (2003). The externalization-internalization deadlock in social representation theory and experimental social psychology. *Papers on Social Representations, 12,* 9.1-9.9.

Branco, A., & Valsiner, J. (1997). Changing methodologies: A co-constructive study of goal orientation in social interactions. *Psychology and Developing Societies, 9*(1), 35-64.

Bruner, J. (1990). *Acts of meaning.* Cambridge, MA: Harvard University Press.

Bushman, B., & Baumeister, R. (1998). Threatened egotism, narcissism, self-esteem, and direct and displaced aggression: Does self-love or self-hate lead to violence? *Journal of Personality and Social Psychology, 75*(1), 219-229

Bushman, B., Baumeister, R., & Phillips, C. (2001). Do people aggress to improve their mood? Catharsis beliefs, affect regulation opportunity, and aggressive responding. *Journal of Personality and Social Psychology, 81*(1), 17-32.

Capezza, N. M. (2003). The cultural-psychological foundations for violence and nonviolence: An empirical study. *Forum: Qualitative Social Research* [Online Journal], *4*(2). Retrieved from January 3, 2006, from http://www.qualitative-research.net/fqs-texte/2-03/2-03capezza-e.htm

David, C., & Kistner, J. (2000). Do positive self-perceptions have a dark side?: Examination of the link between perceptual bias and aggression. *Journal of Abnormal Child Psychology, 28*(4), 327-337.

Diriwächter, R., & Valsiner, J. (2005, December). Qualitative developmental research methods in their historical and epistemological contexts [53 paragraphs]. *Forum Qualitative Sozialforschung/Forum: Qualitative Social Research* [Online Journal], *7*(1), Art 8. Retrieved January 18, 2006, from http://www.qualitative-research.net/fqs-texte/1-06/06-1-8-e.htm

Dodge, K. A., & Crick, N. R. (1990). Social information-processing bases of aggressive behavior in children. *Personality and Social Psychology Bulletin, 16*, 8-22.

Flavell, J., & Douglas, J. (1957). A microgenetic approach in perception and thought. *Psychological Bulletin, 54*(3), 197-217.

Geen, R. G. (1990). *Human aggression.* Pacific Grove, CA: McGraw-Hill.

Gergen, K. (1999). *An invitation to social construction.* London: Sage.

Heine, S. J. (2005). Where is the evidence for pancultural self-enhancement?: A reply to Sedikides, Gaertner, & Toguchi (2003). *Journal of Personality and Social Psychology, 89*, 531-538.

Heine, S., Lehman, D., Markus, H., & Kitayama, S. (1999). Is there a universal need for positive self-regard? *Psychological Review, 106*(4), 766-794.

Kakar, S. (1996). *The colors of violence.* Chicago: University of Chicago Press.

Kelman, H., & Hamilton, V. (1988). *Crimes of obedience: Toward a social psychology of authority and responsibility.* New Haven, CT: Yale University Press.

Lewin, K. (1936). *The principles of topological psychology.* New York: McGrow-Hill.

McCauley, C. (1989). The nature of social influence in groupthink: Compliance and internalization. *Journal of Personality and Social Psychology, 57*, 250-260.

Milgram, S. (1974). *Obedience to authority.* New York: Holt.

Molenaar, P. (2003, July 7-10). *A manifesto on psychology as idiographic science: Bringing the person back into scientific psychology—this time forever.* Invited talk at the 13th International Meeting of the Psychometric Society, Cagliari.

Nisbett, R., & Wilson, T. (1977). Telling more than we can know: Verbal reports on mental processes. *Psychological Review, 84*, 231-259.

Pepper, S. (1961). *World Hypotheses,* Berkeley, CA: University of California Press. (Original work published 1942)

Rokeach, M. (1984). Generalized mental rigidity as a factor in ethnocentrism. *Journal of Abnormal and Social Psychology, 43*, 259-278.

Strube, M. (1989). Evidence for the type in type A behavior: A taxonometri analysis. *Journal of Personality and Social Psychology, 56*, 972-987.

Valsiner, J. (1987). *Culture and development of children's action*. Chichester, England: Wiley.

Valsiner, J. (2003a). Beyond the social representations: A theory of enablement. *Papers on Social Representations, 12*, 6.1-6.16.

Valsiner, J. (2003b). Enabling the theory of enablement: In search for a theory-method link. *Papers on Social Representations, 12*, 12.1-12.8.

Valsiner, J. (2005). Les risques d'une psychologie sociale appliqué. *Hermès, 41*, 91-99.

Zillmann, D. (1983). Cognition-excitation interdependencies in aggressive behavior. *Aggressive Behavior, 14*, 51-64.

PART III

SYMBOLIC SELF-SOOTHING

CHAPTER 5

PROCESSING PROCESS

A Microgenetic Look at the Microgenetic Analysis of Toddlers' Affective Processing

Valerie M. Bellas and James P. McHale

BALANCING BIDIRECTIONAL PROCESSES: MICROGENESIS IN ACTION

Microgenetic analysis requires that the researcher hold present in her/his work the phenomena as a whole greater than the sum of its parts in the tradition of *Ganzheitspsychologie*, while sharpening focus on the movement of the component aspects of the phenomena. The whole is built of these component parts at the same time that it necessitates and organizes them. This simultaneous top-down and bottom-up meaning-making process is the phenomenon in action. Navigating the tentative balance of the bidirectional relationships between whole and part is the delicate task of the microgenetic researcher.

The dynamic relationship between part and whole becomes, in itself, a force of reorganization and transformation. Here, innovation is born of the bidirectional processes within a self-regulating system as it moves forward in time. Thus, through a series of tentative new relationships

Innovating Genesis: Microgenesis and the Constructive Mind in Action, pp. 109–138
Copyright © 2008 by Information Age Publishing

between parts and wholes, new temporary stabilities are achieved. Accordingly, development proceeds from tentative homeostasis to uncertainty to transformation to a new tentative homeostasis (see Figure 5.1.) The microgenetic researcher situates her-/himself to track this movement and recognize these moments of transformation, a process that requires a flexibility of awareness of component parts and tentatively organized wholes.

Microgenetic Method and the Methodology Cycle

Just as a phenomenon develops within the dynamic relationship between part and whole, microgenetic analysis proceeds via the bidirectional interplay of all aspects of the methodology cycle (see Branco & Valsiner, 1997; Valsiner, 1998, Valsiner, 2000). In this formulation, the

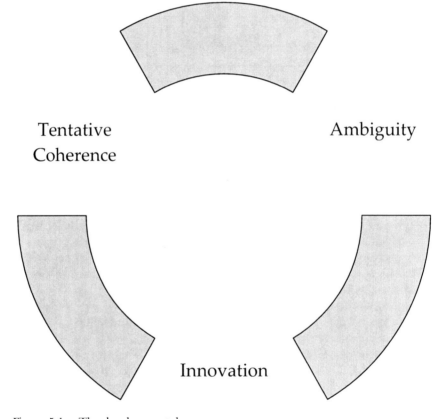

Tentative
Coherence

Ambiguity

Innovation

Figure 5.1.   The developmental process.

researcher's assumptions about the world, the theory guiding the work, the phenomena, the method-data interaction, as well as the researcher's intuitive experiencing are themselves in constant dynamic bidirectional relation to each other. In this active research process, the researcher, immersed in this dynamic instability, remains vigilant, maintaining and developing foresight, hindsight, and metaunderstandings while noting the movement of meaning within the phenomenon-theory-researcher relationship.

Method is understood to be one aspect of the methodology cycle. Method may be the sequential procedure of the research process, but it can never be understood outside its dynamic interconnections to the researcher's assumptions about the world and the interplay of theory, research and the intuitive experiencing of the researcher. The method is intimately linked with the data, as the phenomenon has been unavoidably manipulated when isolated and made accessible to the researcher's method. In this way, the method dictates the kind of data obtained by carving out units of that which is observed (or dismissed) through its explicit or implicit positioning vis-à-vis content, measurement and analysis. The method-data component of the methodology cycle contributes to the research process as it is created and recreated by the ongoing and newly developed understandings of the interaction between active components of the methodology cycle. It is this movement between method (that decision around the "what" we are "doing" to analyze the data) and methodology cycle (the bidirectional relationships among assumptions, theory, phenomenon, and data-method) that is at issue as we consider microgenetic methodology.

Processing Process: Bringing Data to Bear

In this chapter, I will examine three sets of microgenetic studies I have conducted on observations of toddlers participating in a laboratory waiting-task. The data were gathered within the emotion regulation research paradigm of Grolnick, Bridges, and Connell (1996) as part of longitudinal study of families. Within this research paradigm, parents and their toddlers were observed and videotaped in the laboratory setting in order to code and quantitatively analyze the behaviors they engage in to regulate their frustration while waiting for a desired object. In the waiting task, 30-month olds and their parents wait for 6 minutes for the experimenter to return to give the child a present wrapped with shiny paper and bows or a snack of crackers popular with toddlers. The child's parent is asked to remain busy with other work and interact only nominally during the session in order to observe how the children regulate themselves when they are offered little parental support.

The session begins as the experimenter enters the room where the child and parent have been waiting, playing and interacting together on other tasks during their laboratory visit. The room has a limited supply of developmentally appropriately play materials, such as cars, dolls, puppets, and picture books. The experimenter shows the child the attractive object and says that the child will receive the object when the experimenter returns. The experimenter places the object in the room on a small shelf, out of reach of the child, but within the child's sight, and exits the room. The child and parent then "wait" for 6 minutes for the experimenter to return. As the session progresses, the children may engage with the play materials in the room, attempt to engage the parent, explore the room, soothe themselves physically or remain fixated on the object they will receive. There is also variability within parent responses. Parents may take their instructions to "remain busy" quite seriously and rebuff all their child's attempts for contact. Alternatively, they may engage in a limited way or may break the protocol and fully interact with their child. After 6 minutes, the experimenter returns and gives the child the object as promised.

This research protocol has been used to examine the emotion regulation strategies of toddlers in correlational analytical designs (Grolnick et al., 1996). In previous such work, the sessions above are coded at 5-second intervals for child behaviors (Bakeman & Gottman, 1997). These child behaviors are conceptualized as "strategies" that function to regulate emotion. In this way, certain emotion regulation strategies, such as independent play, serve to distract the child from the emotional arousal, and other strategies, such as focusing on the unattainable object of desire, lead to the acceleration of the emotional arousal. Previous work within this perspective includes the analysis of correlations between child strategies and expressed emotion in the session (Grolnick et al., 1996) and parental and child behaviors (Bridges, Grolnick, & Connell, 1997). (For a review see Cole, Martin, & Dennis, 2004 and Grolnick, McMenamy, & Kurowski, 1999.) I have, myself, coded and analyzed these sessions within a quantitative framework in previous projects which examine the relationship between family processes and child strategies (Haskell,[1] DiLallo, DeCourcey, & McHale, 2003) and child strategies and parental ratings of their child's social competence (Haskell, DeCourcey, & McHale, 2005). For the current analysis, however, I will draw upon three microgenetic studies of session content.

My aim in this chapter is to reflect on the process of microgenetic research as I have experienced it across three microgenetic studies of toddler-parent dyads in a waiting task. The narrative is an effort to pause over moments of uncertainty within the research process as it unfolds and to begin to look into the decisions I made throughout this work. The final piece is a microgenetic look at the research process—a dialogic narrative of my own development as a researcher.

The Dialectic of Research Methods: Finding a Place to Start

As I begin this analysis (in the same way as in any microgenetic research), the question arises as to where to begin. How does the researcher break into the ongoing flow of the phenomenon and find a starting point, which is always arbitrary even if one's perspective may make it seem a given or necessary point of departure? What components present in the process preceding the selected starting point will be lost? How do our assumptions about what constitutes the whole bounded by its "beginning" and "ending" change the phenomenon that could be more broadly conceived? This identification of the whole, in part through delimiting where we will begin, may be our first parts-and-whole dilemma. (Although, I am sure that it is not the first because I have eliminated earlier such dilemmas by definition.) Thus, even as we define a whole we are breaking experience into its component part, as we strive to keep the next greater whole in mind.

Accordingly, I hesitate before I start, as possible ways of approaching the work branch out before me. In discussing the process, I can begin at a point when the decision to carry out microgenetic research has been made. I can begin with the uncertainty that created the impetus to bring in a new method to understand the phenomenon. I can begin at the somewhat certain state before the uncertainty from which that innovation sprang. I can begin by outlining the theory of development underlying my conceptualization of the process.

I am aware of the heavy hand that will come down and cut off experience that is integral to this process. I wonder if I can weave these lost characteristics of my experience into the analysis despite a decision to start further along in time. Can I weave the past into the discussion of phenomenon in time? Moreover, knowing that time has passed after the completion of these studies, and that my approach has developed since, I wonder what of this future orientation I can integrate. I approach this pragmatically, knowing that these cuts are temporary. I also approach this moment with great seriousness, as defining the whole is a result of this process, even if I include in the narrative the ambiguity that surrounds the decision.

Microgenetic analysis in its ideal form must embark upon a process of defining a whole while keeping the next greater whole in mind. This next greater whole continues to influence the manner in which the newly and temporarily defined whole is understood. Therefore, as I do not lightly begin to carve out the whole by defining its initial boundary, I hold as part of this *practical whole* those components of the next greater more *ethereal whole* not highlighted within these arbitrary boundaries.

Experiencing the Whole, Breaking it Into Pieces: Finding a Reason to Innovate

I am drawn to start this narrative looking in on me in a university basement laboratory. I am sitting in front of a large video monitor with a remote control in hand, as I have for hours for many days. I stop the video every 5 seconds and record the behaviors of the toddlers I am watching. I subsequently code the sessions for variety of "emotion regulation strategies" including independent play, physical self-soothing, and interactive bids, noting each individual behavior in which the child engaged for the 6 minutes in which they were asked to wait (Grolnick et al., 1996). (Drawing on the above model, I believe I am starting at the tentative homeostasis that preceded the impetus to turn to a new method. Here, as well, I begin to turn to method within the methodology cycle while trying to hold the other aspects of the cycle constant.)

While charged with the task of identifying discrete behaviors, I was experiencing the whole of these waiting sessions. I was watching as each child moved through the task, noting to myself the rise and fall of activity in time, the arc of emotional reactions and the meaning that this task assumed for each child as it began, continued and drew to its conclusion. As I watched and coded, an internal dialogue about the nature of the work in which I was engaging and the nature of the phenomenon I was observing developed. (In terms of the methodology cycle, here we see an interaction between the phenomenon and the intuitive experiencing of the researcher.)

I would vacillate in ambivalence, seeing the utility of demarcating measurable units of behavior in terms of analyzing the relationships between that which I was coding and other variables of interest, yet I was uncertain what the static bits of behavior I was culling from this dynamic experience could tell us about the broader phenomenon I was observing. At this juncture, I was experiencing an incongruity between my method and an implicit assumption that I held (that behaviors were meaningful as they participated in processes that moved us along developmental trajectories.)

It was this uncertainty born of a consequential incongruity that gave way to innovation. I would continue with my analysis of emotion regulation strategies, but I also wanted to employ a method that would allow me to examine more holistically some of the processes I was observing. At this point, I may not have realized the entirety of restructuring that would come along with this change in proposed "method." However, I was soon to learn that one could not just tweak method without influencing all aspects of the methodology cycle.

Shifting to a Microgenetic Perspective: Redefining the Construct, Focusing on a Process

As indicated above, much of the work on emotion regulation conceptualizes child behaviors as strategies that function to regulate emotion. As I watched the toddlers waiting, I began to feel that the notion of *regulation,* in the sense of controlling or directing emotion, did not always best suit my understanding of what was happening within these sessions. It seemed to me that in particular segments, the emotion was *processed,* that is, that during the session the child came to a novel understanding of the world and had used the emotional impetus and semiotic means to bring them to this new relationship with self and environment.

Contained in this shift of perspective was a new understanding of affective processes. In my previous conceptualization of emotion within the emotion regulation paradigm, affect was (in practice if not in theory) treated as an entity contained within the child, analyzed as a component of a child's larger experience separate from behavior, cognition, and the broader organization of the child's regulatory systems. My shift to a process orientation was a movement toward understanding affective experience as integrated in the relationship between child and parent and child and environment. The affect was a part of the child's experiencing of the world around her/him.

In addition, I wished to shift focus from the idea that the toddlers were employing an emotion regulation *strategy,* a discrete functional behavior, to a perspective by which the toddler's actions could be understood to be meaningful within a developmental *process.* This more ontogenetic framework was one where the child's social, emotional, cognitive and physical development were being shaped by her/his activity, instead of this previous understanding of their behaviors as more deterministic and self-contained. This movement in perspective, from a more mechanistic and deterministic conceptualization to a more transformative and ontogenetic understanding of the phenomenon, is essential to my microgenetic work.

With this newly developed theoretical perspective, I returned my focus to the data and became particularly interested in segments of the sessions where toddlers used symbolic resources, such as language (e.g., talking to the parent about the waiting or the awaited object) or symbolic play, (e.g., acting out or representing in play a waiting or returning sequence) to represent their experience within the experimental situation. In our coding system, we had identified this behavior as *symbolic self-soothing*. This was understood as symbolic activity which helped the child manage the emotion arousal that arose when waiting for the experimenter to return with the desired object. Thus, when engaged in symbolic self-soothing, toddlers talked about or acted out some aspect of the experimental situation (e.g., leaving, returning, receiving the object) in order to soothe themselves in the face of intense or intensifying emotional experience generated by the experimental situation.

My experience was beginning to shape my theoretical perspective on the function of semiotic mediation within a regulatory system. I began to consider the notion that when toddlers used symbolic means to process their circumstance, these means functioned neither as a distraction from the emotional impetus nor represented an unbridled pursuit of this state. What semiotic mediation seemed to allow children to do was remain goal directed (to remain focused on the desired object) but not become disorganized by the momentary frustration of their desire. When engaged in productive symbolic processes, the toddlers' experiences were reorganized and sometimes transformed by the experience of a new perspective constructed via the distancing from the present that semiotic mediation allows.

The process, here, appeared to be better described as moment of learning about the parameters of the interaction between child, parent and experimental situation than one serving the function of "soothing" as previously developed in the emotion regulation literature. Therefore, as a child began to experience the disorganizing effects of a frustrated goal pursuit, s/he would call upon language to help make sense of the self in relation to the environment. This new understanding would serve to reorganize this relationship, moving the child toward developmental goals. For example, a toddler repeatedly sings out "Someone's knocking! Someone's knocking!" to reorganize the experience of the withdrawal of the desired object toward an understanding of the experience as waiting for the moment in which the experimenter announces her/his return.

The Process Begins and Questions Arise: The Relationship Between Theory and Analysis

I now had a process of interest and some goals for the way I wanted to look at this process. At the same time, this decision to apply a microgenetic perspective opened up a field of uncertainty. One area of uncertainty is the essential and sometimes uncomfortable relationship between theory and analysis. I experienced this as a dilemma. Perhaps analysis should be leading the theory or instead should theory emerge from the completed analysis of the phenomenon as observed? My fear was that when analyzing my data I would find the processes I had begun to identify because I set out to find them. Wasn't the process of looking to confirm my hypothesis the pseudoscience that Karl Popper (1963/2002) cautioned against? I would, therefore, not know if these processes were present in phenomenon or if I had "created" them by their pursuit. Of course, this separation of theory and method disregards the necessarily constructive process of any engagement with data. The bidirectional nature of the phenomenon-theory relationship allows moments of freedom for the phenomenon and innovation for the theory to occur in active relation to the presence of the still developing counterpart.

The theoretical perspective that was arising by virtue of my experience of being immersed in the phenomenon was shaping the construct and my understanding of nature of the process. At the moment, I felt that I must "return" to the phenomenon, setting to the background my theoretical perspective and pulling to the foreground the children and their waiting activities. Going back through many tapes, I focused on instances of symbolic self-soothing that seemed to unfold as a sequence and selected three sessions that have served as the data I have analyzed across the three studies presented here.

Method: Searching in the Toolbox

Further uncertainty arose around choosing or designing a "method" to analyze these sessions. I understood that time was more important *within* the sequences than my previous methods had allowed me to explore. Semiotic mediation was not simply an entity that could be "coded" as either present or not present in any given 5-second interval. Instead, it was a process that needed to be examined as it was unfolding across time. Thus, I decided that a time-analysis method best suited this project (Molenaar, 2004; Molenaar & Newell, 2003).

I was, next, confronted with the question of what to pay attention to in time. I decided to code the 6-minute sessions on a 5-point Likert scale for the following categories: emotion expressed, regulation, soothing, and intensity of anticipation and frustration. As I sat down to make sense of this time analysis, I encountered one of the great crises of the project. I did not know exactly what the data I had gathered meant or how to use them. At the start of the time analysis, I had envisioned that some pattern would emerge from the data. However, at the end of the coding what I had was approximately 80 subjective ratings for each of my 5 amorphous and subjective categories. These ratings went up and down, but what exactly, if anything real, was increasing or decreasing? Had I tried to quantify the unquantifiable? I had a more detailed picture, but of what?

It is entirely possible that in efforts to "find a method," I had quite clumsily used a "tool-box" approach to method (Branco & Valsiner, 1997 Diriwächter & Valsiner, 2005). In this way, I had just applied a method in absence of a relationship with the other aspects of the methodology cycle. The codes in my time analysis were not born of my new assumptions, burgeoning theory or the phenomenon as a process. Time series analysis, therefore, did not serve as a dynamic and connected approach to understanding the data. In fact, the phenomenon was lost in the presence of this method.

Theory Reemerges

I was at loose ends in terms of data analysis. I sought clarity and purpose through the writings of the central developmental theorists of symbolic and interpersonal development: Bowlby, Piaget, and Vygotsky.

As I read Bowlby, I recognized the sessions' dynamic structure to look more like a control system and less like a more singularly determined drive focused event. Bowbly (1969) wrote,

> Past discussions of instinctive behavior have tended to concentrate on sequences that have a dramatic and time limited outcome, such as orgasm, and to neglect **the behavior the outcome of which is an ongoing relationship,** such as maintenance of a specified distance over a comparatively long period. There can be no doubt that the latter sort of behavior is of great frequency and vital importance to most animals. (pp. 71-72, emphasis added)

I focused in on the toddler's semiotic mediation process as a negotiation of distances within the ongoing relationship between child and parent and child and the experimental paradigm/environment guided by a child's dynamic connection to (or loss of connection with) her/his affective experience and the intentions contained therein. It seemed to me that the symbolic process worked in relation to various set-goals of the system, which I identified as the goal of receiving the desired object, maintaining a relationship with parent and mastering the challenge set by the environment. Symbol, here, represented feedback to the system to monitor the relationship between experience and goal.

Reading Piaget (1962, 1975/1985) highlighted the dynamics of equilibration, reequilibration, and reorganization in the waiting sessions I had observed. Piaget (1975/1985) posits,

> Since every re-equilibration involves actions with a teleonomic character we must explain how goals, new as well as old, are chosen and account for **how the means used to reach a goal are improved** or why the means applied succeed. (p. 139, emphasis added)

In relation to Piaget's perspective, I began to understand the process as moving from one relatively homeostatic state toward another new state of relative homeostasis that was fundamentally reorganized by virtue of the child's negotiation of distances to goals (as recognized above). In this framework, learning was occurring in these sessions within moments of disequilibrium, and in these moments, the child turned toward symbolization as a means to reorganize the experience.

Vygotsky and Luria (1930/1994; and Vygotsky, 1934/1986) elucidated the nature of "symbol as a tool" to organize the experience. Vygotsky and Luria (1930/1994) suggest,

> Direct manipulation is replaced by a complex psychological process, where inner motivation and **the creation of intentions, postponed in time duration**, stimulate (children's) own development and realization. (p. 111, emphasis added)

With this notion of symbolization as a means of providing children psychological distance from the here and now, I was able to focus on a child's use of symbol as a tool to examine and better understand the parameters of the situation and place the present in relation to past events and future possibilities. Via semiotic mediation, conceptual objects that are not concretely available to the child in the immediate environment can be directed to the solution of the problem that presents itself to the child.

Modeling the Phenomenon

One of my goals for the study was to model the process I had observed. Although I had come to my first analysis with a time focus, as I began to further understand the process, I came to realize that my linear analysis did not match my conceptualization of the nonlinear process in which the toddlers were engaged. I realized the model that I was trying to build would not be the result of my analysis, but would have to be built through the analysis and theory building aspects of the project. The full model would have to show the movement among ongoing relationships, the equilibrium, reequilibrium, and reorganization of development and the use of elements not concretely available to the child. I needed to integrate a nonlinear microgenetic process to a goal oriented ontogenetic unfolding.

With my experience of the phenomenon as I had more closely observed it in my time analytic work, a more dynamic theoretical understanding built from my reading of classic developmental theories and the creation of a model of the process that I had observed, I was ready to reenter the analysis anew. I no longer wished to add a theory or add a method, but instead was focused on the interrelationship between them. In order to hold present the theory in the analysis, I developed a narrative of each of the three sessions, keeping in mind the theoretical structure as I closely described the phenomenon (the activities of the children in time). Within this narrative, I integrated the categories I had coded in the time-series analysis, but removed its point-by-point temporality.

The resultant narrative analysis, locates moments of symbolic self-soothing in the larger sequence of the 6-minute session. It chronicles the child's verbal and nonverbal activities and outlines emotions expressed and bodily arousal, as it reports on exploratory and soothing behaviors. The narrative marks the child's integration of possible future states, shifts in perspectives that are currently unavailable to the child, as well as apparent moments of equilibrium and disequilibrium (Haskell, Valsiner, & McHale, 2003).

Empirical Examples: Study 1, Symbolic Self-Soothing in Toddlers

In these segments below, 29-month-old, Caitlin, is waiting for crackers while her mother is filling out questionnaires. In this session, Caitlin's mother addresses her only when there are safety concerns.

Excerpt 1: Knocking

Frustration grows as Caitlin waits. She kicks the furniture. She hears the knocking sound that results from her kicking and yells, "Who's that!" Caitlin smiles and runs to the door and knocks. "Who's that?" she inquires. The pretense of the knock signifying the experimenter's return is a symbolic representation allowing Caitlin to imagine the future (perhaps hoping that this will accelerate the process), and momentarily her frustration turns into anticipation. Caitlin is certainly still focused on goal attainment (getting the crackers), as she remains well integrated and regulated (does not become dysregulated by frustration).

In this first excerpt, the analysis attempts to capture arousal (kicking), the discovery of a symbolic tool (knocking) and the transformation of affect (frustration to anticipation). The analysis notes the ongoing commitment to the goal (having the experimenter return) without loss of the ability to self-regulate.

Excerpt 2: Locking and unlocking

With clear hand movements mimicking locking from top to bottom, Caitlin says, "Lock. Lock. Lock. Lock." She is transforming the unpleasant lack of autonomy to a decision to be locked in. She waits a few seconds and then says, "Unlock. Unlock. Unlock." She moves her hands more broadly now, from bottom to top. She jumps out of her space, no longer scowling. Caitlin has not only turned around the loss of autonomy, she has released herself from its boundaries triumphantly.

Here, the analysis centers on the transformational power of the semiotic mediation. Caitlin is exploring the experimental paradigm and taking on the position of the experimenter to lock and unlock the door (the door through which the experimenter exits and will return). Equilibrium is reestablished, but the desired object remains salient to the child. This analysis focuses on how the child is processing her relationship to the environment, not in the way she is regulating her emotion.

Overall, in this narrative analysis, I aimed to pinpoint the moment when the toddlers had regained a sense of equilibration, and yet seemed fully activated by the emotional impetus (anticipation or frustration) that they were processing. I concluded with the suggestion that this reorganization was central to the ontogenetic goal of processing emotions, that is, to be better able to work in relation to individual, interactional, and environmental set goals without being overwhelmed by one's affective reaction or distracted from the goal orientation the affective reaction serves.

This first study achieved some of the project's original goal to understand children's activities as a developmental process. Nonetheless, it left me with many areas for further inquiry, including, the nature of the reorganization, means of the transformation and the process by which new relationships between self and other and self and environment were negotiated within the system. These questions would come to bear in my next studies.

Narrative and Generalizability

The truth is I was feeling that this work was not rigorous, and at this point in the research, I was deeply uncertain about what I had achieved. I am still conflicted about narrative as an analytic method. Of course, narrative is the medium that I am utilizing in this current microgenetic analysis of microgenetic research. Nevertheless, I have to admit dialogicality within myself about this issue.

My values fall along the lines that narrative is truth, and that it is the skilled interweaving of subjective experience that ultimately all psychological research is about (Valsiner & Diriwächter, 2005). However, I cannot escape the feeling that my goal as a microgenetic researcher is not to describe experience, but instead to model processes. These models, at their best, will stand as a metaphor for some mediated experience between myself, as a researcher, and my subject/participant, perhaps no more connected to objective reality, but yet operating differently than narratives.

This tension between describing individual experience and generalizing data by some means (some more quantifiable than others) remains open in microgenetic work. Generalization from a single case, whether analyzed with narrative methods or by other means, may come about as the methodology cycle is transformed and innovated in time. In this way, generalization may require multiple steps from the analysis of a single case, to the development of a model, to testing and modifying that model on new individual cases (Molenaar & Valsiner, 2005; Valsiner, 2003). Correlational researchers face a parallel issue regarding generalization when they move from group to individual, which requires the assumption of homogeneity in groups which is never, in actuality, the case (Valsiner, 1986).

The Next Study: Uncertainty and Transformation

My next project was a result of an invitation to participate in a symposium at the 18th biennial meeting of the International Society for the Study of Behavioural Development in Ghent, Belgium, titled "Beyond Uncertainties: Symbolic Processes And Change" (Zittoun & Abbey, 2004). Because of the focus of the symposium, my study was bounded by these three compelling concepts: uncertainty, symbolic processes and change. Thus, the frame of my work shifted again. It moved from an exploration of soothing (which remained mired in the more drive-focused emotion regulation paradigm) to one of negotiated relationships and the nature of conceptual and experiential reorganization in social, emotional and cognitive development.

From Goals to Needs: The Focus Becomes Intention

Contrary to the understanding that the toddlers in the waiting-task were primarily aroused by the blocked goal of retrieving the desirable object, it seemed to me that more diverse and essential needs motivated the children that I had observed. I had begun to study self-determination theory, which posits three essential psychological needs: autonomy, relatedness and competence (Deci & Ryan, 1985). Autonomy is the need to freely determine one's own course of action. Relatedness is the need to have close relationships with other people. Competence is a need to be effective in interactions with the environment. I embraced the assumption that these psychological needs were always present to the children while participating in the task and could be tracked as a source of motivation.

Furthermore, I began reading the work of Brentano (1874/1995). I was inspired by his formulation of intentionality as directed toward both an object and the subject itself. As well, I read von Uexküll (1934/1957). I was influenced by his conceptualization of an object, not appearing to the subject as such, but instead one "transformed into perceptual cues and perceptual images and invested with a functional tone" (p. 72). In this way, "objects" (people, boundaries, ideas, and materials) in the child's environment were functional and dynamic points of active intention. They were understood in relationship to the child and imbued with properties of both self and other.

Drawing on the work of Lewin (1931), whereby the situation assumes as much importance as the object, I began to look at the child's relationship to environmental affordances and limitations and the psychological forces that shape her/his vector or direction for action. In short, I began to conceptualize the session's movement as a field, that is, an uncertain territory to be negotiated. In this territory, the child must not only navigate her/his own intentions (as outlined above), but also the parent's intentions (perhaps to follow the guidelines of the experiment or finish the paperwork provided) and those of the experimenter (which may be to be absent and unavailable to explain the situation or deliver the desired object). This move toward understanding the session through a field orientation marks a shift in understanding, whereby I was no longer viewing the child and the environment in opposition to each other, separate and reactive, but instead was now able to bring them together within a shared integrated experience.

With this new perspective on intentionality, the nature of a perceived object and field orientation, I began to reconceptualize set-goals as *positions of intent.* Here again, we see how each aspect of the methodology cycle participates in a bidirectional interaction, thereby shifting meanings. I moved between the phenomena (transformation through symbol in relationship with self, other and environment) and my assumptions about the world (need based motivation in active participants) to build theory (identifying the dynamics of intentionality and the integration of relationship between self and objects in the environment within the phenomenon as experienced).

Consequently, I posited that in the waiting task, the toddler may experience the need for relatedness (e.g., comply with the parent's wish to not to be bothered when s/he is busy) and experience the need for autonomy (e.g., to pursue the desired object.) The children may experience frustration or yearning in relation to the satisfaction of psychological needs. The motivation to satisfy these needs gives rise to intentional positions, which provide direction for action. The child negotiates various internal and external positions of intent, which may, at times, lie in opposition to each other.

Thus, I began hypothesize that, in part, what the child might be organizing and reorganizing in this developmental process was an understanding of the *positions of intent* both within and outside of her-/ himself. Therefore, in an uncertain situation, the various positions of intent remain ambiguous to the subject. The dynamic negotiation of positions of intent within a field gives rise to developmental processes by clarifying intentions and transforming previous organizations of intention, thereby creating opportunities for innovation.

Process and *das Ganze* (the Whole)

As I write about the development of the notion positions of intent and my growing understanding of transformational means, I feel I have become less unsuccessful at continuing to pursue and document my microgenetic process. This turning point in the research was experienced as an entity in itself. I am less aware of the components of the process as it unfolded. This may be a moment that each researcher confronts as s/he follows a microgenetic process. There may come a point of transformation, a coming together of a whole that is greater than the sum of its parts, a moment when the process cannot be followed because of some fundamental reorganization of the components, the emergence of a new phenomenon (Diriwächter, 2004a, 2004b, 2004c). Marking these moments of transformation is part of the microgenetic process.

Empirical Examples: Study 2, Uncertainties, Intention, and Transformation in Toddler's Processing

In the segments below, 31-month-old, Becky, is waiting for a present while her mother is filling out questionnaires. In this session, Becky's mother is busy, but interacts in a minimal, yet warm, manner when she approaches.

Excerpt 1: Going away and coming back.

Segment: Becky says, "I'll just go away for a minute and think about it," and turns to face the wall. Becky turns quickly, facing out to the mirror and the room and says, "I got some juice!" She pushes through the small space (where she has been playing), pretending to carry a cup in her hand. Becky walks over to her mother and gives her the pretend juice.

Analysis: The (position of) intent Becky most centrally reckons with in this segment is that of the researcher. Through her pretend play, Becky transforms the ambiguous intent of going and promising to return, to a clarified intent of going, returning and delivering on the promise by bestowing the desired object.

I was, further, interested in exploring the means by which semiotic mediation clarified and reorganized the intentions within the field. I organized the work around three *transformational means*, which were the mechanisms of change, (1) movement from the real to the imaginary, (2) repetition and creation and 3) evocation of past and future orientation. I returned to the data looking for instances of these mechanisms in action. As I watched for these moments, I built a theoretical stance as to the manner in which these mechanisms functioned.

Excerpt 2: Repetition—Transforming the return.

Segment: Becky repeats the pretend sequence (bringing juice to her mother) and then covers the opening where she has been preparing this sequence with a blanket. She goes under the blanket, steps out into the room and exclaims with a big smile, "Here I am!"

Analysis: Becky brings the pretend juice once slowly, returns and brings it again more rapidly. In this repetition, she is creating the separation of spaces from the "away" and the "coming back" and establishing a regularity to the sequence. Not long after this repetition, an additional element is integrated into the symbolic sequence. Becky brings over the blanket to cover her "away" space, hiding it from the view of the other side. She then pops out with a "Here I am!" becoming visible and returning in a more dramatic and unexpected way than in her previous transitions from "away" to "back" which lacked a gate or surprise entry. By virtue of this repetition, the entry portion of the symbolic sequence is broken off and further explored. Indeed, it is this that Becky is waiting for, the "here I am" moment of the researcher's return. She understands now that this is what the researcher intends to do.

An important aspect of this second study was the creation of visual models. I modeled the three transformational means as they were represented in the data. Moreover, I created a visual model of each of these transformational means as an abstract process. We can now test these models in multiple individual subject designs and identify to what extent the process, as it was found to occur in these segments, may be generalizable to other contexts (see Figures 5.2a. and 5.2b).

Losing Contact With the Intention

I presented the completed analysis of the second study at the 18th biennial meeting of the International Society for the Study of Behavioural Development in Ghent, Belgium, including both narrative analysis and visual models of the uncertain territory, ambiguous, and clarified positions of intent and transformational means (Haskell & McHale, 2004). After the presentation, I asked the conference audience if there were any questions. I looked up to meet a soft but direct gaze. The

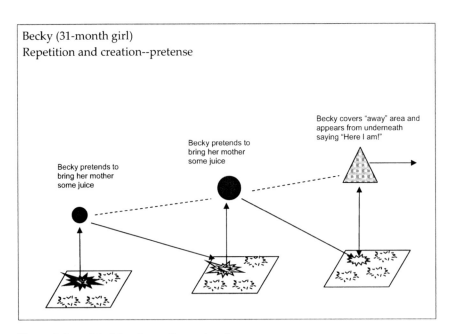

Figure 5.2a.   Models of transformational means.

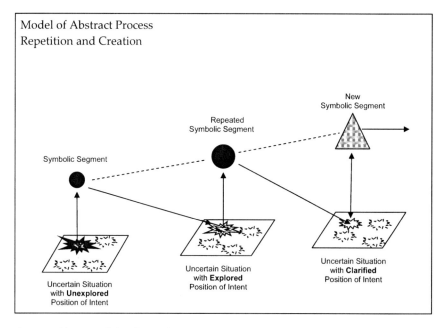

Figure 5.2b.   Models of transformational means.

audience member asked me something to the effect of, "But what about emotion? Don't you think this process is an affective process?"—"Oh yes," I responded, "This work began in questions about the processing of emotion. I believe emotion is integral." Time was up for questions.

The audience member was right. I had made it through my analysis without ever looking at emotional processes. The project above had outlined a symbolic/cognitive process and focused on perspective taking and learning, but what I had wanted to understand was emotion. This second study was an important step toward understanding the process, but clearly, I needed to refocus my efforts on social and emotional development. In my next project, I kept the audience member's question present in my mind, as I never again wanted someone to point out to me that emotion mattered.

Voices in Development

I entered the next study with a renewed motivation to analyze emotion processing in the waiting sessions, specifically the manner in which affect participated in the shifting of meanings within this system. Moreover, I wanted to better understand the role of the processes I had examined in terms of a person's development across the lifespan, that is, to more directly understand the role of microgentic processes in ontogenetic development. In addition, I entered this project determined to sharpen my focus on the relational system.

I had become interested in work on the dialogical self (Hermans, 2001; Hermans & Hermans-Jensen, 2001, 2003). The sense that the self is not unitary but instead constructed via multiple I-positions, seemed closely related to my own conceptualization of interactional territories populated with a multiplicity of positions of intent. A colleague, Kaya Ono, and I became interested in how the dialogical self developed and the manner in which the multiple I-positions were taken into the developing self (Haskell, Ono, & McHale, 2004). Ono had language data from a child 22-27 months of age. My data were gathered through observations of a 30-month-old. We wanted to use the two data sets to begin to explore these processes at two time points with the goal of providing a preliminary framework by which we might investigate the role of microprocesses in ontogeny. We began with questions of *what* was developing across time. As a toddler learned to cope with the present circumstances, how would this contribute to processes in later childhood or adulthood? Together, we conceived of the ontogenetic goal as building a more complex and complete sense of *self-in-relation* to other and environment, as opposed to the development of a bounded self (Haskell, Ono, & McHale, 2004).

We became quite interested in the notion of intersubjectivity. This was not just an *interactive* space that we were observing between parent and child, but it was an illustration of *intersubjectivity*, a process defined by Trevarthen (1992) as "the child's mental adjustments to the mental activities of the cooperative other" (p. 119). This perspective posits that the infant "possesses a sort of consciousness, imagination and expressive motility and coordination" (p.1 27). The microgenetic understanding of the process of developing self-in-relation (to others, objects and the environment) we were building was one where voices were made conscious, imagined, expressed, and coordinated within relationships.

Furthermore, this work maintained the centrality of affective experience in development. We set out with the assumption as proposed by Valsiner (2005) that "mental processes are themselves generated by the differentiation of feelings" (p. 1). In addition, we conceived of the relationship between cognition and affect, along the lines of Lewis and Ferrari's (2001) notion of the "synchronization of appraisal and emotion" which they describe as the "macroscopic coupling of cognitive and emotional systems that give rise to emotional interpretation" (p. 148). Thus, emotion and cognition, in a coordinated relationship, produce the higher order level of organization necessary for meaning.

In my analysis, I wished to focus on emotional dialogs and the interactive space in which movement toward a goal of self-in-relation emerged. The concept of *voice* in multivoicedness expanded the concept of *position* that I had used in the previous study. Voice was by its very nature social and affective. As I focused on embodied voices, I was able to identify the mode by which perspectives were taken in and internally processed as the enactment of voice. Specifically, in my analysis, I looked at how the toddler took on the role of the experimenter, "feeling through" this enactment the experimenter's intention in the situation he faced.

Empirical Example: Study 3, Multivoicedness in Development

In the segments below, 30-month-old, Verne, waits for crackers with his father. Verne's father breaks the protocol and interacts with Verne, helping him to understand the nature of the situation in which they have found themselves.

Segment transcript:

Verne: (addressing his father, inquiring about the cup of crackers) "Daddy you can't get it? Daddy you can't get it."

Father: (seemingly distracted) Why can't I get it?

Verne: (commanding) Just Get It!

Father: I'm going to get in trouble if I get it. She (the researcher) is going to yell at me, 'Why'd you get it?'" (He says the researcher's words in a softly gruff and scolding voice.)

Verne: (turning around and smiling broadly) "She has to get it!" (He then looks half in the mirror and half at his father) "Now she gonna say...." (Assuming the role of the researcher with a scolding tone and posture, he screeches) "Aaaaaagh!" "Why'd you do that?"

Analysis: Verne explores his father's position of intent, trying to bring the obstacle to the surface "You can't get it? You can't get it," he inquires of his father. His entreaties again thwarted, Verne demands that his father "just get it!" In response, Verne's father offers a dialogical explanation for his recalcitrance. He tells his son that the researcher will get mad and yell at him if he gets the crackers. Not only does he explain *this, but he* enacts *her voice, saying "Why'd you do that?" in a scolding tone. Verne quickly takes on the researcher's persona and in an emotionally expressive, activated moment, he transforms the situation into a concrete representation of the relationship between the researcher and the father. Verne comes to understand self-in-relation, in that his relationship to his father and the researcher can now be understood as nested in his father's hierarchical relationship with the researcher.*

The redramatization of the affective reaction, as in Kaplan's (1983) genetic dramatism, is a process of co-construction, which aids the child in entering the experience in a new way, helping the child to cope with the stressor. The "taking-up" of voices that I intended to mark was in this case literal. The connection was between the taking-up of a voice and the taking-in of an I-position. This new dialogical thread within the self formed a more relational self—a step toward the development of understanding self-in-relation (contrary to the notion of development self which is unitary and self-regulated).

Ontogenetic Analysis

Because we looked at two different participants across time, Ono and I could only begin to address the issue of the ontogenesis of self-in relation. Furthermore, our work at time one was not microgenetic by method, so I will report only briefly what we concluded. In this first analysis, Ono looked at a 2-year-old's use of mental state verbs, such as "*want*" and "*know*," in relation to her reference to self and others in subject position. She found that the toddler tended to couple "*I*" with mental state terms in both monologue and dialogue. We suggested that this was a process was nested within the process of the development of I-positions within the developing child. We termed these functionally developed subject symbols "objects of reflection." We posited:

> Objects of reflection give rise to a flexibility of intentions, allowing children not only to step away from their own desires, thoughts and feelings as if they were a third person, but to take on the role of the other, whose psychological experiences are never directly available to them. These objects are mental representations with personal meanings, which not only allow one to be distanced from "here and now" subjective experiences and social interactions, but to offer *a possibility to be with or without* one's own, (as well as projecting others,) innermost feelings, desires, and thoughts. (Haskell, Ono, & McHale, 2004, p. 4)

Thus, we suggested that this ability to manipulate intention was a step in the development of the I-positions which were voiced in ongoing development of the dialogical self. This step in our research process allowed us to begin to understand the manner in which "dialogical regulation" contributed to the development of the understanding of self-in-relation. We are now at the point in our understanding where we can begin examine the heart of my original questions about the processing emotion in social relationships understood as a goal oriented ontogenetic process.

Models and Dialogical Analysis

For this study, I decided not to visually model the processes we were examining. My colleague had told me that, in essence, she found the models incomprehensible. This is not the first time I had heard this complaint about the visual models of microgenetic processes that I have created. Although I endeavored to do the meta-analysis without this visual representation, I found it difficult to move to the level of generalization (as discussed above) with the narrative analysis as the foundation. The role of visual models as a means of analysis and the nature of those models is an important issue for microgenetic research and one that must be further explored.

Furthermore, although I was continuing to pursue microgenetic analysis, I took on dialogical analysis a bit naively. I thought I could just add dialogicality to my model. However, through this study I have come to realize the complexity of dialogical analysis. Dialogical theory needs to serve as the framework of the analysis. I had aimed to identify moments in which voices were taken in, but I found that I could not use the theory to cull the process from the data. I, essentially, had no dialogical method. I wonder if I have not yet made a cycle from theory, to phenomenon to method within the methodology cycle. Returning to theory or to the phenomenon may give me the grounding I need to develop a method which will honor the bidirectional relationships of the other aspects of the cycle.

Bringing it all Together: The Process of Microgenetic Research

Following the model of development in Figure 5.1 that proposes that development proceeds from tentative homeostasis to uncertainty to transformation to a new tentative homeostasis (see Figure 5.1), I would like to suggest that the microgenetic research process unfolds in a like manner. Methods of analysis move from a tentative coherence to ambiguity to innovation to a new tentative coherence.

We can see this cycle replayed in the studies above. For example, at the end of the second study, I had felt a sense of coherence regarding my analysis of the transformational means that I had outlined. I had shown in my analysis how these means moved a child from a state of uncertainty to one of more clarity in relation to the previously ambiguous positions of intent she was encountering. This sense of coherence gave way in the face of the question I received from the audience when I was presenting the work reminding me that this was an affective and social process. I realized that I had not addressed this issue, and the field became ambiguous to me again. Hence, I was again unsure what was transpiring in my 6-minute sessions! Innovation arrived in my synthesis of my readings about the dialogical self and particularly in the notion of the essential multivocality of the experience. As I shifted my focus, to the analysis of voice and the embodiment and enactment of an essentially emotional and social experience, I found a new tentative coherence around the process by which development was proceeding (see Figure 5.3).

This cycle is also illustrated in the process of writing this chapter (a microgenetic account of microgenetic research). I began with a tentative coherence stepping through my process in a systematic narrative in time. As I described the theoretical perspective of the second study, I found that I was unable to determine how I had come to this new understanding of the phenomenon. This was a moment of loss of clarity as I entered an ambiguous field as a writer. The innovation occurred when I recognized

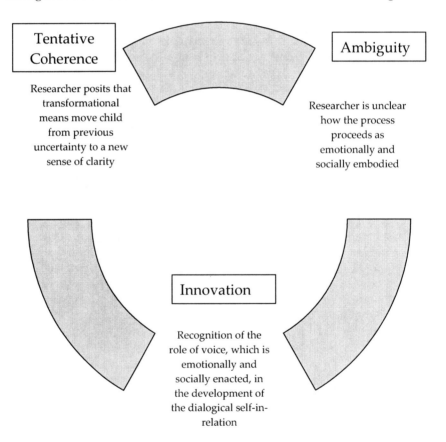

Figure 5.3.   Example of developmental process in the microgenetic research of toddler's use of symbolic means in emotion processing.

that I was experiencing a moment of emergence when the whole was present as greater than the component parts. I returned to a relative state of coherence as I realized that this process would naturally occur in the analytic process (see Figure 5.4).

Conclusion: Honoring the Uncertain

I will conclude with a brief review of the issues that remain full of rich ambiguity and innovative potential within the development of microgenetic methodology. The areas I will address are:

1. the relationship between the empirical and the theoretical
2. noting emergent wholes while examining microprocesses

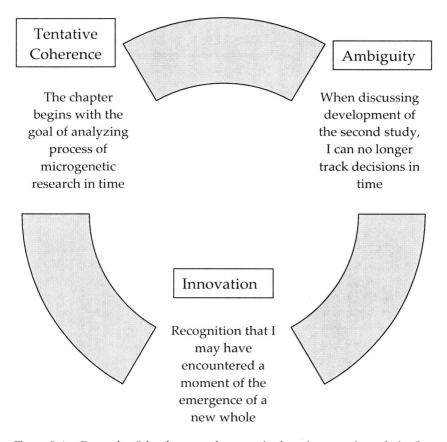

Tentative Coherence

Ambiguity

The chapter begins with the goal of analyzing process of microgenetic research in time

When discussing development of the second study, I can no longer track decisions in time

Innovation

Recognition that I may have encountered a moment of the emergence of a new whole

Figure 5.4.   Example of developmental process in the microgenetic analysis of microgenetic research.

3. making decisions to resolve or not resolve ambiguities in the research and writing process
4. managing multilevel systems

The Tension Between the Empirical and the Theoretical

Theory drives our research, yet we look to phenomena to tell us its story as a process unfolds. These two positions, equally valid, lie in relation to each other. The researcher is charged with the responsibility to hold on to the theoretical impetus of the analysis while s/he listens intently. This process is much like that of ethnographic work, where two cultural perspectives come together within the subjective experience of the ethnographer.

The ethnographer brings the perspective of her/his native culture to the field (similarly, we bring our assumptions and theoretical biases). The ethnographer sits with her/his participant in participant observation (in a similar way to our empirical analysis of the data) and engages in thick description (Geertz, 1983) of that which s/he is observing. This process of description lies in the coming together of the investigator's original cultural lens and that which is discovered through a process of curiosity and a willingness to pursue an understanding of that which s/he can not comprehend looking solely through the framework s/he has brought to the field. Embedded in this process is an oscillation between a process as it is currently unfolding and a retrospective process which includes the benefit of—not suffers from, as Popper (1963/2002) might suggest—"hindsight bias." The researcher has some experience of a whole as "completed" as well as that which was and is in a state of movement, transition and transformation.

What emerges from fieldwork is a mediated experience of individual idiosyncrasies, previous cultural framework and new understandings of different ways of life, as well as the movement between retrospective and developing processes. In this way too, must the researcher hold all aspects of the methodology cycle simultaneously—mediating subjective experience with theoretical framework with the questions that arise from the phenomenon as honestly as possible. This is not a linear movement, but instead a weaving of theory and empirical data with parts and wholes of each—oscillating in various time frames and states of development across a variety of trajectories—that fit and do not fit together and may emerge as a greater whole.

Recognizing Emergent Wholes and Analyzing Microprocesses

The researcher must remain aware of moments of transformation and innovation as the whole is greater than the sum of its parts. The researcher must take responsibility for the fact that s/he will neither be able to keep entirely anchored in a process nor be able to speak about a phenomenon as an entity without looking inside. As aspects of the process resist scrutiny, these may be moments of emergence. Again, this process proceeds in a nonlinear, unpredictable way, with both parts and wholes rising and falling as we follow the phenomenon in time.

Acknowledging Ambiguity

The process of noting ambiguity and uncertainty in the process of research is essential although very difficult. Moments of ambiguity may be experienced as a failure of understanding by the researcher, and much energy may be applied to resolving or dissolving them. This process of pursuing clarity is productive when the moment of confusion gives way to innovation or transformation. However, embracing ambiguity is a necessary and productive aspect of the research process.

In a similar way, there is the question of how to write-up research with the rich ambiguity of the process in tact. It may be a more compelling and useful text, one which includes the places of ambiguity essential to the process, however, if all the ambiguities that remain unresolved are reported, the clarity of communication and the emergent understanding itself may be lost.

The Challenge of Analyzing Multilevel Systems

In some ways, calling this work microgenetic research is a misnomer. The research that I believe we are endeavoring to do is microgenetic, ontogenetic, and cultural-genetic in nature. We must look at microprocesses with a developmental, and thus contextual, eye, wondering about and pursuing the larger developmental trajectory that this process is serving. Furthermore, a level I have not been able to reach in the above described research, is perhaps, the very level of interest in this series, cultural-genesis. The editors of this volume have asserted that the process (much like developmental processes outlined above) of emergent cultural meaning proceeds cyclically by way of the individual internalizing societal meanings, transforming them and externalizing these interpretations. This level too must be included in microgenetic research.

NOTE

1.   This author's name was changed to Haskell to Bellas in 2006.

REFERENCES

Bakeman, R., & Gottman, G. M. (1997). *Observing interaction: An introduction to sequential analysis*. Cambridge, MA: Cambridge University Press.

Bowlby, J. (1969). *Attachment and loss: Attachment* (Vol. 1). New York: Basic Books.

Branco, A. U., & Valsiner, J. (1997). Changing methodologies: A co-constructivist study of goal orientations in social interactions. *Psychology & Developing Societies, 9*(1) 35-64.

Brentano, F. (1995). *Psychology from an empirical standpoint* (A. C. Rancurrello, D. B. Terrell & L. L. McAlister, Trans.) New York: Routledge. (Original work published 1874)

Bridges, L. J., Grolnick, W. S., & Connell, J. P. (1997). Infant emotion regulation with mothers and fathers. *Infant Behavior and Development, 20*, 47-57.

Cole, P. M., Martin, S. E., & Dennis, T. A. (2004). Emotion regulation as a scientific construct: Methodological challenges and directions for child development research. *Child Development, 75*(2), 317-333.

Deci, E., & Ryan, R. (1985). *Intrinsic motivation and self-determination in human behavior.* New York: Plenum.

Diriwächter, R. (2004a). Editor's preface. *From Past to Future, 5*(1), 1-2.

Diriwächter, R. (2004b). Ganzheitspsychologie: The doctrine. *From Past to Future 5*(1), 3-16.

Diriwächter, R. (2004c). Völkerpsychologie: The synthesis that never was. *Culture & Psychology, 10*(1), 85-109.

Diriwächter, R., & Valsiner, J. (2005, December). Qualitative developmental research methods in their historical and epistemological contexts [53 paragraphs]. *Forum Qualitative Sozialforschung/Forum: Qualitative Social Research* [Online Journal], *7*(1), Art 8. Retrieved December 1, 2005, from http://www.qualitative-research.net/fqs-texte/1-06/06-1-8-e.htm

Geertz, C. (1983). *Local knowledge: Further essays in interpretive anthropology.* New York: Basic Books.

Grolnick, W. S., Bridges, L. J., & Connell, J. P. (1996). Emotion regulation in two-year olds: Strategies and emotional expression in four contexts. *Child Development. 67*, 928-941.

Grolnick, W. S., McMenamy, J. M., & Kurowski, C. O. (1999). Emotional self-regulation in infancy and toddlerhood. In L. Balter & C. S. Tamis-LeMonda (Eds.), *Child psychology: A handbook of contemporary issues* (pp. 3-22). New York: Psychology Press.

Haskell, V., DiLallo, M., DeCourcey, W., & McHale, J. (2003, April). *Family processes at infancy and the use of play as an emotion regulation strategy in the toddler years.* Poster presented at Conference for the Society for Research in Child Development, Tampa, Florida.

Haskell, V., Valsiner, J., & McHale, J. P. (2003, June). *Toddlers' processing of affect in symbolic self-soothing: The early development of symbolic play skills.* Poster presented at the 33rd annual meeting of The Jean Piaget Society: Play and Development, Chicago.

Haskell, V., & McHale, J. P. (2004, July). *Symbolic processes in a toddler's efforts to move forward in the face of uncertainty.* Paper presented 18th biennial meeting of the International Society for the Study of Behavioural Development, Ghent, Belgium.

Haskell V., Ono, K., & McHale, J. P. (2004, August). *Multivoicedness in early child-hood regulatory processes: A developmental perspective.* Paper presented The 3rd annual conference on the Dialogical Self, Warsaw, Poland.

Haskell, V., DeCourcey, W., & McHale, J. (2005, April). *Cross-parent consistencies and differences in toddlers' emotion regulation strategies.* Poster presented at Conference for the Society for Research in Child Development, Atlanta, Georgia.

Hermans, H. (2001). The dialogical self: Toward a theory of personal and cultural positioning. *Culture and Psychology, 7*(3), 243-281.

Hermans, H., & Hermans-Jansen, E. (2001). Affective processes in a multivoiced self. In H. Bosna & S. Kunnen (Eds.), *Identity and emotion: Development through self-organization* (pp. 120-140). Cambridge, MA: Cambridge University Press.

Hermans, H. J., & Hermans-Jansen, E. (2003). Dialogical processes in the development of the self. In J. Valsiner & K. J. Conolly (Eds.), *Handbook of developmental psychology* (pp. 534-559). London: Sage.

Kaplan, B. (1983). Genetic-dramatism: Old wine in new bottles. In S. Wapner & B. Kaplan (Eds.), *Toward a holistic developmental psychology* (pp. 53-74). Hillsdale, NJ: Erlbaum.

Lewin, K. (1931). *A dynamic theory of personality.* New York: McGraw-Hill.

Lewis, M. D., & Ferrari, M. (2001). Cognitive-emotional self-organization in personality development and personal identity. In H. Bosna & S. Kunnen (Eds.), *Identity and emotion: Development through self-organization* (pp. 177-201). New York: Cambridge University Press.

Molenaar, P. C. M. (2004). A manifesto on Psychology as idiographic science: Bringing the person back into scientific psychology, this time forever. *Measurement, 2*(4), 201-218.

Molenaar, P. C. M., & Newell, K. M. (2003). Direct fit of a theoretical model of phase transition in oscillatory finger motions. *British Journal of Mathematical and Statistical Psychology, 56,* 199-214.

Molenaar, P. C. M., & Valsiner, J. (2005). How generalization works through the single case: A simple idiographic process analysis of an individual psychotherapy. *International Journal of Idiographic Science*, Article 1. Retrieved August 27, 2005 from http://www.valsiner.com/ articles/molenvals.htm

Piaget, J. (1962). *Play, dreams and imitation in childhood.* New York: W. W. Norton.

Piaget, J. (1985). *The equilibration of cognitive structures: The central problem of intellectual development.* Chicago: The University of Chicago Press. (Original work published 1975)

Popper, K. (2002). *Conjectures and refutations: The growth of scientific knowledge.* London: Routledge. (Original work published 1963)

Trevarthen, C. (1992). An infant's motives for speaking and thinking in the culture. In A. H. Wold (Ed.), *Dialogical alternative: Towards a theory of language and mind* (pp. 99-137). Oslo: The Scandinavian Press.

Valsiner, J. (1986). Between groups and individuals: Psychologists' and laypersons' interpretations of correlational findings. In J. Valsiner (Ed.), *The individual subject and scientific psychology* (pp. 113-151). New York: Plenum Press.

Valsiner, J. (1998). *Guided mind: A sociogenetic approach to personality.* Cambridge, MA: Harvard University Press.

Valsiner, J. (2000). *Culture and human development.* London: Sage.

Valsiner, J. (2003). Culture and its transfer: Ways of creating general knowledge through the study of cultural particulars. In W. J. Lonner, D. L. Dinnel, S. A. Hayes, & D. N. Sattler (Eds.), *Online readings in psychology and culture* (Unit 2, chapter 12). Bellingham, WA: Center for Cross-Cultural Research, Western Washington University.

Valsiner, J. (2005). Soziale und emotionale Entwicklungsaufgaben im kulturellen Kontext [Social and emotional developmental tasks in their cultural context]. In J. Asendorpf & H. Rauh (Eds.), *Enzyklpädie der Psychologie* (Vol. 3). *Soziale, emotionale und Persönlichkeitsentwicklung*. Göttingen: Hogrefe.

Valsiner, J., & Diriwächter, R. (2005). Qualitative Forschungsmethoden in historischen und epistemologischen Kontexten [Qualitative developmental research methods in their historical and epistemological contexts]. In G. Mey (Ed.), *Qualitative Forschung in der Entwicklungspsychologie*. Köln, Germany: Kölner Studien Verlag.

von Uexküll, J. (1957). A stroll through the world of animals and men: A picture book of invisible worlds. In C. H. Schiller (Ed.), *Instinctive behavior: The development of a modern concept* (pp. 5-82). New York: International Universities Press. (Original work published 1934)

Vygotsky, L. S. (1986). *Thought and language* (2nd ed.). Cambridge, MA: MIT Press. (Original work published 1934)

Vygotsky, L., & Luria, A. (1994). Tool and symbol in child development. In R. Van Der Veer & J. Valsiner (Eds.), *The Vygotsky reader*. Cambridge, MA: Blackwell. (Original work published 1930)

Zittoun, T., & Abbey, E. (2004, July). *Beyond uncertainties: Symbolic processes and change*. Symposium presented at the 18th biennial meeting of the International Society for the Study of Behavioural Development, Ghent Belgium.

CHAPTER 6

A RESEARCHER AT THE CROSSROADS

A Commentary Upon Processing Process

Carla Cunha

Valerie Bellas and James McHale (this volume) approach their chapter as a dialogical narrative of a developmental research process, written in the present to retrospectively achieve an analytic view of the past while developing several sequential microgenetic studies. In this commentary, I will maintain dialogism as a semiotic and theoretical tool to guide my reflections upon their questions and their work. In this sense, it seems useful to start by outlining some of the general principles that guide the dialogical framework as a specific approach to epistemology, psychological science, and professional ethics. Following this, I will focus and elaborate on some of the questions raised by Bellas and McHale about the scientific developmental process of an investigator, the values for psychological theory and practice within this approach and the guidelines for microgenetic methodologies. Having highlighted some of the challenges and theoretical difficulties that need to be overcome in order to create meaningful and innovative research and theory, I will take the chance to

Innovating Genesis: Microgenesis and the Constructive Mind in Action, pp. 139–156
Copyright © 2008 by Information Age Publishing
All rights of reproduction in any form reserved.

present some of my personal decisions regarding these issues in my own developing process of a microgenetic psychological study.

DIALOGUE AS THE PROCESS AND THE CONTENT

With its strong emphasis on the rejection of a representational epistemology which characterized modern science, postmodernist thinking, in particular the social constructivist movement lead the way to a profound and relevant critique concerning the social sciences. In turn, this aspect draws attention to the social, relational, and dialogical features of meaning making, in particular the creation of scientific knowledge (Salgado & Hermans, 2005). However, the extreme versions of this critique (e.g., Gergen, 1994) which argued in favor of the refusal of any kind of private and internal psychological experience lead to a social solipsism that created a few problems to psychology (Marková, 2003b). Namely, what could be the role of a science that aimed to study subjectivity, if there are no such things as subjective experiences? Are psychologists left to accept that this science has an impossible object of study? Are we to resign to only what exists between people? As Salgado (2003) has questioned before:

> If someone uses introspection and tries to know himself, he is turning into an interior world that was socially constructed; when he symbolizes a certain body state with an emotional label, the same happens. Does this mean that you are relating to someone? Yes and no. In a certain sense, you are alone; in another you are accompanied by all of those who share the same sphere of intelligibility. But, independently of it, you are having a private and personal experience. (p. 189)

Dialogism seems to create a solution to this dilemma. Subjectivity is still a viable object of study for psychology with the "admittance that, once familiarized with some particular language, the individual has authentic private (in opposition to public, explicitly shared) experiences" (Salgado & Hermans, 2005, p. 7). It is my belief that, in a dialogical epistemological stance, we can admit having private and subjective experiences, without needing an essentialist foundation to that subjectivity or to psychology. According to Marková (2003b), the necessary developments for psychology to achieve its goals are: to stop being mute to ontology and to commit to an ontological stance on the nature of human beings and human change, thus allowing the impasse between the individual solipsism of foundational epistemologies and the social solipsism of social constructionists to break. If we characterize the mind "as the capacity of human beings to communicate, to make sense of signs, symbols and meanings" (p. 23), "a situated and historically constituted phenomenon in communication, tension and change" (p. 24), we have an ontological commitment of the human being as a dialogical, communicational, and relational being, in an unavoidable and temporally irreversible change process that is at every time rooted in history and culture. In sum, dialogism implies a necessary ontological commitment of the human existence as a communicational existence, since "*to be* means to *symbolically communicate.*" (p. xiii).

Following this argument and in an approach clearly inherited from Mikhail Bakhtin, Salgado and Gonçalves (2007) assume four main axiomatic principles for dialogism: (1) the principle of relational primacy; (2) the principle of dialogicality; (3) the principle of alterity; and (4) the principle of contextuality.

The relational primacy draws attention to the human life as a relational life with an *Other* (being this other person, other dimensions of self, the social realm, etc.). The other is always considered to be intrinsically connected to an *I* since "Being is simultaneity; it is always *co*-being" (Holquist, 1990, p. 24). Subjectivity is only possible because relationships with other human beings allow it: "Nobody exists alone—in fact, every human being is, from the very beginning, involved in a relational and communicational process" (Salgado & Hermans, 2005, p. 8). For some decades now, the field of developmental psychology has been presenting increasing evidence that argues in favor of an innate intersubjectivity as the most powerful developmental tool—a specific social awareness and orientation towards the other that allows babies to establish relationships (Trevarthen & Aitkin, 2001).

The principle of dialogicality sends us to the necessary simultaneity of at least two responsive dialogical participants in the dialogical encounter creating a communicational interchange (Salgado & Gonçalves, 2007). At this point we are faced with the concept of dialogue both as metaphor and metonymy for dialogism. In this sense, if human existence is dialogue and happens through dialogue, psychology has to necessarily deal with it as a process and a product. The concept of dialogue has an abstract sense and it refers to several different conditions (Linell, in press): (a) to the meaning that is produced during the dialogical encounter; (b) to the communication that is produced through a semiotic device—like language; (c) to the social *praxis* that provide the specific context to the communication; and (d) to the difference of the participants in interaction. However, if in our discussion we talk about dialogical relations, we necessarily and simultaneously invite the (dia)logical opposite—monologue. Hence, we might ask: can we have a monological relation with an *Other*? By axiomatic assumption, an encounter between two individuals is necessarily dialogical (while an encounter between a person and an object is usually monological), since it is an encounter with two responsive interlocutors and the relation is the absolutely inseparable unit. However, Salgado and Gonçalves (2007) state that the monologicality versus dialogicality dilemma is more dependent on the sort of interchange that occurs and least on the kind of entities relating. If one interlocutor tries to exclude and annihilate the other, treating him like a nonresponsive object (an *it*), we can categorize this act as monologization of the *Other* (Holquist, 1990). In this sense, I will later argue on how traditional psychology has sometimes created a monological account of human beings, treating their research participants as monological entities, instead of persons. Nevertheless, according to dialogism, the simultaneity of the dialogical *Other* is so fundamental that it moves us to the third principle.

In a Bakhtinian reasoning, the principle of alterity emphasizes that, a subjective existence is a consequence of the irreducible and necessary relation of tension and difference between an *I* and an *Other*, an *Ego* and an *Alter* (Marková, 2003b; Salgado & Gonçalves, 2007). As we have seen, a dialogue implies simultaneity and responsiveness between participants in an irreversible time and space; however, communication and addressivity can only occur in the inevitable difference that exists between both dialogical elements (Holquist, 1990). Alterity implies, above all, difference and tension. "Through tension, the self is not attempting to fuse with the other but, instead, to set his own position and to assimilate strangeness" (Marková, 2003a, p. 257). This principle draws attention to a striking difference between this point of view and the social constructionist focus: while the latter focuses on what is common and emphasizes what is shared, dialogism emphasizes this radical difference and the never-ending tension between interlocutors. It goes further than sharedness, by putting emphasis on the assumption that subjectivity emerges from a position of outsidedness: "to communicate means to be for another, and through the other, for oneself" (Marková, 2003a, p. 257). The self can only author itself by the subjective appropriation of the *Other*'s view—and the view of the *Other* is marked by the radical difference that exists in-between. For dialogue to occur there has to be a difference that keeps meanings in motion: any meaning can only emerge from its difference towards an(other).

The last axiomatic principle in this discussion is the principle of contextuality, which relates us to the specific social-historical-cultural context that surrounds a particular dialogical encounter and gives it its intelligibility. The context situates the discourse: there are no independent messages from its context and so, contexts would not be what they are in the absence of a given construction of meaning which thus, situates them (Linell, in press). In this sense, dialogism and social constructionism share the view of local "truths" and situated historical, social and cultural "realities"—the social construction of phenomena. Nevertheless, it admits, above all, that this kind of dialogically created reality is subjectively appropriated by individuals—and this should not be ignored by the psychological science.

A Dialogical View of the Scientific Process

Bellas and McHale's chapter, in my view, illustrates how the scientific process of a specific investigator is a dialogical process, built out of tension and dissatisfaction that makes the researcher move further from one study to the next. This sincere narrative shows us not a logical and cumulative sequence that usually appears in the dominant narratives characterizing the scientific process and acquisition of knowledge, but instead a tensional sequence, a series of attempts to surpass difficulties and improve on limitations, that at some point in time where recognized or valued by the investigators. Though this narrative presents a personal reflection of an individual process, I personally recognize and identify myself with some of the feelings and doubts presented here, and it will probably lead to the same outcome in the minds of other young researchers reading this in the future.

In this sense, Bellas and McHale's chapter is a narrative of the scientific process that humanizes it because science is above all a human process which, like any other, is dialogical in my point of view. Perhaps this chapter, more than describing the scientific process itself, is a narrative that characterizes the process of a human being involved in a scientific investigation of a certain area. Most of the time, this development is not a rational, linear, and logical one, but tensional and affective as well—and this clearly contrasts with the popular versions of how to "make" science. In their chapter, we can see how imagined interlocutors or specific scientific audiences were involved with them in a communicational interchange that invoked the conflict, tension, and disagreement of other points of view, alternative explanatory positions and profitable criticisms, and how these internal and external dialogues kept creating the transformation and further inquiry that led to the different studies.

Science is an unfinished process—always in mutation and transformation that generates the kind of dissatisfaction in the investigator that Bellas and McHale communicate to their readers. This may be related to an effort in achieving some other place, some other point in knowledge—an orientation to the future, to the next question and the next challenge in the anticipatory integration of the future in the present that characterizes human existence (Abbey & Valsiner, 2004). Like any effort of meaning-making science is always incomplete, unfinished, in motion—this never-ending human/social/historical/cultural context that is the scientific endeavor is always demanding further creation and innovation. Any researcher who was well-acculturated within this sphere of intelligibility suffers from the same ambition, which is at the same time his/her motive and his/her anguish.

Thus, the researcher lives in a dynamic between what is already created and what is not-yet understood, in which any point of departure has already been a point of arrival. However, in his effort to subjectively incorporate the knowledge already created and build novel knowledge in an innovative and creative act (with all the contingencies this holds, historical and accidental), the researcher has to comply with the rules and values of this communicational encounter between scientific participants like peers, supervisors, faculty, and scientific community in general. Obviously, the creative process is not totally free—the scientific community has its constrictions, values, language, and action codes like any other dialogical and communicational arena. So, this pressure for creativity and innovation is a rather constricting one—new findings have to be situated in the careful yet challenging balance between previously accepted intelligibility discourses and novel ones to be assimilated and approved.

Some of these novel scientific products (for example, new theories) may not be accepted immediately by the scientific community, or not accepted at all. Psychology has several examples of creative minds not readily acknowledged by their scientific peers and whose ideas waited a long time for delayed or eventual recognition (e.g., Lev Vygotsky, Jean Piaget, Mikhail Bakhtin). Nevertheless, once these scientific products and constructs are accepted by the scientific community and become usual in their discourse they are exported *a posteriori* to the general community in the shape of practical speeches about everyday common phenomena (we could think about the enormous amount of self-help books about motivation, emotional intelligence, and personal relationships that are found in bookstores).

If we take the methodology cycle (Valsiner, 2006) as a structuring lens and make a brief reading of this process, we can see how our general common sense assumptions enter the scientific field as an intuitive experience of researchers that in turn elaborate methods that capture certain aspects of the phenomena, collecting some data that becomes comprehensible in scientific theories that, then return to the general public transforming (or not) their general assumptions and/or creating new ones. So, if we assume an epistemological stance that true scientific knowledge is the one that is accepted by a specific scientific community in a given social, cultural, and historical time, in this sense, is always situated in that linguistic community that considers it valid, I pose this question: From an ethical point of view, should our knowledge and methodologies also be exposed to the scrutiny of its lay participants—the first and the last targets of this cycle of knowledge? Generally this sensitive question is usually put aside by the argument of, lack of expertise of these participants with the scientific terminology and technical discourse that we use, but in this line of reasoning, we have to admit that scientific knowledge is a form of power that separates the educated and the ignorant—and the latter will not be heard in this knowledge production cycle. This possibility certainly leads me to reflect on alternatives.

I can speculate that a possible solution for this problem could be to also make this knowledge production cycle dialogical: the researcher should be involved in an emphatic active effort to understand the subjective position of the *Other* (being this other the coparticipant in the investigation). After all, if we as psychologists want to make of subjectivity our object of study and we, as humans, are always constricted by the radical difference that exists between us, it is necessary to hear the voice of our participants— because our theories will be about them. Psychological science has already produced an enormous amount of knowledge that was deaf to the subject's point of view. In this traditional way of doing research, the researcher monologically dominates the subjectivity of the *Other*: it reduces the participant to the passivity and nonresponsive status of an object (instead of a person). In my perspective as a psychologist and researcher, I believe that a dialogical, epistemological, theoretical and ethical point of view, are valuable, and so it is important: to engage in dialogue with the *Other*, and let my initial assumptions, categories of analysis and latter theories be influenced and enriched by the participant's subjective position.

Accepting the Challenge of *Microgenesis*

Bellas and McHale mention several challenges a microgenetic researcher has to face and places the demand for innovation in every step of the scientific process: in the definition of the phenomena to be studied, in the link between theories and methods of investigation, in the tracking of a constantly changing object of study, in the analysis of data and in the writing of the results.

The Ambiguity of the Starting Point

One of the first challenges they faced as microgenetic researchers was the dilemma of how to find a starting point (which is arbitrary since it is the product of a human decision) and how to grasp the phenomena (while discarding what is not important for our purposes). These questions lead us to the first challenge of the microgenetic process, common to any other scientific process, which is the definition of the phenomena. The definitions, or better, the descriptions of the phenomena are multiple, polysemic—or, in a Bakhtinian terminology—endowed of *heteroglossia* (Bakhtin, 1981). Trying to describe a certain phenomena, or deciding how, places the investigator in the center of the ambiguity created by the multiplicity of ways to describe something (the specific phenomena), by different (theoretical) points of view, different (theoretical or empirical) intentions, different interlocutors or contexts. Ambiguity is "an emergent and continuously present property of selfhood and meaning-making processes" (Ferreira, Salgado, & Cunha, 2006, p. 10). However, this ambiguity has to be (at least partially) overcome if we want to communicate something. The scientific descriptions of phenomena occur, thus, in a complex communicational space that forces its participants to a reduction of ambiguity while changing to a symbolic level of linguistic exchange. As such, this is an inevitable and irreversible transition to a different level from the one where the target phenomena occur—the level of experience. Placing something in this communicational space implies a dialogical interaction with an *Other* (supervisor, peers, etc.) and even if it may potentially create other sources of *heteroglossia*, it is restricted by the rules that mediate this scientific interchange and the need to be understood by the interlocutor. In this reasoning, a starting point in a microgenetic investigation is never orphan of others, especially, the voices of other theories.

Thus, from my point of view, microgenetic research should start by the articulation of a theory that allows a description of phenomena in its process of transformation (Valsiner, 2006), which is the intent behind this kind of research. In this sense, it should be framed within a theory that provides adequate linguistic devices to the characterization of becoming. This is actually a challenge in itself since language tends to be static and lack the adequate terminology to describe a constantly changing object of study (Valsiner, 2006). Referring to this issue, Valsiner emphasizes the vertical consistency between axiomatic assumptions, theories, concepts, methodologies, collected data, and descriptions of phenomena as the adequate way to accomplish scientific knowledge—especially in the field of developmental science. Microgenetic intentionality will probably lead the investigator to situate in this field—a general orientation that focuses particularly in "the dynamic interplay of processes across time, levels of analysis, and contexts." (Carolina Consortium on Human Development, 1996, cited in Valsiner, 2006) in contrast with a large tradition of developmental psychology that has been unfortunately focused mostly on outcomes and in tracking the differences between individuals. Aiming to look for microgenesis within the focus of developmental science will probably lead the investigator to engage in the creation of innovative methods "tailored" to the study of phenomena within that vertical methodological consistency and that specific research(er) point of view, instead of using prescribed or "ready-made" methods supposedly "correct" to access any given developmental process. In sum, finding an adequate semiotic-organizing-system is imperative in this field of microgenesis, since it is not the microgenetic method by itself that allows us to achieve the previously mentioned research ambitions.

Constructions Versus Constraints of the Objects of Study

In this moment of the discussion, Bellas and McHale's concern about the possibility of constriction and "creation" of phenomena and data (since every study implies that some decisions will be made about which descriptions and analytic categories will be privileged over others), needs to be reflected upon. This question has different implications when it is asked within a representational epistemology, where it enquires if our knowledge represents the world, and consequently, the essence of things or objects of study it intends to explain. In this epistemological framework, even if it were necessarily implicit, the "construction" and constrictions upon the descriptions would be denied. This rising concern would inevitably lead to an exclusion of this theoretical knowledge, since this framework allows no ambiguity or doubt (Ferreira, Salgado, & Cunha, 2006).

On the contrary, the epistemological line of reasoning that I have been using derives from an epistemological framework which is aware that the linguistic games we choose to play will necessarily constrain our vision of the phenomena. In this sense and however pertinent it may be to argue upon the implications of these "constructions" and constrictions, they do not necessarily lead to the elimination of knowledge. Another important remark to note is that, when we are describing something, we are at the level of meaning-making, which is like I said before, a different level from the one where experience occurs. This is an inevitable gap that will always be present in our psychological science, and this distance can never be overcome because these two levels (experiential vs. semiotic/linguistic/meaning-making) will never coincide. In this line of reasoning, the issue turns out to be whether or not our descriptions are open to the subjective experience of the *Other*. This openness to the *Other* will necessarily present some obstacles to psychology because we will never reduce the radical difference that separates and differentiates two unique human beings (Jacques, 1991). However, in my view, this effort of openness and attunement with the *Other* needs to be intentional and pursued in psychological research, instead of mistakenly taken for granted.

Hence, our ambitions as psychologists and researchers may shift to the construction of such adequate descriptions that respect the subjective experience of other human beings—dialogical descriptions. What I mean with this, is that, we may want to construct scientific knowledge as the product of a dialogical interchange between the investigator and the interlocutors (the research participants), played with an effort of achieving some kind of empathic understanding in this process. In this dialogical encounter the rejoinders will both be enriched and modified by each other's positioning (with their own background and preferential linguistic games). The scientific endeavor is to seek a "surplus of seeing" (Holquist, 1990) emergent of this dialogical encounter that enhances the possible description of the *Other*: the researcher's vision needs to be added to the vision of the *Other*, so that a complemented perspective of the whole is created combining both points of view. Consequently, psychology would come closer to subjectivity.

When referring to the data analysis stage, Bellas and McHale state that for a process of meaning-making to occur from the collected data, a new look at the theories has to be done—as we can see, this shows how the process of meaning-making is never a orphan of theories. This is so, because, "the world does not speak; only we do" (Rorty, 1989, p. 26) and, like the world, data requires efforts of meaning making that emerge generally from the semiotic field of theories, even if these are opposite ones (in an A vs. Non-A relationship; see Abbey & Valsiner, 2004).

Finally, the writing of results is played again in the linguistic and communicational arena. This step of the investigative process is another one where innovation comes into action. However, like I have mentioned before, the products of the investigative process are the somewhat challenging equation of the empathic movement of the investigator towards the subjectivity of the other and his/hers return to his/hers own yet already different subjectivity and the norms and rules of the linguistic community (interlocutors and audiences) where they are to be communicated. Acceptance of these products, either immediate or delayed, imply a new semiotic device that opens the horizon to further possibilities of (linguistic) action, creation of theoretical alternatives, referential concepts and novel psychological "realities" or constructs. Innovation always involves a re-description of the phenomena and it is always played in the semiotic, linguistic field—so this should be our ultimate goal and achievement as microgenetic researchers. Thus, the innovation required in this step of the process is a linguistic one—played at the meaning-making level.

The Riddle of Psychological Time

Another important challenge for microgenetic research highlighted by Bellas and McHale is the tracking of a constantly changing object of study. If "The central descriptive unit of dynamic focus is the notion of trajectory—movement through time" (Valsiner, 2002b) we are left with a problem concerning the adequacy of a given arbitrary decision on how to deal with time or how to construct the adequate temporal units to capture an evolving psychological phenomenon, especially subjective experience. If "A person creates signification by way of a sign in a here-and-now-to-future context" (Josephs, Valsiner, & Surgan, 1999, p. 258), how can we capture the meaning-making process that is happening "now?" The question about what is the nature of "now" has intrigued some authors (e.g., Stern, 2004). I have been particularly interested by the possibility of human beings experiencing a discontinuous flow of experience in time. Stern uses an ancient distinction of time to address this issue: the Greek view of *chronos* (the objective view of continuous time, as measured by our clocks) and *kairos* (which is the subjective time experienced as a whole in discontinuous lived moments, different and independent "present moments of lived experience"). This distinction allows us to address the recognized differentiation relating to the incompatibility of the perception of our subjective experience with an objective passing of time (when we are anxiously awaiting for something, we have all been surprised by the experience of the prolonging of time rather than the experience of its objective measure). It seems to me that, if we want to adequately describe the subjective experience, we need to focus on *kairos* or the "present moment." This author presents some necessary characteristics of the "present moment" (Stern, 2004) and I have selected a few for this illustration: (a) "Awareness or consciousness is a necessary condition for a present moment" (p. 32), (b) "The felt experience of the present moment is whatever is in awareness now, during the moment being lived" (p. 32), (c) "Present moments are of short duration" (p. 33), (d) "Present moments are holistic happenings" (p. 35), (e) "Present moments are temporally dynamic" (p. 36), and (f) "The experiencing self takes a stance relative to the present moment" (p. 39).

The "present moment" of subjective experience is the feeling of what happens and implies the recognition of myself as the centre of that experience (characteristic *a*) and what is now in my awareness (*b*). For example, I may now be thinking about how to finish writing this idea, but if I am suddenly interrupted and someone asks me what I was thinking, I shift to a different present moment, which is trying to objectively explain my past experience to someone. The subjective experience of "now" is an independent experience, a gestalt (*d*) and is usually compared to the duration of a musical sequence, since they are both units of meaning-making as a whole (*c*). However, their short duration accompanies the dynamics of our affective field (*e*)—always shifting according to changes in the level 1 of processes of generalization and hyper-generalization in affective regulation of the flow of experience (general immediate presemiotic feeling) (see Valsiner, 2005). The experiencing self may also be more or less involved in the present moment, since it can distance itself or become closer, or even evaluate what is happening (*f*) (Stern, 2004).

In this line of reasoning, the notion of our temporal units will be shaped out of the developmental process that we are studying (always with the background of our assumptions and theories that conceptualize the subjective psychological process as a whole). In this framework, we can select phenomenological events instead of mere parts of an experience to focus on our studies—and this is, in my view, substantially different from a methodological device that leads us to divide the process into a chronological sequence. In this last case, we are placed in the heart of the parts-and-whole dilemma, without ever constructing a solid view of the gestalt phenomena we want to grasp.

I am becoming increasingly fascinated by the possibility of studying the present moment of lived experience, because it is my understanding that it may be nicely combined with the Bakhtinian notions of positioning and event of the self (Holquist, 1990): everything is experienced from a certain position in existence and the meaning of experience is necessarily influenced by the position from where it is being apprehended by the person; this position is always experienced as an event, an event of being a self (a self in that specific position) in space and time.

My Ongoing Personal Dialogues With *Microgenesis*

My interest in microgenesis started, like any other microgenetic researcher, by the possibility of keeping a persistent involvement with psychological processes constantly evolving and changing. Emerging in the background of an interest in the dialogical self theory (DST, e.g., Hermans, 1999; Hermans, Kempen, & Van Loon, 1992) and dialogism (with its implications to psychology—see Marková, 2003b; Salgado & Hermans, 2005), I wanted to grasp the imaginary dialogues and movements between *I-positions* in an interview with a participant (Gonçalves & Cunha, 2004). This interview is assumed as a semiotic tool (or a complex set of successive semiotic devices) to create the possibility of meaning-making by fostering internal dialogues (between *I-positions* in the participant) and external dialogues (in the interaction of interviewer and interviewee).

Dialogism (e.g., Holquist, 1990; Salgado & Hermans, 2005) allowed me to arrive at a conceptualization of human beings as intersubjective and relational beings, always in interaction with an *Other*, and the DST gave me the possibility to depict the self as a relational, social, cultural, and dialogical process and product (Hermans, Kempen, & Van Loon, 1992; Salgado & Hermans, 2005). I was, however, unsatisfied with some empirical versions of the DST (see Ferreira, Salgado, Cunha, Meira, & Konopka, 2005, for an analysis of different levels of multivoicedness in DST research) and increasingly more interested in the concept of *I-position* as a given center of experience in the self (Salgado & Ferreira, 2005)—a Bakhtinian event of the self (Holquist, 1990). In this sense, subjectivity is constituted by a dynamic flow and succession of *I-positions*, each one engaged in dialogue and creating novel meaning-making throughout the passing of each lived moment. Daniel Stern's (2004) view on the "present moment" gave me the unit of analysis to track the shifting of one *I-position* to another. I assumed that this novel conceptualization allowed me to bring the dialogical approach nearer to the phenomenology of experience.

Emerging from these theoretical decisions, the intentions of this microgenetic study became: (1) to depict and characterize the dynamic flow of *I-positions* in the dialogue and, (2) to keep track of the subjective meaning-making processes that accompany the flow of the lived experience during a research interview (Cunha & Gonçalves, 2005). This study also has other specific goals, it aims to achieve in the articulation between the microgenetic and the mesogenetic levels of analysis (Valsiner, 2002a), like: (a) the description and modeling of specific autoregulation processes in the dialogical self that maintain a dynamic stability in the meaning-making processes through time; (b) the description of how specific semiotic devices may introduce innovation and change; and, (c) the characterization of the dialogical change processes that may appear (Cunha & Gonçalves, 2005). However, the last three research objectives will not be discussed here, since their elaboration would "distract" us from our illustrative purposes in this commentary.

So, with the first and second objectives in mind, my transcripts of the interviews became a pathway of changing *I-positions*, involved in specific meaning-making processes at each given "present moments." I decided to cut the entire transcript into different utterances—which I conceived as different *I-positions* in time and analyze each utterance with different parameters (this was also inspired in the work of Leiman, 2004). With dialogism and DST in the background the following parameters of analysis seemed important to me in light of the purposes of this study: The agent (*who* is speaking); The interlocutor (or specific audiences *to whom* he is speaking); The content (*what* is being said, the contents of speech); The intentionality (*why* is it being said); and the "storytelling-event" (in a terminology borrowed from Stanton Wortham, 2001) that refers to *how* is it being said, as the intersubjective positioning towards the interlocutor. I believe these to be the important criteria for a truly dialogical account of the phenomenology of subjective experience: the dialogical interchange between an *I* and an *Other*.

The transcripts, being the result of a dialogical encounter between the participant and the interviewer, already identify the interlocutors in dialogue. However, Bakhtin (1981) argues for a *double addressivity* in communication: "each utterance is always addressed toward an object (or, more precisely, addressed toward the specific available discourses about a given object), but it is also addressed to an interlocutor" (Salgado & Hermans, 2005, p. 8). In this sense, the participant is not only addressing the present interlocutor, but also addressing the possible alternative ways of meaning-making, possible contents of speech, or his past *I-positions*, at each "present moment." The intentionality implicit in the meaning-making process allows me to grasp different intersubjective positionings or orientations of the participant at each point of the interview, simultaneously creating unique "storytelling events" by the succession of the participant's different attitudes towards his audience in the dialogue.

An Illustration of the Microgenetic Analysis of the Transcripts

To allow a better clarification of the microgenetic methodology of analyzing the transcripts, I will now illustrate with a specific excerpt of a transcript.

This transcript refers to an interview with a research participant that chose to discuss his professional situation as a significant personal problem which causes him a certain amount of distress and worrying in his daily life. Throughout the interview, the participant talked about his dissatisfaction with his present professional situation and the possibility of changing jobs. However, this option elicits concern with the unknown future and the risk of making a mistake. As the interview continues, the participant brings forth different ways of positioning himself in face of these personal concerns and worries, expressing a dynamic stability in a conflict between being "too worried" or "too indifferent" about his professional situation and considering the implications between being "passive" or "active" towards a decision that would bring uncertainty to his future. Throughout the interview, we can also depict the proliferation and escalating of these positions (Valsiner, 2002a), while he proceeds in further elaborating and describing his problem (e.g., "me as worried" vs. "me as excessively worried," "me as apparently unworried").

In the specific excerpt that is being presented here, the participant is reflecting on what he would think about this present problem if he was to project himself in a positive future, 10 years from now. Looking back from this point in the future into his present concerns and fears, he says:

Participant: Perhaps, I would ask... (utterance 123) *Why so much worrying?* (utterance 124) *Because, after all, everything was solved!* (utterance 125)

According to the microgenetic methodology that I have been describing, this question presents three *I-positions*, connected to three "present-moments" (identified by these different utterances). Each one of these utterances is analyzed according to the referred parameters of analysis, as the Table 6.1 presents.

In this small excerpt, we can see how the participant shifts from one *I-position* to the next, semiotically (re)organizing himself in face of the specific task and his meaning-making elaborations. While doing this, he speaks from different phenomenological points, to specific interlocutors and audiences. What he says accompanies and reflects his flow of experience and places him with different intersubjective orientations towards the interlocutor, himself and the specific contents of his speech and thinking, while creating the first glimpse of a novel way to view the present situation—"I as an Optimist," that becomes further elaborated in the rest of the interview.

A Researcher at the Crossroads: Concluding Remarks

Being a psychologist or a psychological researcher is dealing with ambiguity and uncertainty as a way of life. Microgenesis is a particular

Table 6.1.   An Example of the Microgenetic Analysis

Parameters	Utterance 123	Utterance 124	Utterance 125
Who?	I as in the present	I as if I was the positive future	I as if I was the positive future
For whom?	The interviewer + the positive future	The interviewer + I as in the present	The interviewer + I as in the present
What?	He states that he would ask	He asks why so much worrying	He states that after all everything was solved
Why?	Complying with the request of the interviewer: imagining and explaining the dialogue between present and a point in the future where he looks upon this moment	Performing the same task: imagining and explaining the dialogue between present and a point in the future where he looks upon this moment	Performing and developing the same task, this time realizing that this future is associated with the resolution of this specific problem and its absence
How?	Repeats the task he has to do to organize himself to imagine	Becomes involved in an imagined position of the future, using the direct speech	Starts presenting himself as an **optimist** about the problem

ambiguous field that presents unique challenges to the investigator at every step of the way, sometimes confronting him/her with multiple directions and crossroads. In these decisive stages of the scientific process, the need for innovation and creativity is almost an imperative. Process, change, development and transformation are the ambitions and seldom attainable goals. However, the chance to observe a psychological phenomenon in its irreversible unfolding and transformation in time is a fascinating area of investigation. Many are the challenges and the anguishes experienced at every step of the way. Nevertheless, since I have been involved in this field, I have caught myself paying attention to the little things in life, the little unrepeatable moments of everyday experience that fade away if unnoticed.

Throughout this commentary, I have tried to highlight some of the scientific challenges in general and those associated with microgenesis in particular. I have argued that psychology has to make an ontological commitment to the nature of human beings and human process so that subjectivity reenters the psychological arena of investigation with a renewed impetus. At this stage of my work, I have been satisfied with the possibilities that the dialogical epistemological, theoretical and ethical framework have given me and with the conceptualization of human beings as essentially relational beings. Hence, the dialogical perspective was always present as the guiding structure of my comments and my reflections, just like it is present in my work. Some decisive periods of the research process were highlighted and discussed: challenges in the definitions/descriptions of the phenomena, the vertical methodological consistency between assumptions, theories, and methodologies, some of the questions that appear while making sense of the data and, again, the redefinition of phenomena while describing the results.

The reflection presented here, although quite challenging to me, also helped me to organize my thoughts and theoretical stances around my work. Since all this was written for the always present audience of my (possible) future readers, I hope this work can be useful and potentially inspiring to other young researchers.

REFERENCES

Abbey, E., & Valsiner, J. (2004, December). Emergence of meanings through ambivalence [58 paragraphs]. *Forum Qualitative Sozialforschung/Forum: Qualitative Social Research* [Online Journal], 6(1), Art. 23. Retrieved July 15, 2005, from http://www.qualitative-research.net/fq-texte/1-05/05-1-23-e.htm
Bakhtin, M. M. (1981). *The dialogic imagination: Four essays by M. M. Bakhtin* (C. Emerson & M. Holquist, Trans.). Austin, TX: University of Texas Press.

Cunha, C., & Gonçalves, M. M. (2005, September). *Changing problems while exchanging positions: A microgenetic case-study.* Paper presented at the First ISCAR Congress (International Society for Cultural and Activity Research), Seville, Spain.

Ferreira, T., Salgado, J., & Cunha, C. (2006). Ambiguity and the dialogical self: In search for a dialogical psychology. *Estudios de Psicología, 27*, 19-32.

Ferreira, T., Salgado, J., Cunha, C., Meira, L., & Konopka, A. (2005). Talking about voices: A critical reflection about levels of analysis on the dialogical self. In P. Holes & H. J. M. Hermans (Eds.), *The dialogical self: Theory and research.* Lublin, Poland: Wydawnictwo, KUL.

Gergen, K. (1994). *Realities and relationships: Soundings in social construction.* Cambridge, MA: Harvard University Press.

Gonçalves, M. M., & Cunha, C. (2004). *Identity positions interview.* Unpublished interview, University of Minho, Portugal.

Hermans, H. J. M. (1999). Voicing the self: From information processing to dialogical interchange. *Psychological Bulletin, 119*, 31-50.

Hermans, H. J. M., Kempen, H., & Van Loon, R. (1992). The dialogical self: Beyond individualism and rationalism. *American Psychologist, 47*, 23-33.

Holquist, M. (1990). *Dialogism: Bakhtin and his world.* New York: Routledge.

Jacques, F. (1991). *Difference and subjectivity: Dialogue and personal identity* (A. Rothwell, Trans.) New Haven, CT: Yale University Press.

Josephs, I. E., Valsiner, J., & Surgan, S. E. (1999). The process of meaning construction. In J. Brandstätder & R. M. Lerner (Eds.), *Action & self development* (pp. 257-282). Thousand Oaks, CA: Sage.

Leiman, M. (2004). Dialogical sequence analysis. In H. J. M. Hermans & G. Dimaggio (Eds.), *The dialogical self in psychotherapy* (pp. 255-269). Hove, East Sussex, England: Brunner-Routledge.

Linell, P. (in press). *Essentials of dialogism: Aspects and elements of a dialogical approach to language, communication and cognition.* Unpublished manuscript.

Marková, I. (2003a). Constitution of the self: Intersubjectivity and dialogicality. *Culture and Psychology, 9*, 249-259.

Marková, I. (2003b). *Dialogicality and social representations.* Cambridge, England: Cambridge University Press.

Rorty, R. (1989). *Contingency, irony and solidarity.* Cambridge, England: Cambridge University Press.

Salgado, J. (2003). *Psicologia narrativa e identidade: Um estudo sobre auto-engano* [Narrative psychology and self-identity: A study on self-deception]. Maia, Portugal: Publismai.

Salgado, J., & Gonçalves, M. M. (2007). The dialogical self: Social, personal, and (un)counscious. In A. Rosa & J. Valsiner (Eds.), *The Cambridge Handbook of Socio-Cultural Psychology* (pp. 608-621). Cambridge, England: Cambridge University Press.

Salgado, J., & Hermans, H. J. M. (2005). The return of subjectivity: From a multiplicity of selves to the dialogical self. *E-Journal of Applied Psychology, 1*, 3-13.

Salgado, J., & Ferreira, T. (2005). Dialogical relationships as triads: Implications for the dialogical self theory. In P. Oles & H. J. M. Hermans (Eds.),

Proceedings of the 3rd International Conference on the Dialogical Self (pp. 141-152). Lublin, Poland: KUL.

Stern, D. N. (2004). *The present moment in psychotherapy and everyday life.* New York: Norton.

Trevarthen, C., & Aitken, K. J. (2001). Infant intersubjectivity: Research, theory, and clinical applications. *Journal of Child Psychological Psychiatry, 42*, 3-48.

Valsiner, J. (2002a). Forms of dialogical relations and semiotic autoregulation within the self. *Theory & Psychology, 12*, 251-265.

Valsiner, J. (2002b, October). *The concept of attractor: How dynamic systems theory deals with future.* Paper presented at the 2nd International Conference on Dialogical Self, Ghent, Belgium.

Valsiner, J. (2005). Affektive Entwicklung im kulturellen Kontext. In J. B. Asendorpf (Ed.), *Enzyklopädie der Psychologie. Soziale, emotionale und Persönlichkeitsentwicklung* (Vol. 3, pp. 677-728). Göttingen: Hogrefe.

Valsiner, J. (2006). Developmental epistemology and implications for methodology. In R. Lerner (Ed.), *Handbook of child psychology: Theoretical models of humandevelopment* (Vol. 1, 6th ed., pp. 166-209). New York: Wiley.

Wortham, S. (2001). *Narratives in action: A strategy for research and analysis.* New York: Teachers College Press.

PART IV

DAYDREAMS

CHAPTER 7

MORPHEUS AWAKENED

Microgenesis in Daydreams

Stacey Pereira and Rainer Diriwächter

Who has not daydreamed at one point or another? The student during a boring lecture, the commuter on his/her ride to work, the girl who cannot fall asleep at night, or the older gentleman silently sitting on a bench along an idle pond—we can all remember those little "adventurous" escapes that breach the boundaries of the external world and take us into the realm of fantasy.

But what are they, these little mental escapades? How is it that at one moment we are trying to solve some given task, only to find ourselves suddenly lost in thoughts that often bear little resemblance to what we were previously pondering? We sought to explore these questions by examining the development of people's daydreams from a microgenetic point of view. Our central aim was to articulate the key characteristics involved in daydreaming and further try to capture parts of the developmental process as it occurs. We believe that such clarification will bring us one step closer to understanding the nature of microgenesis as a whole.

Innovating Genesis: Microgenesis and the Constructive Mind in Action, pp. 159–185
Copyright © 2008 by Information Age Publishing

WHAT IS A DAYDREAM?

There seems to be no universal definition of what a daydream is. Smith (1907) once suggested that daydreaming is a "rest" for the mind from the tiring act of attention. Its key characteristics can be described as "a withdrawal of the attention, more or less complete, from the external senses, and a greater or less degree of mental automatism" (p. 53).

For our present purposes, we opted to borrow Singer and Antrobus's (1970) definition of daydreams, which is operationally clear and understandably concise in its usefulness: A daydream is anything one may be thinking about that does not pertain directly to the task in which one is currently involved. This definition allows for a great variety of people's responses while clearly being able to maintain the distinction between daydreaming and thinking about a task that is presently being performed. Yet defining a phenomenon in one sentence provides little insight into its underlying processes, actual content, and functionality. Hence, we shall continue our investigation by examining some past research on daydreaming in order to crystallize the main trends.

The Content of Daydreams

What do daydreams really consist of? According to Smith (1907), the content of a daydream is believed to be chiefly determined by environment, though its forms are influenced by age, health, and the degree of mental development.

More recently, Singer and McCraven (1961) conducted a study involving some 240 participants between the ages of 10 and 50 years. Participants were given a daydream questionnaire and asked to provide specific examples of daydreams. Results showed that 96% of the participants reported that they engaged in some sort of daydreaming daily; and, that these daydreams generally consisted of clear images of people, objects, or events. The daydreams often involved practical and more private concerns, with strong sexual, altruistic, or good fortune themes. At first glance it appears that daydreaming involves a large degree of visual imagery with a strong orientation towards future interpersonal behavior. As for when and where daydreaming generally occurs, the study reported that participants most often daydreamed when alone and usually daydreamed right before sleep, while in bed. Daydreaming was found to be least frequent when first waking in the morning, during meals, and while engaged in sexual activity. Nonetheless, the conclusions drawn by Singer and McCraven were that, overall, daydreams vary widely in type and content for different people.

The Function of Daydreams

Given that daydreams vary widely in type and content, what is their actual function? Antrobus and Singer (1964) proposed that a function of daydreaming is to help people maintain arousal rather than get drowsy or fall asleep during boring tasks. The researchers instructed participants to watch a blinking light and press a button whenever the light blinked at a brighter intensity during a 90 minute period. Half the participants performed this task while they engaged in verbal free association, while the other half carried out this task as they counted continuously out loud. The results of the study showed that those participants who were allowed to verbally free associate during their activity were more awake, less ill tempered, more comfortable, and more alert. Those participants who were restricted to continuous counting while performing the task were more likely to be uncomfortable and even fall asleep. As already noted, Antrobus and Singer concluded that daydreaming could serve the function of maintaining arousal. However, this maintenance seems to come at a cost: while those participants who verbally free-associated were more alert, more comfortable, and less ill tempered overall, they made more errors than those participants whose verbalizations were limited to counting. Though, when considering that those participants who counted were more likely to fall asleep, there was not much of a difference in accuracy between the two groups.

Generally speaking, Gold and Reilly (1985) suggest that, "the underlying mechanism of daydreaming content is current concerns," (p. 124). In their study, participants were asked to keep daydream logs over a period of 2 weeks. The researchers were interested in learning if personality traits and current concerns were potential influences on daydreams. While no relationship was found between personality traits and daydreams, they found that more than one-third of the participants' daydreams related to their top two reported current concerns. We thus can anticipate that the function of a person's daydreams could have direct relevance to his/her current life circumstances or even immediate context.

The Process of Daydreaming

While the above studies nicely illustrate some prominent daydream characteristics, they seem to contribute little towards understanding the actual processes that underlie the phenomena of daydreaming. In an attempt to further refine our knowledge on the actual development of daydreaming, we shall now turn our attention to some theoretical considerations that help clarify the complex qualities involved in daydreaming.

Consciousness

One thing that greatly separates daydreams from night-dreams is the fact that daydreams can be consciously altered by the dreamer. That is, the dreamer can influence the direction in which his/her dreams proceed. At one point the dreamer may be thinking about a movie recently watched, only to find him/herself in the role of the film's hero. The apperceptive shift is often subtle, without much advanced planning, yet predominantly interconnected with the past and/or present environment (or *Umwelt* in the sense of von Uexküll, 1909, 1940/1982—see also Smith, 1907). In order to understand these apperceptive shifts that occur through daydreaming, we must first come to terms with its governing principle: consciousness. As understood by Wilhelm Wundt (1922),

> Every psychical compound is composed of a number of psychical elements which do not usually all begin or end at exactly the same moment. As a result, the interconnection which unites the elements to a single whole always reaches beyond the individual compounds, so that different simultaneous and successive compounds are united, though indeed somewhat more loosely. We call this interconnection of psychical compounds *consciousness*. (p. 246)

Wundt's general idea of consciousness was that it is the combined whole of parts of our immediate experience. While Wundt did place emphasis on psychical elements (such as the contents of our immediate experience—ideas, emotions, and/or volitional acts) through his physiological psychology, for the purposes of our current report we need to keep in mind that for Wundt, the actual whole of mental phenomena is qualitatively different from the sum of its parts (see Diriwächter, 2003, 2004a, 2008). During a creative act (such as daydreaming) the whole takes on new characteristics that are not contained in its elements (i.e., an idea becomes more—or different—than just an aggregate of simple sensations and feelings). Thus, Wundt's principle of creative synthesis (*schöpferische Synthese*), which pays tribute to the qualitative change of the whole over its parts, is vital and a necessary axiom for understanding the actual processes that govern the direction of daydreams.

Wundt's Apperceptive Synthesis

According to Wundt (1922), there are predominantly two types of processes of the interconnection of psychical elements: apperceptive synthesis (or combination) and association. Wundt's theory of apperceptive synthesis explains that some elements that are brought forth by associations are purposely emphasized and interconnected through the process of apperception, while others are left in the background. Apperception is

"the process through which any such content is brought to clear comprehension" (p. 252). According to Wundt, the motives of choice can be
explained only from the whole previous development of the individual
consciousness.

Memories in particular may play an important part in active imagination since they interfere and help shape the voluntary images that we con-
jure up. Thus, it may be feasible to assume that the development of
daydreams continues through a sequence of continuous synthesis transformations. That is, apperceptions synthesize, often creatively, to a new
whole mental configuration that in return gives rise to new perceptive and
apperceptive acts.

William James' Notion of Stream of Consciousness

William James also emphasizes the important role of apperceptions
as one of the complex qualities of consciousness. It is not just the awareness of sensations and objects that make up consciousness, but also the
relations of discriminative attention associated with particular sensations and objects. Furthermore, consciousness for James is not static;
rather, it undergoes a constant stream of development. It is an axiom
that humans never stay the same, or as James (1893, p. 154) put it: "No
state once gone can recur and be identical with what it was before."[1]
While some states of mind can hold some sort of time span, thought
overall is forever changing from one state to another. As James (1890)
wrote:

> Such a description [of changing thought] can awaken no possible protest
> from any one. We all recognize as different great classes of our conscious
> states. Now we are seeing, now hearing; now reasoning, now willing; now
> recollecting, now expecting; now loving, now hating; and in a hundred
> other ways we know our minds to be alternately engaged. (p. 230)

As one state transforms into the next, we may well encounter thoughts
that have characteristics similar to those previously conceived. But are
they identical? If one were to experience the same object twice, are the
cognitions associated with that object identical with the initial thoughts?
We do not think this to be the case. Each experience with that same object
requires a fresh look, possibly seen from a different angle or in relation to
different thoughts. This may well be part of an inherent "problem-solving" component involved in daydreaming; something that our present
studies further aimed to explore. Thoughts are not static; and therefore,
the whole of the stream of consciousness preceding the current focus of
the daydream affects it. Each thought, according to James, is actually partially determined by the thoughts before it.

Yet these changes do not happen abruptly. As already indicated, con-sciousness is perceived as a stream that flows continuously without break. A break in consciousness would imply "losing" consciousness! But even so, such breaks in consciousness are seldom felt as interruptions; people are largely unaware of these so-called "breaks." James (1890) compares this phenomenon to that of the blind spot in the eye; even though there are no light receptors where the optic nerve connects to the eye, people do not notice any interruption in sight. Certainly, there is the possibility of interruptions; ongoing cognitive processes can be interrupted by environ-mental factors. However, these interruptions tend to cause confusion between thoughts, not actual breaks in the stream of consciousness. In studying daydreaming, such potential outside interruptions will be referred to as *triggers* since every interruption necessitates a "restart" in the cognitive process.

The Microgenesis of Daydreams

We believe that any attempt at understanding the *process* of daydreaming must be undertaken from a microgenetic vantage point. Since the days when microgenesis (then under the term *Aktualgenese*) was first articulated by Wohlfahrt (1925/1932) in relation to visual Gestalts, it has become a general area of interest in "capturing" the instant-by-instant developmental changes in the "here-and-now" (Diriwächter, 2004b, 2005a). The microgenetic orientation is particu-larly helpful in understanding the transitions of thought, and thus, the development of daydreams. We can hereby draw upon three predomi-nant characteristics while observing microgenetic processes (Siegler & Crowley, 1991, p. 606):

1. Observations span the entire period from the beginning of the change to the time at which it reaches a relatively stable state.
2. The density of observations is high relative to the rate of change of the phenomenon.
3. Observed behavior is subjected to intensive trial-by-trial analysis, with the goal of inferring the processes that give rise to both quan-titative and qualitative aspects of change.

Hence, instead of examining development through "before" and "after" observations and then inferring the development through these particular moments in time (as is often done via questionnaires), the microgenetic approach allows the researcher to collect and analyze a rich amount of data about development as it happens.

Traditionally, the microgenetic approach has been used mostly when studying changes in which the direction of the change is predictable (see

Diriwächter, 2008). However, the direction of change from one focus to another during daydreaming is anything but predictable and is dependent on the whole of the daydreaming person's life experience, which of course is largely unbeknownst to the researcher.

In that regard, Valsiner (2000) describes the microgenetic orientation as a strategy that not only triggers, but also records and investigates phenomena as they emerge. It has three main components: the initial state, the intermediate forms where new forms are being created, and the final state where there are newly created forms. The most important part of the microgenetic orientation is the focus on the "unfolding of the intermediate forms," (p. 78). These forms can be the beginning of what will eventually be a final form or forms that transpire but never actually develop to the point of a final *Gestalt*.

As Valsiner and Van Der Veer (2000) illustrate, *Vorgestalts* ("pre-forms," or "preformulations," see Sander, 1930) can form a particular sequence before reaching their *Endgestalts* ("final form"):

$$A\text{-}ab\text{-}B\text{-}bc\text{-}C \rightarrow \text{leads to final} \rightarrow X$$

The importance in this illustration lies on the ability to capture the development as it is occurring. It places its "focus on the transformation from one unit (A, B) to another (B, C), through an inherent transformative process that binds both the previous and the subsequent unit (ab, bc)" (p. 305). It is precisely the intermediate forms that shed insight into the developmental process as it is taking place.

This orientation is particularly relevant for the study of daydreams, as it may help shed insight into how we progress from one dreaming state to another. Although dreaming entails a certain degree of automatism, we believe that daydreaming is nevertheless a creative act. Hence, the process of daydreaming may proceed synthetically through constructive elaborations of previous daydream states.

Constructive Elaboration

The transitive nature in the stream of consciousness during microgenesis need not be a passive event. In fact, many transitions take place in form of constructive elaborations of past and present experience. According to Josephs, Valsiner, and Surgan (1999), once a meaning is established, it is not stable and may be changed through the emergence of new meanings. One way this can happen is through constructive elaboration, in which a new structure can emerge within the previously structured field, thereby entirely changing the meaning of the preexisting structure. For example, let the original meaning be defined as A, and let anything that is not contained in the original meaning be defined as non-A. In this tension, a new focus, B, can emerge within the non-A field. Next, the new focus, B, begins to stand in opposition to that which is non-B. At this point, the new apperception of the B versus non-B tension can take over the previous structure, thereby replacing the A versus non-A tension. In effect, we can see that the original meaning has transformed into something novel: a new meaning!

How to "Capture" a Daydream?

If not explicitly shared, each person's thoughts belong only to him or her and cannot come into the view of another person's consciousness. This, of course, makes studying daydreaming difficult since we cannot look into someone's thoughts and follow their progression. In order to solve this dilemma, we proposed two ways[2] to study daydreaming. One way was to examine peoples' reconstructions of their daydreams. In this approach, participants were asked to report their daydreams via daydream-journals (see "Understanding the Process of Daydreaming: The Daydream Journals" section).

A second approach was to focus on daydreams as they unfold. The immediate phenomena itself, of course, can hardly be captured. For what is left in the researchers hands is always a mere shadow of what it once was. Direct observation is one thing; fully capturing the moment is another. One way to try to capture that which seems intangible (i.e., thoughts) is to have research participants think aloud. Antrobus and Singer (1964) used a similar method when study daydreaming; they instructed participants to free associate out loud as a way to replicate inner cognitive processes otherwise unknown to researchers.

Karl Duncker (1945) also suggested that participants "think aloud" while they are dealing with a particular problem in the context of an experimental setting. Duncker states that "the subject who is thinking aloud remains immediately directed to the problem, so to speak allowing his activity to become verbal" (p. 2). It is clear that the participants' overt thoughts (i.e., spoken) do not necessarily correspond with the immediate experience of a given phenomena. What it does allow us to see, however, is the restructuring of this original phenomena—a mediated experience. The originally experienced phenomena genetically precede the specific properties expressed; the latter are developed out of the former. The process of "think aloud" can provide a large amount of information about the microgenesis of daydreams. It is through that information that we were able to consider the synthetic and analytic thought processes during expressed daydreams (see next section).

Understanding the Process of Daydreaming: The Daydream Journals

Our first approach towards understanding the process of daydreaming involved data from 14 participants (3 male, 11 female), all of whom were solicited from undergraduate psychology classes at Clark University in Massachusetts. The participants' ages ranged from 18-22 years ($M = 19.64$ years, $SD = 1.28$), and were labeled P1-14 for identification purposes.

The participants were instructed to record one daydream per day during a period of 2 weeks. Four aspects were to be recorded about the daydreams: (a) the daydream itself, (b) the feelings before, during, and after the daydream, (c) the meaning, if any, that the participant attributed to the daydream, and (d) where the participant was and what he/she was doing when the daydream began. A total of 133 daydreams were collected.

Analysis

Let us begin by examining the following excerpt that stems from an 18-year-old female participant's daydream journal entry:

Example 1

P5: "I was in my dorm room watching a taped episode of *American Idol* with my boyfriend. When we were finished, I was sitting on my bed, imagining what it would be like if I became famous, like the people on *American Idol*.

I dreamed that my quartet (a group of girls I sang with often in high school) was performing in my hometown. We were overheard by someone who worked for a record label, and he wanted to give us a contract. We were flown to Hollywood where we immediately started work on our album (we were writing most of the songs and recording them a cappella). We each had personal trainers. And we all had stylists who did our hair and makeup and helped us pick out new clothes. By the end of the daydream, we were all looking amazing and performing live onstage.

My quartet and I have been singing together for years, and we have gotten pretty good. I've always had the distant dream of being a music performer, and singing with my quartet seems like a good way of doing that. Now that we're all in college, I miss singing with them almost every day. I miss the experience and I wish I could sing with them all the time, like we used to."

This excerpt nicely illustrates the apperceptive shifts and associative links that are expressed during the reconstruction of the experienced daydream. For example, the participant sets the stage (context) by writing that she had been in her room watching the TV show *American Idol* when her daydream started. The perceptive act of the show (*a*) and what she attended to (*a'*) establishes the initial direction of the emerging daydream: she began thinking of herself as being famous (like the people on the show). One cannot become famous without a social environment. Interestingly, at this point the expressed memories of a quartet (i.e., social) she sang in (the past) affected her ongoing apperceptions (of watching the show) so that she began shifting her thinking towards the direction in which her quartet was to become famous. It seems this creative act, the repeated process of apperceptions that develop synthetically (e.g., from singular—"just me"—to multiple persons—"my quartet") as well as analytically (e.g., we've been singing for years and *we are good!*), each represent a fundamental daydream unit. That is, the daydream continues through the construction of what we hereby coin "*daydream-monads*," the fundamental qualities of the daydream complexity.

Furthermore, we are able to orient this analysis along the previously discussed model of constructive elaborations: Daydream monads start with an apperceptive act ("A": herself being famous like the people on *American Idol*). This apperceptive act, "A," stands in opposition to "non-A" (e.g., not being famous and/or not *American Idol*). The daydream monad transforms—whereby "B" (the quartet becoming famous) emerges within the overlap of field "A" (famous) and opposite field ("non-A": not this show). The new focus becomes the center of attention, thereby shifting the development into a new direction, thus giving rise to a new *daydream-monad*. This new monad (now B) is also defined in opposition to what it is not (non-B). The process repeats itself as the stream of monads transform from thinking about being famous, to performing in her hometown, to being discovered, to getting a contract for an album, to personal trainers and stylists, to performing live onstage.

Establishing a Daydream Model

At this point we would like to summarize and visually represent the central ideas upon which we touched in the above example. Figure 7.1 is to be understood in generic terms, and is meant to help clarify the systemic complexes during the microgenesis of daydreaming. (1) shows the reconstructive process of daydreams. Apperceptive acts allow for the emergence of daydreams within a specific context. Often an environmental trigger (*a*) that has been apperceived will "jump-start" the daydream. The particular focus becomes internalized[3] (*a'*), that is incorporated as part of the agent (or the "I") who does the daydreaming. He/she in return then undertakes further creative manipulations of the initial apperception. Frequently,

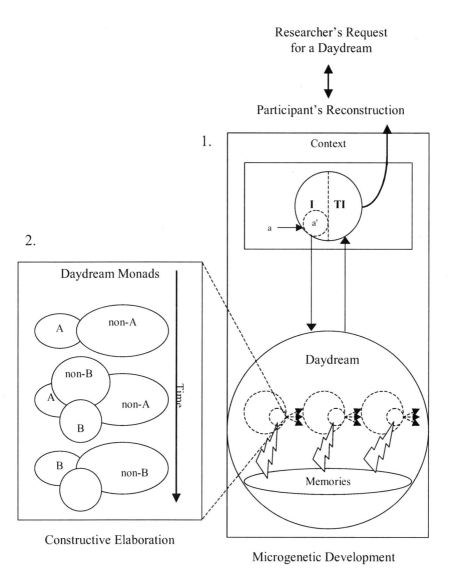

Figure 7.1.   Model of systemic aspects of daydreaming.

daydreams take "a life of their own," as exemplified through the active and conscious "daydream monads" (circles), which are subject to new associations, memory interference, and subsequent apperceptions. The daydream monads transform and progress further through the process of constructive elaborations (see section 2 of the model). These elaborations translate into a new focus (small circle within the daydream monads) that has been brought forward within the original apperceptive fields. As the daydream proceeds, it is subject to various "interferences," such as emerging memories (represented as lightning bolts). At the end of the entire daydream sequence, the participant is asked to reflect upon the daydream and to reconstruct it for the researcher. Both the daydream and the reconstruction of the daydream take place in their given "here-and-now." The "lived-through" daydream leads to a transformed "I" ("TI") or agent, which in effect does the daydream reconstruction. Naturally, the transformation is to be understood on the microgenetic level.

This model (Figure 7.1) depicts the systemic aspects of daydreaming. (1) shows the reconstructive process of daydreams. Apperceptive acts allow for the emergence of daydreams within a specific context. Often daydreams take "a life of their own," as exemplified through the active and conscious "daydream monads" (circles), which are subject to associations, memory interference, and apperception. The daydream monads go through the process of constructive elaborations (2). Here, the daydream monad (the particular focus of the daydream at a given moment) is changing as a new focus (small circle) is being brought forward within the original field. The daydream continues in this way with the individual's memories also playing a role in the train of thought. The daydream leads, microgenetically speaking, to a transformed "I" (TI) or agent, which in effect does the reconstruction of the daydream. With this model in mind, let us place the illustration (Figure 7.1) into another concrete example given to us by a 19-year-old female participant:

Example 2:

P11: "I was in class, in a bad mood.

Before this dream I was frustrated. The girl behind me was snapping her gum. Someone near the front was loudly reciting the notes from last class. And the professor was clapping his hands to get people's attention. I must have been in a bad mood cause it was all ticking me off.

In science class today I saw a velociraptor amble through the doorway of the classroom. Its body was stooped over, scaly and green and it raised its snout to sniff at the air. It snarled and everyone in the classroom began to shriek. It was chaos, desks and tables were overturned and people tried to get up and run. As soon as they moved the raptor was upon them, pulling at their flesh, tearing it apart and devouring them. I stayed still and watched the horror. Each person reacted differently some fainted others tried to fight back. Their bones snapped and their bodies collapsed to the ground in bloody heaps. I alone remained unharmed. When everyone else had been maimed and eaten. The raptor gave me a wink and left.

[This daydream] definitely stems from watching the Jurassic Park trilogy."

In the above entry of the participant's daydream journal, we can detect (1) the individual daydream monads as well as (2) some key-components involved in the transition of monads. The participant indicates that she was in a bad mood while sitting in class when her daydream began. Her unpleasant apperceptions can be seen as the initial triggers for her later solution: a velociraptor eating her classmates.

Section 1 of Figure 7.1 visually represents the context in which the participant is situated. The perceptive act of the annoying classroom events (*a*) around her and those she eventually attended to (*a'*) gave rise to actual daydream. The participant began thinking of a velociraptor entering the room (for surely it can get rid of these annoying distractions in the classroom). As the participant later indicates, memories of the *Jurassic Park* trilogy affected her current focus when she began thinking about the velociraptor and the details of its appearance.

(2) The daydream continued through construction of new monads whereby the participant repeats the processes of perceptive and apperceptive acts. Again, the process of constructive elaboration can be shown here: The daydream starts with a focus, or monad (A: the velociraptor entering the classroom). This *Vorgestalt* soon becomes more concrete as a new monad (B) forms within the overlap of field A and non-A of that first monad: the velociraptor entering the classroom is defined at this point in opposition to anything that is not the velociraptor entering the classroom (A). The new focus (B: the velociraptor snarling and sniffing the air) forms within the "anything that is not the velociraptor entering the classroom" field (non-A). Note that there is an overlap, for the velociraptor exists both in A and non-A. This new focus then takes over the previous one, allowing for a new monad to be formed. This new monad (B) again becomes defined in opposition to what it is not (non-B). Subsequently, this process repeats itself as the monads transform from thinking about the velociraptor entering the classroom, to its sniffing the air and snarling, to its killing of all the people in the classroom but herself, to it winking at her and leaving her unharmed (*Endgestalt*).

Understanding the Process of Daydreaming: The Think-Aloud Approach

The purpose of this second approach was to try to reduce the time continuum from the immediate to the mediated experience as much as possible by having participants continuously thinking aloud. We further wanted to use their narratives to explore the possible functions of daydreaming.

Our second approach towards understanding the process of daydreams involved data from 19 participants (5 male, 14 female), all of whom were solicited from undergraduate psychology classes at Clark University in Massachusetts. The participants' ages ranged from 18-46 years, $(M = 21.9$ years, $SD = 6.51)$. The participants of our second approach were numbered P101-119 so as to distinguish them from the participants of our first study. Participants were asked to watch and report on randomly moving vector graphics displayed on a laptop computer screen (model Enpower ENP-601) for 7 minutes while the researcher left the room. We considered this ambiguous task to stimulate boredom in the hopes that participants would more readily be able to engage in daydreaming. Participants were asked to speak any thoughts aloud during this period of time. All overt thoughts were audio recorded. Lastly, participants took part in a short interview session. In this interview, participants were first asked to recall what they were thinking about during the past 7 minutes. Participants were also asked to elaborate on some more general questions:

(a) How often would you say you daydream?
(b) In what settings do you usually daydream?
(c) Are your daydreams often triggered by something in your environment?
(d) Are there certain themes that often come up in your daydreams?
(e) Do you feel a daydream can change your mood?
(f) Do you feel that your daydreaming has a purpose for you?

Analysis

An important objective of this study was to further explore how daydreams begin. It was thought that by linking the objective with the subjective world (an approach that goes back to the days of Wundt), we could not only better determine the procedural nature of daydreaming, but also more readily explore the possible functions of daydreaming. As mentioned earlier, Smith (1907) writes that, "The content of daydreaming is chiefly determined by environment" (p. 81). Hence, according to Smith, the environment can help trigger daydreams in one way or another, thereby representing a form of daydream catalyst.

A particular situation can trigger peoples' memories via the laws of association. The context often comes to "life" through some action or some particular object in the person's environment that he/she apperceives. We see these particulars located in the person's *Umwelt* (see von Uexküll, 1940/1982) as directional triggers of daydream development. It is important to note that participants' values and meanings associated with these triggers help determine the particular direction.

The Notion of *Triggers*

Let us examine the following "think aloud" transcript excerpt that not only helps illustrate a daydream trigger, but also provides valuable information about the microgenetic process involved in daydreaming:

> P106: "Green and some color I can't quite describe, tan-orangey, white kind of thing … whatever. *There's a lot of writing on this desk. I haven't written on a desk since I was like, in 6th grade.* It's so *annoying to me that people, like, put their gum under their desk.* And then *it ends up sticking on my leg* and then I got random different colors all over my jeans throughout the day just because of all the different desks that I used to go to."

We can draw particular attention to the upper half of section 1 of our general model displayed in Figure 7.1 (see also Figure 7.2). While concentrating on the moving vector graphics on the computer screen, this 20-year-old male participant notices inscriptions on the table in the laboratory (= a). This particular apperception triggers the daydream "I haven't written on my desk since I was like, in 6th grade" (= a'). We can further see concrete stages of the transformation from "writing on top of the desk" (is not nice), to "gum under the desk" (not nice either) to "gum on the participants leg" (is very unpleasant). These different stages (from one *Gestalt* to another) of microgenetic development do not only display the transformational outcome from desk to leg, but also a link (or loop) to the general impression of the current context in the "here-and-now" (random different colors on my jeans—random different colors are being displayed on the computer screen in form of vector graphics). Thus, the apperceptive shifts that occur are first linked to the environment, but then further develop through the actual daydream, thereby partially "removing" the participant from the task at hand (to observe and report on the vector graphics being displayed on the screen). Nevertheless, we can still detect environmental components (e.g., different colors) of the current context emerge throughout the participant's narrative. That is, the general impression (or *Gesamteindruck*) of the current context does not "perish" entirely, rather reemerges microgenetically in the form of transformed relationships. Hence, daydreams (as any form of development) can proceed synthetically, yet not without developmental loops to initial triggers or other impressions already preconceived. New development is not linear, but rather proceeds through frequent stages of

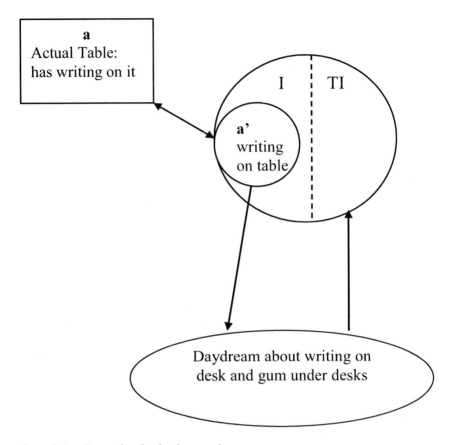

Figure 7.2.   Example of a daydream trigger.

loop-backs to prior developmental achievements (or secure anchor points).

Daydreams as "Cognitive Jumpstarts"

In our follow-up interviews, participants often reported that daydreams tended to occur at times when they were feeling bored or lethargic. The daydream provided a means to escape reality:

P105: "Yeah I think [daydreaming] has a purpose. I think you need to relax a lot, so it's just, well, I don't want to call it escapism, but something; and it gives me a more interesting internal landscape or something."

P7: "I imagine Palm Pilot (annoying student in my English class) crashes into the wall while leaning back in his chair and lodges his little pointer pencil in his eye. The aftermath includes ambulances, fire trucks, and general chaos. *During the daydream I was granted a respite of amusement.*"

P4: "I daydreamed that I was out shopping with my roommate for shoes and we were in a shoe store with tons of shoes all around us, and we could have any of the shoes we wanted in the store. I got a bunch of summer shoes and sandals, and we left carrying big handled bags full of shoes. *I felt bored before this daydream, but during the daydream I felt happy and less bored.*"

But daydreams are more than just escapism—they are reported to revitalize and energize the person. For example:

P12: "I had a daydream about sledding. I wanted to go sledding and daydreamed about the last time that I did. I was with my brothers and we had a lot of fun.... I hit the jump that all of them could not get for the life of them. It hurt. I wanted to go again and I daydreamed about where I could go out here in Worcester ... and who would go with me. I was with a boy but he was faceless. I was having a very good time though. *I was very tired struggling to keep awake before the* [day] *dream. Then I felt better, more energized.*"

In other words, daydreams seem to serve as a form of "cognitive jump-start" that allows the person to process new information that lie outside the persons immediate situation, thereby providing a mental "break" from the current environmental context. The apperceptive shift from *here* (the situational context in which I find myself "struggling to keep awake") to *there* (the daydream that takes me on an exciting sled-ride) "revitalizes" the mind.

This increase in perceived energy goes beyond thoughts per se, and incorporates the entire being. The daydreamer *lives* through these dreams and thus *feels* their properties. That is, the daydream can become more than just some random thoughts "out there," rather the person as a *whole* (in the sense of *Ganzheit*—see Diriwächter, 2004b) experiences the daydream in all its complex qualities. Feelings are of particular relevance to the complexity of the experienced phenomena, as no experience comes without the coloring effect of feelings. These complexes help distinguish the before and after states which we so readily report on. It is not just about what a person does, but also how he/she experiences the "doing." In short, feelings help define our experiences.

Daydreams as "Mood Adjusters"

Some participants reported feeling tense or aggravated before their daydream and more relaxed afterwards. For example, one 20-year-old male participant mentioned that he was feeling very frustrated and was having a hard time writing a school paper before his daydream. He then started daydreaming about being on a beach in Mexico, focusing on many different aspects of sitting on the beach, such as the white sand between his toes, the sun beating down and tanning him, a cold beverage with condensation built up on it, and the clear, light blue waves crashing up in front of him. In the following excerpt, he highlights his feelings during and after the daydream:

> P13: "During the [day]dream I felt relaxed, peaceful, and a warmness came over me. All the frustration had left my body and I was just lying back in my chair completely relaxed. After, I felt disappointed that I wasn't there anymore, but *I felt a lot more relaxed and ready to refocus on my paper.*"

While the end of the daydream brought disappointment, the relaxing aftermath of sitting on the beach allows the rejuvenated mind to refocus the attention to the actual task at hand: writing the paper. In other words, the apperceptive shifts throughout the daydream not only serve to embark on a "mental adventure," but also to withdraw from concentrating on the strenuous task that one is confronted with in the "real world."

We further found that daydreaming may help alleviate mild depressive feelings, as exemplified through the following excerpt by a 20-year-old female who recounted a daydream about being with her boyfriend, whom she does not see often:

> P14: "My feelings before the daydream were a feeling of light depression. I have been very stressed lately with the end of the semester approaching and I feel so trapped with responsibility and I feel like I have been lacking attention to myself (like relaxing and doing things I enjoy) and to my boyfriend (we have opposite schedules so we don't see each other a lot). So I would say I felt pretty sad, disappointed and trapped. During the daydream however I felt very free of responsibility and could just enjoy the time that we were having together. *After the daydream I didn't feel AS upset as I did before the dream because I had a little hope that the end of the semester is near.*"

Also, many daydreams served to help reduce or alleviate anger, as the following excerpt by a 20-year-old female participant shows:

> P8: "My mom had just called to tell me about my cousin Lisa. She ran away to live with my ex-boyfriend—they have been dating for a few months now, and since then, she has not spoken one word to me. Her sister says it's

because she's scared to actually say it to me. Lisa hates me, because of all the things my ex had said to her about me (all lies). I was really upset. I had a daydream that I was standing in my kitchen (at home) with my cousin. She had her back to me. All of a sudden, I say, "So, Lisa, how's my ex-boy-friend???" She turns around, shocked, and sarcastically says, "Great!!!" Then, I punched her in the face. *I felt very mad and frustrated both before and after having this daydream, but I guess I was a little less mad afterwards.*"

Some participants actually described daydreaming as a way to release aggression without actually acting the aggression out. As one participant wrote, "it just kind of [lets me] do things that I wouldn't really do in my life; get out aggression." The structural configuration of aggressive feeling states transforms as the situation that "ought not to be the way it is" becomes manipulated abstractly by the daydreamer to result in "now things are the way they should be."

This goes to show that daydreams are more than just a series of random thoughts—these dreams are lived-through! They are experienced with all the colors that feelings can provide, and in the end often supply a resolution that real-life may not readily allow for. In effect, the feelings one experiences during the act of daydreaming seem to help lead to a momentary catharsis that leaves the participant relieved of certain unpleasant mood states. If the unpleasantness prior to the daydream is seen as a problem, then we can say that daydreams are a means of solving that dilemma (at least on a short-term basis)

Daydreams as "Problem Solvers"

Singer and McCraven (1961) once indicated that daydreaming might have a problem-solving function. If we follow the stream of consciousness and the idea that nothing reoccurs exactly the same, then this lack of 'sameness' must necessarily lead to different outcomes. Confronted with a problem, a daydream may serve to attain a desired outcome that is different from those previously conceptualized.

We found this notion confirmed in quite a few of our recorded daydreams. For example, one 20-year-old male participant began to focus on the laptop screen (on which he was watching the vector graphics) and noticed that it was an older computer. Perplexed by this antiquated equipment, the participant began conjuring up possible reasons of why the researcher would have an older computer:

P106: "She has a Pentium. This is actually kind of an *older looking laptop*, a little bit thick, but hell, *she's a college student.* She *probably got this her first year* and she's probably fixing to graduate and *going to get a new computer* as soon as she's done. *Or maybe she has another computer."*

In this excerpt, we can see the participant engaged in a self-imposed problem: Why does the researcher have an old computer? The series of apperceptions during this microgenetic development are again proceeding analytically (e.g., she is a college student) as well as synthetically (e.g., she probably got this her first year) away from the actual task of observing the vector graphics. The complex quality of the general impression (*Gesamteindruck*) to which these apperceptions find their anchorage consist of (a) "computer is old" and (b) "she is a college student." Figure 7.3 displays the stream of generated solutions during this process of meaning-making:

Note that each generated *daydream-monad* of new meaning is intricately linked (or looped) to the general impressions first articulated. This constant motion of cross referencing is a necessary component for daydreams to progress and transform: It is the "cognitive fuel" that the

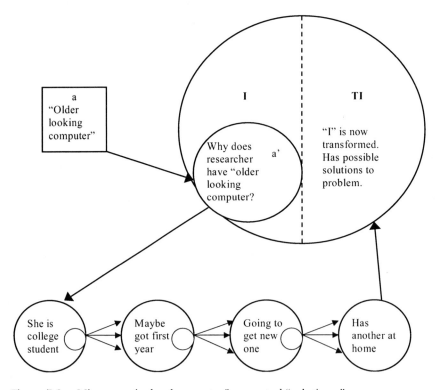

Figure 7.3.   Microgenetic development of generated "solutions."

person needs to have so that the microgenetic development does not become stagnant (see also "Cognitive Jumpstarts" above). Heretofore we can also say that the development does not proceed in a strict linear fashion; rather, the loop-like referencing makes the development incorporate simultaneous characteristics, (general impression and ongoing apperceptive shifts) which produces a web-like structure.

We can further illustrate the process of problem solving during day-dreaming by taking a closer look at the following transcript stemming from a 24-year-old male participant:

> P119: "Sitting at this computer makes me think about how I have to e-mail someone about my stupid loan. I was supposed to get a student loan this semester, well the semester that just went by, for school, but someone screwed it all up. They said that the bursar's office messed up, but I don't know if they will, like, help me now. I really need that money to pay my stupid bills that I put off because they told me I was going to get this money. I don't know what I'm going to do without that loan.… I should e-mail somebody, but I don't really know who. Maybe I should talk to someone in the, um, the bursar's office; they are the ones that screwed it all up. Someone else, I think it was my step-dad, told me that I could call the Board of Higher Education since they sent me letters saying that I had the loan and now they won't give it to me. That would be good, I think. They told me that I should try to get a, um, a personal loan. That's what the financial aid office said. They won't help me now and they're just trying to blame everything on the other office. But maybe I should get a personal loan. Or I could try getting a loan from my grandmother; she always helps me when I need something. But I really don't want to ask her. Maybe I should just get another job for the summer and work a ton while I'm not in classes. But then that doesn't leave me any time for baseball and I really want to keep playing. I keep thinking there should be someway for me to make money doing something with baseball. I wonder if I could do a baseball camp or something like that. This is so annoying; they are the ones that screwed up. Well, that's what the financial aid office says at least. I'm going to call the bursar's office first before I try anything else, I think."

The transcript again highlights the situational trigger (computer—a) of which a particular characteristic is apperceived (e-mail—a'). This is brought forth in connection (e.g., association) with a particular problem ("where is my student loan?") the participant has to deal with. This problem is articulated in a manner that places blame on situational circumstances (as opposed to dispositional factors) in which "others" (e.g., bursar's office) have neglected their duties in making sure that the participant would receive his money. What follows is a renewed series of synthetically oriented apperceptions that aim to develop a viable solution to this dilemma: (A) I could e-mail someone to get my money; (B) I could talk to someone; (C) I could call someone; (D) I could get a personal loan; (E) Maybe even a loan from my grandmother; (F) I could also get another job for the summer; (G) or perhaps I could earn money through my baseball hobby; (H) It's probably best if I try one of my original solutions before trying something else, so I will call the bursar's office.

We can see that the developmental progression of generated solutions to the originally stated problem (where is my loan?) again does not necessarily proceed in a strict linear fashion (i.e., from A to C), rather finds its course progress over several options attended to, some of them rather far removed from current feasibility (e.g., turning baseball hobby into money), only to return back to something more viable (H C). We would like to draw further attention to the individual *daydream-monads*, which seem to help bring a level of concreteness to the uncertainty of the originally stated problem. It is one of the fundamental properties that humans aim to rid themselves of any diffuse state and instead strive to attain clarity in their lives (see Diriwächter, 2008). Hence, any *daydream-monad* represents an attained level of concreteness that will serve as the basis for further mental explorations into the presently unknown. These steps, so to speak, are the essential revelations that have become objectified during the microgenetic process. The daydreamer can use these objectifications as anchor- or reference points while searching for additional solutions to a given problem. In the end, the list of generated solutions has transformed the ambiguous situation of stated problem into one that now allows for concrete action (e.g., "I will make a phone call").

Reflections on our Findings

We have tried to illustrate the nature of microgenetic development in daydreams (see Figure 7.1) and provide a handful of examples of key qualities essential to the process of daydreaming. We placed most of our investigative efforts into the role of apperceptions, which are the fundamentals to the shift in the microgenetic trajectory. That is, the progression of a sequence of dynamic *Gestalts* operates hierarchically under the principle of simultaneity, since the general impression is present throughout the process of reconstruction.

Thus, microgenetic development involves a complex interplay (hence, complex qualities) between a series of apperceptive shifts (both analytically and/or synthetically oriented) with frequent referencing to the general impression of the phenomena. The nonlinearity of microgenetic development has also been reported in another study by Diriwächter (2005b) who highlighted a particularly interesting process he coined "recycling" in which participants narratives "circle" around already established levels of concreteness (i.e., previous apperceptions) and from there eventually "break-through" to an instance of novelty-creation (synthesis). Yet, there is no "new" without the "old." Each instance where novelty became visible on the narrative level, we see it simultaneously embedded in the layers of the general impression previously expressed. Hence, we can speak of fluid *Simultangestalten* (or simultaneous Gestalts) whereby one (the general impression) incorporates the other (a sub-whole or *Unterganzes*).

While the flow of time is irreversible (Bergson, 1907/1945), the nature of an experience need not be confined to the present moment: an experience can extend into the future (as well as into the past). The hypothetical possibilities of *what could be* or *what could have been* serve to make the present field of experience larger (i.e., by extending its components beyond the present moment in time) and thus allow for multiple microgenetic trajectories in the here-and-now context. These trajectories represent the "pathway" along which the synthesis formations become noticeable during daydreams and are colored by the feeling-tone, which the person has expressed. Of course, the developmental trajectories themselves bring possible shifts of feelings expressed as the person "feels into" (*Einfühlen*) the new (hypothetical) situation that was set up by that person.

The notion that a person's thoughts during synthesis formation of a microgenetic event need not be confined to the context of the immediately given (e.g., what can be evidently heard or seen in the physical surroundings by the person), but can venture into a hypothetical realm of future directives, has been proposed by Volkelt (1959/1962) some time ago. He saw that the process of *Einfühlung* into an immediately given also implies a certain degree of anticipation of future developmental directives so that our feeling into the situation is also guided by our expectation of what the future holds for us. It is important to note that we do not just "project" our feelings into the event, nor (and that should be clear by now) do we keep our feelings and thoughts differentiated during the future oriented developmental progress. Instead, we place ourselves totally (*Ganzheitlich*) into the anticipated trajectories in order to make them come "alive."

What have we learned from our applied methods?—Both of our approaches (daydream journal and "think aloud") resulted in a rich amount of data. The greatest shortcoming of using daydream journals as the source of data is, of course, that the data is far removed from the original phenomena. Participants had sufficient time to choose what aspects of the daydream they would write down and what they would leave out. Furthermore, there is a complete absence of readily noticeable and reliable intermediate or transitional forms of the daydreams' microgenetic progression. Hence, we took that data to represent the highlights of participants' daydreams, the fundamental apperceptions that evolved during the entire developmental process. Nonetheless, we believe that the data obtained was sufficient to develop not only a generic model representing the systemic aspects of daydreaming, but also to identify key characteristics involved in daydreaming.

In a sense, this form of data collection results in what is comparable to James' (1890) description of *substantive thought*. In his discussion of the continuous nature of thought, James identifies two types of thought: one is of slow change. With this type of thought, the person is aware of each object that is the focus of consciousness—it is a restful and stable type of thought. On the other hand, when the thought is of rapid change, the person is aware of the transitions between the thoughts; this thought has a flight-like nature. The restful and relatively stable thought in which these resting places are noticed is referred to as the *substantive thought*, while the flight-like thought is referred to as the *transitions*. According to this notion, the substantive part of thought is considered to be the goal or conclusion of thought. The transitions exist to bring us from one substantive thought (conclusion) to another.

In that regard, we had hoped that the "think aloud" approach would be well suited to capture the transitive nature of the microgenetic process. In fact, the "think aloud" approach seemed to lend itself best for capturing microgenetic data of the "original" phenomenon since there is a minimal time delay between immediate and mediate experiences. That is, compared to the daydream journals that encompassed a carefully crafted reconstruction of the daydream, the "think aloud" approach allowed for daydream construction as it was occurring. Generating data in such a way more adequately guarantees closeness to the original phenomena, whereby it must be restated that the person expressing his/her thoughts can still choose to omit certain information he/she does not wish to share. Nevertheless, some key aspects of the complex quality of daydreaming became readily clear through the "think-aloud" approach, most noticeably the revelation of the step-by-step process of coming to a solution of a stated problem. It showed how a problem was presented, the different solutions considered (transitions), and which solution was decided upon.

Researcher, Methodology, and Guiding Theory

We find it important to briefly inject some words on the researcher's role while trying to make sense of daydreams. Just like there is no such thing as a "neutral" object in our *Umwelt*, the analysis of daydreams has been undertaken through the lenses of particular axioms that were outlined earlier in this chapter. For one, we adopted Wilhelm Wundt's notion of the concept of consciousness that would govern people's daydreams—and more importantly, the implications from creative synthesis. This allowed our analysis to dive into particular and fundamental qualities of daydream progression (e.g., apperceptions) while maintaining an overall *Ganzheits*-approach (along the lines of "no parts without the whole"). Our study looked at the complex qualities believed to be central during daydreaming. We purposely gave the participants a large "playing" field in which they could allow their thoughts and feelings to flow freely. It was believed that this fairly unstructured design would not hinder the psychological development of the participants. Our analysis sought to establish the relationships not from an elementaristic (that is, isolated factors) point of view, but rather from a holistically, all-encompassing outlook that highlighted the "interwovenness" of central components that are all too often overlooked or even forgotten.

We opted to follow the axiom outlined in the section on James' "Stream of Consciousness," which emphasizes that humans are ever-changing, and thus we tried to focus on the systemic aspects (field-like) of daydreaming. That is, we highlighted some fundamental qualities of daydreaming and traced their most basic processes via means of participants' written daydream-journals as well as live, overtly expressed thoughts in the context of microgenetic development. We thus see our descriptive approach guided by theory (including our own assumptions about daydreams), yet at the same time restricted by the boundaries that the previously stated axioms imply.

This, of course, should not come as a surprise. The developmental process of knowledge construction by the researcher is not free from restrictions, nor is any form of development for that matter. Restrictions allow for goal-directedness and thus "true" development (as opposed to mere changes *per se*). In that regard, we adopted our method (daydream-journal and "think-aloud") not as if we reached into a readily-made "toolbox" (see Valsiner, 2000 for a discussion about this problem), rather we constructed and tailored our approach to the specific assumptions and consequent requirements we believed necessary for our investigation of daydreams: Their microgenetic development.

To some people the intangibility of subjectivity while experiencing the world may make our analysis of daydreams seem "unreal." But if we deny the existence of synthesis formation and transformation in every one of our moments, then we will face difficult times in trying to explain the emergence of novelty. We reconstruct our experiences daily. We seek clarity in an otherwise diffuse world. Thus, in trying to come to understand ourselves, let us start again from the lived experiences, from the top down, from the *Gesamteindruck* to the ever-shifting apperceptions, from the *Gefühlston* to the sensations; for it is the experience that make the seemingly "unreal," real:

> The physicist's atoms will always appear more real than the historical and qualitative face of the world, the physico-chemical processes more real than the organic forms, the psychological atoms of empiricism more real than perceived phenomena, the intellectual atoms represented by the "significations" of the Vienna Circle more real than consciousness, as long as the attempt is made to build up the shape of the world (life, perception, mind) instead of recognizing, as the source which stares us in the face and as the ultimate court of appeal in our knowledge of these things, our *experience* of them. (Merleau-Ponty, 1962, p. 23)

NOTES

1. An idea that naturally has been echoed throughout the ages, as far back as the days of Heraclitus (ca. 540-480 B.C.)
2. By no means do we imply that these are the only valid approaches to studying daydreaming.
3. Whereby it must be emphasized that such internalizations are not assumed to be on a 1-1 ratio, as indicated by $a \rightarrow a'$.

REFERENCES

Antrobus, J. S., & Singer, J. L. (1964). Visual signal detection as a function of sequential variability of simultaneous speech. *Journal of Experimental Psychology, 68*(6), 603-610.

Bergson, H. (1945). *L'Evolution créatrice*. Geneva, Switzerland: Éditions Albert Skira. (Original work published 1907)

Diriwächter, R. (2003, June). *What really matters: Keeping the whole*. Paper presented at the 10th Biennial Conference of International Society for Theoretical Psychology, Istanbul, Turkey.

Diriwächter, R. (2004a). Völkerpsychologie: The synthesis that never was. *Culture & Psychology, 10*(1), 179-203.

Diriwächter, R. (2004b). Ganzheitspsychologie: The doctrine. *From Past to Future 5*(1), 3-16.

Diriwächter, R. (2004c, August). *Learning from Ganzheitspsychologie: Overcoming the "blind spot" of complexity in psychology's methodology*. Paper presented at the 28th International Congress of Psychology, Beijing, China.

Diriwächter, R. (2005a, March). *Aktualgenese: Development in the "here-and-now."* Paper presented at the Clark University Multidisciplinary Conference, Worcester, MA.

Diriwächter, R. (2005b). *Ganzheit & Feelings: An investigation into the process of psychological synthesis*. Unpublished doctoral dissertation, Clark University, Worcester.

Duncker, K. (1945). *On Problem-Solving* (L. S. Lees, Trans.) Washington, DC: The American Psychological Association.

Gold, S. R., & Reilly, J. P. III. (1985). Daydreaming: Current concerns and personality. *Imagination, Cognition and Personality, 5*(2), 117-125.

James, W. (1890). *The principles of psychology*. New York: Henry Holt.

James, W. (1893). *Psychology*. New York: Henry Holt.

Josephs, I. E., Valsiner, J., & Surgan, S. E. (1999). The process of meaning construction: dissecting the flow of semiotic activity. In J. Brandtstädter, R. Lerner (Eds.), *Action & self-development: Theory and Research Through the Life Span* (pp. 227-282). Thousand Oaks, CA: Sage.

Merleau-Ponty, M. (1962). *Phenomenology of perception* (C. Smith, Trans.). London: Routledge & Kegan Paul.

Sander, F. (1930). Structure, totality of experience, and gestalt. In C. Murchison (Ed.), *Psychologies of 1930* (pp. 188-204). Worcester, MA: Clark University Press.

Siegler, R. S., & Crowley, K. (1991). The microgenetic method: A direct means for studying cognitive development. *American Psychologist, 46*(6), 606-620.

Singer, J. L., & Antrobus, J. S. (1970). *Manual for the imaginal processes inventory*. Princeton, NJ: Educational Testing Service.

Singer, J. L., & McCraven, V. G. (1961). Some characteristics of adult daydreaming. *The Journal of Psychology, 51*, 151-164.

Smith, T. L. (1907). The psychology of daydreams. In G. S. Hall & T. L. Smith (Eds.), *Aspects of child life and education* (pp. 53-83). Boston: Ginn.

Uexküll, J. von. (1909). *Umwelt und Innenwelt der Tiere*. Berlin, Germany: Verlag von Julius Springer.

Uexküll, J. von. (1982). The theory of meaning. *Semiotica, 42*(1), 83-87. (Original work published 1940)

Valsiner, J. (2000). *Culture and human development*. London: Sage.

Valsiner, J., & Van Der Veer, R. (2000). *The social mind: Construction of the idea*. Cambridge, MA: Cambridge University Press.

Volkelt, H. (1962). Simultangestalten, Verlaufsgestalten, und "Einfühlung." In F. Sander & H. Volkelt (Eds.), *Ganzheitspsychologie* (pp. 147-158). München, Germany: C. H. Beck'sche Verlagsbuchhandlung. (Originally presented in 1959 for the Festschrift für Friedrich Sander in Göttingen)

Wohlfahrt, E. (1932). Der Auffassungsvorgang an kleinen Gestalten. Ein Beitrag zur Psychologie des Vorgestalterlebnisses. *Neue Psychologische Studien, 4*, 347-414. [*Dissertation, Leipzig-1925*]

Wundt, W. (1922). *Grundriss der Psychologie* (15th ed.). Leipzig, Germany: Alfred Kröner Verlag.

CHAPTER 8

THE MICROGENETIC STUDY
OF DAYDREAMING

Jeanette A. Lawrence and Agnes E. Dodds

Stacey Pereia and Rainer Dirwächter (this volume) have chosen a common, but largely neglected psychological phenomenon to submit to microgenetic analysis. Daydreaming is an everyday experience, has been approached from different psychological perspectives for over a hundred years, and continues to present researchers of the mind with methodological challenges. Pereira and Diriwächter have taken up the specific challenge of developing a microgenetic account of changes in daydreaming activities. They set themselves the goal of analyzing the processes and characteristics of daydreaming, and showing how it is amenable to microgenetic analysis. They provide evidence of changes in daydreaming in experimental situations and their participants' reports of their daydreaming experiences. Their goal is not simply a smart exercise in applying microgenetic analysis to an unusual domain. Essentially Pereira and Diriwächter are asking questions about the how and why of daydreaming, proposing that a microgenetic approach makes a unique contribution to our understanding of this common, but enigmatic phenomenon, by revealing how daydreaming experiences emerge and are elaborated.

Innovating Genesis: Microgenesis and the Constructive Mind in Action, pp. 187–204

Our focus on daydreaming follows along the track that Pereira and Diriwächter have carved out of what has potential to be a theoretical and methodological quagmire. We follow in their steps by discussing the characteristics and functions of daydreaming, taking careful note of their claims. Then we examine some of Pereira and Diriwächter's data and method of analysis, focusing on their aim to capture the emergent and elaboration processes involved in daydreaming experiences, and the accompanying methodological issues. In particular, we address the use of think-aloud verbalizations of daydreaming episodes and their suitability for tracking the evolution of undirected thinking, suggesting some modifications and additions to the method that may make it more suitable for tracking daydreaming as a special kind of private mental processing.

IDENTIFYING DAYDREAMING PHENOMENA

Daydreaming belongs to a range of mental activities that are distinguishable from the usual activities of psychological experiments, by not being oriented to a particular task in the environment. By concentrating on the "off-task" characteristics of daydreaming, Pereira and Diriwächter bring to the fore a particular methodological concern—the long-debated concern of how to investigate an activity that is essentially covert and essentially undirected. This concern reiterates for the contemporary researcher long-standing issues about access—access by participants to their own mental processes and access by the investigator to those processes without editorial gloss by the participants. Out of the control of the researcher, then, daydreaming takes the investigator into the underworld of personal mental activity.

Pereira and Diriwächter add the specific methodological concern of investigating microgenetic change in how daydreaming *evolves*, especially how it emerges in consciousness and how it is elaborated within a single daydreaming episode. The issue of the evolving nature of daydreaming naturally raises the vexing question of what this evolving activity can or does achieve for the daydreaming person. Their interest is tied to the conviction, that we endorse, that daydreaming does serve purposes in people's experience, and therefore deserves the search for appropriate methods.

Daydreaming is strongly linked to current concerns and life circumstances, and does more than provide relief from boredom, or distraction from an undemanding task. In light of the significance of daydreaming as a common experience, we find that the "off-task" way of conceptualizing daydreaming that Pereira and Diriwächter follow becomes a little constricting, and we wish to open up the discussion, suggesting that investigators treat daydreaming as a specific, directed task in psychological experiments, rather than as a serendipitous side product.

We find Singer's (2003, p. 462) position compelling, in incorporating daydreaming into a wider set of closely related mental activities, "the phenomena of our ongoing stream of thought, daydreams and interior monologues." His conceptualization importantly imbeds daydreaming phenomena in the larger domain of private, ongoing thought.

At this point, it is useful to clarify that the phenomenon under investigation is the mental process of daydreaming: a point Pereira and Diriwächter make throughout their chapter. Neither they nor we are concerned about a stand-alone entity "the daydream" that may or may not belong to one or more persons. We are concerned about the mental activity that is described as "daydreaming." It is that sense of an activity that justifies Pereira and Diriwächter's interest in how that process develops, and therefore, is amenable to microgenetic analysis. Drawing on Pereira and Diriwächter's account, an investigator will use a microgenetic analytic technique only if the phenomena under investigation is assumed to evolve over time, with the possibility for the investigator of observing its emergence and development, especially in terms of transitional states and transformations.

Daydreaming is a Personalized Activity—Conscious, Personal, and Private

Being conscious, and able to be given attention makes daydreaming accessible to the daydreamer. Accessibility is a corollary of consciousness and attention, although of itself that does not imply infallible monitoring. There are good grounds for distinguishing conscious, attended mental processing from the automated variety (Mandler, 1985). While the daydreamer may give full attention to her daydreaming, her experience is open to inspection, but not anyone else's in the natural course of events. She also is able to manipulate the daydreaming experience: calling it up and changing its content and direction in response to environmental and internal triggers.

We associate fantasizing with this category of mental activity, believing it to be an important component in the discussion of people's manipulation of their daydreaming. People have reported to us their reoccurring daydreams in which a central theme is elaborated and embellished in succeeding episodes. Thus, by revisiting my continuing vision of "my tennis triumph" or "my wedding to the man of my dreams"

I may add features at will. For instance, a different Grand Slam tennis tournament with a fresh opponent, or a few more bridesmaids and vows of undying devotion can be added as I play out my fantasy. I can also pile up the horrors that may await me in a nasty reoccurring daydreaming experience in which I play the leading role in a *Jurassic Park*-type adventure, or lose my job. This notion of a familiar, revisited, and reworked daydreaming scenario is significant for a developmental approach to the subject, where the existential link of daydreaming to action comes to the fore. We see this as a dimension of the activity that could well be added to the Pereira and Diriwächter account.

Consciousness naturally implies more than control. It also speaks to the personalized nature of the daydreaming experience and its private qualities. While it may seem trite to comment about the privacy of a mental activity, it is extremely important when the researcher attempts to investigate it. Daydreaming is not accessible to the observer. As Mandler (1985, p. 55) argued;

> Events and objects in consciousness can never be available to the observer without having being restructured, reinterpreted, and appropriately modified. The content of consciousness, as philosophers and psychologists have told us for centuries, is not directly available as a datum in psychology.

Once the person expresses his daydreaming experience, that expression becomes part of the interactive, social world in which the audience plays a central role and takes up a particular stance, affecting the report. The expression becomes an act of communication and as such has an interactive function. The trace of the daydreaming is externalized as the daydreamer reports it for audience understanding, edification, confusion or a host of possible purposes. The experience may be reduced, embellished, edited, or corrected, but at least it is expressed in a form suitable for communication rather than for internal experience. Pereira and Diriwächter acknowledge this constraint: "If not explicitly shared, each person's thoughts belong only to him or her and can not come into the view of another person's consciousness." However, the privacy and accessibility issue goes further than whether or not thinking is "shared."

From the perspective of internalization-externalization processes, personal thoughts, including daydreams, are not among the entities that can be strictly "shared." Once one person expresses his thoughts, they are moved from the intrapersonal realm to the interpersonal realm and become part of the phenomenal field taken up by another person. "Shared" thought is elusive and illusory. Communicated thought makes it possible for people to interact with each other without interrogating their meanings (Lawrence & Valsiner, 2003). Communication allows people to engage in the same activity and to communicate with each other about it (e.g., singing patriotic songs and reciting religious creeds) while their different meanings and reservations remain intact and aside. A person may report daydreaming experiences, but the experience cannot be transported to another person's consciousness. Even if it triggers that new person's daydreaming on the same theme, the daydreaming will be different, because it belongs to the experience, memory, and internalizing activities of that person.

Daydreaming has a Stream-Like, Ongoing Quality

Pereira and Diriwächter appropriately link daydreaming to James' stream of consciousness and Heraclitus' once-only experience. This temporal situatedness of "little mental escapades" (p. 157 this volume) has two implications for analysis. First, the activity evolves within each daydreaming episode, and Pereira and Diriwächter's account is valuable in demonstrating that evolving quality. There is concrete evidence of the immediate, ongoing flavor in the sizeable portion of verbalized think-aloud report obtained from P119, and then in Pereira and Diriwächter's tracing of the sequential $\underline{A}$ to $\underline{H}$ apperceptions within that episode. They show the initial rising to consciousness of P119's financial concern, along with the environment trigger that "jump-starts" the episode. The computer used in the experimental presentations acts as a trigger, suggesting e-mailing—an e-mail that is related to a current concern for P119. Then subsequent sequenced steps in the daydreaming experience, involved P119 in working through a series of possible solutions to the original problem. There is a sequential flow to the verbalization which loops back to earlier thoughts ("monads" in Pereira and Diriwächter's terminology), and reworks the possibilities.

Now it is this immediate, temporally sequenced development of ideas or monads that makes Pereira and Diriwächter's microgenetic analysis exciting. Tracing through the progressive monads in the daydreaming experience allows them to identify the movement and change in their daydreamers' experience.

They use Wundt's apperceptive synthesis to label the monads and whole experience of the evolving process, but this is not an essential component to the sequential analysis. The essential feature, rather, is that there is movement within the individual daydreaming episode. The person generates the initial idea and develops it, working towards a solution.

That developing daydreaming may be in the form of a story or script (e.g., the reoccurring script of the wedding day), or it may be a soliloquy. The monologue begins in consciousness, triggered by some feature of the environment, by an enduring personal concern or by the coming together of environmental and personal material. The monologue develops, running off like a script with side issues and loops. Alan Bennett's (1998) TV plays *Talking Heads* are wonderful examples of the way such monologues develop, spinning through topics by free association in the midst of revisited and anticipated social encounters. The power of such enacted soliloquies, in part, derives from the frequency and familiarity with which most people lapse into their own constructed scripts. The humor gains from the readiness of people to hear echoes of their own performances of unexpurgated musings.

Alongside its immediate application, each daydreaming experience can be temporally located in the development of the person's life experience. It would appear that the frequency and nature of daydreaming changes according to the person's life period. Giambra (1974), for example, found that although problem-solving daydreaming does not decline with age, sexual daydreaming does decline. While it is likely that people's daydreaming will reflect the kinds of activities that are foremost in their lives, there may not be a one-to-one relationship. In fact, the opposite may occur, and the fantasies that have intrigued psychoanalytic practitioners relate more to the unfulfilled pre-occupations of many patients (Singer, 1976). Daydreaming, after all, is thought for oneself, and fantasy may be anchored in reality or in unreality.

To continue the earlier example, my fantasy may continue across years, uninterrupted by ongoing reality. The wedding daydreaming may persist over time, despite the fact that my chosen wedding partner marries someone else. I may simply add a new, more joyful feature to the wedding script by imagining how he comes to realize that he made a mistake and I am the great love of his love after all. Our reunion and the marriage is changed to accommodate the subsequent real-world phenomena. The daydreaming does not have to agree with what happens, reality can be reinterpreted for the person's own purposes. This kind of link between daydreaming and reality may be uncompelling to the researcher, but it has been shown to be significant for clinicians since the time of Freud.

More theoretically interesting is the link between daydreaming at a particular point in personal time and past and future events. In the case of P119, the run through alternative solutions is colored by his insistence that the bursar's office was at fault. He could, therefore, approach that office first ("first before I try anything else") with a determination generated by his own blamelessness. His long-term relationship with his grandmother also gets a place in the daydreaming episode. In fact, it dissuades him from one possible solution: asking her for the money. In a genuine sense, the single piece of daydreaming is temporally located in an ongoing life.

Daydreaming has Significance for Personal Goals

Just as a daydreaming episode may arise from a person's life goals (as a special form of current concerns), so it also may contribute to the pursuit and achievement of goals. For instance, the Grand Slam daydreaming may, in fact, belong to an aspiring tennis player who is already on the road to tennis success. In contrast, it may belong to a "couch potato" type of tennis player whose fantasy daydreaming bears no relation to his actual life goals. Let us, for the sake of the argument set aside the playful fantasizing that is disassociated from this person's life, although such fantasizing may serve other purposes, such as, release of tension or boredom (Langens & Schmalt, 2002). For the aspiring player, her daydreaming episode can serve the motivational purpose of bringing the distant prize closer and into the realm of the imagined possibilities that Langens and Schmalt (2002) identified in their interviews. Not only does the daydreaming activity arise out of a genuine concern and imagined goal, but it may add to that goal's probability. The present activity, then, is imbedded in the whole of the person's life course, arising from past and continuing desires and helping to shape their attainment. The process works much like the projective, imaginary walk through a mental blueprint that Miller, Galanter, and Pribram (1960) saw as one of the benefits of forward planning.

As we have shown, daydreaming activities are unfettered by environmental constraints. Imagining can assume fantastic dimensions. They also are free of any overt consequences of covert commitments to future activities. The person is free to play out possible scenarios, as well as to try out possible selves (Singer, 2003). In that playing out, she is able to identify personal priorities as well as the priorities and constraints that she can anticipate in the comments and actions of the other people included in the scenario.

Such inclusions may be voluntary, or come from the intrusion of environmental triggers. While Pereira and Diriwächter focus on the initial "jump-start" triggers that get the process going, Klinger (1990) used within-process diversionary triggers in an intriguing experimental technique to investigate the power of external triggers. Before the experiments, he asked people about their current concerns. In the experimental situation, the participant was asked to listen to two tape recordings simultaneously. He modified both scripts, mentioning a participant's current concerns in one recording, and not in the other. He found that participants' verbalized thoughts were more often related to their current concerns than to the other material. Regardless of the source of any intrusion, the person is able to accommodate or adapt the intrusive material, by using it in the constructive process, as in our earlier wedding example.

The goal-directedness of daydreaming within people's current and future-oriented concerns and life circumstances is not immediately obvious in Pereira and Diriwächter's analysis, although the verbal commentary by P119 focuses on his problem solving of how to act to resolve his financial difficulties. His daydreaming episode actually concludes with an intentional statement about how he will act. Further data are needed to determine if the intention came to fruition, but for P119, a solution emerged from the episode, at least for the present.

Daydreaming is Emotionally-Charged

While not all daydreaming experiences are full of emotion, an emotional element appears to be attached to many triggers or to the elaboration of the dreaming. Within the psychoanalytic approach, daydreams are traditionally associated with repressed sexual and aggressive tendencies and regression to child-like impulses (Singer, 1976). An emotional charge is exacerbated or released by certain types of fantasizing daydreaming.

Even if the actual content is not emotionally-charged, an episode may affect the daydreamer's emotional state. Imagining oneself on a sunny beach on a cold winter's day and playing out the pleasure of being warm and relaxed, for instance, is able to change a present mood. If the daydreaming is colored by positive emotion and intent, it helps induce a positive mood-state in the wintry circumstances. The opposite is also possible, depending on how the person goes into the episode and how she works through it. The result may be greater gloom with the juxtaposition of ice and sand. Langens and Schmalt (2002) addressed the opposing valences of the emotion-daydreaming interaction in a series of studies that revealed that positive daydreaming had different consequences for people with strong and weak dispositions towards fear of failure, tension, anxiety and confusion. People with high levels of fear of failure, when asked to imagine attaining a personally-specified goal, reduced their commitment to their goals. It would seem they talked themselves out of their goal because of the negative emotionality attached to the goals. Unfortunately, Langens and Schmalt did not reassess their moods after this unpleasant daydreaming episode.

In experimental situations, emotional accompaniments or over-lays of daydreaming have allowed research participants to rest, to escape boredom, to lower levels of tension and stress. On the other hand, they have been shown to assist arousal and energize activities unrelated to the content of the daydreaming (Antrobus & Singer, 1964; Singer, 2003). One of Pereira and Diriwächter's participants described how he felt more relaxed and energized after daydreaming about the beach, even though he was disappointed that he was not there (p. 174). Another participant described the release of aggression she felt after daydreaming an encounter involving "punching up" her boyfriend-stealing cousin. Her retrospective report of this daydreaming episode includes an imagined dialogue with the cousin. In reporting that instance, she reverted to the present tense, with all the emotional attachments and exclamation marks (presumably hers) pointing to the immediacy and potency of her emotional state. She felt better after the episode. Thus, the affective dimension may be triggered, maintained, or diverted through an episode. How to capture it, along with the processing, is a major task for researchers.

Daydreaming is Functionally Useful

It can be seen from the above that daydreaming serves several functions in people's lives. Klinger (1990), for instance, refers to its usefulness in promoting organization beyond the immediate context.

> Daydreams are so much a part of you that what you experience in them affects what you do in the real world. Paradoxically, daydreaming is one of the ways in which you keep your life organized, a way to milk your experiences for the lessons they hold, and a way of rehearsing for the future. It is a natural way of improving the efficiency with which we use our brains. (p. xii)

Klinger's (1990) perspective resonates with the connection we make between goals and daydreaming, and likewise, with Pereira and Diriwächter's willingness to describe it as a form of problem solving. Developmentally, goal-directedness, with its intentions for future action, and with the retrieval and review of past encounters has significance for ontological development. Pereira and Diriwächter demonstrate in P119's data the useful of daydreaming processes for problem solving. They also ascribe to these processes the facilitation of immediate, microlevel changes in the development of the self during a single episode. Once an episode has been jump-started by an environmental trigger, "The particular focus becomes internalized (a') that is incorporated as part of the agent (or the "I") who does the daydreaming." Although this self-changing dimension is not developed, it connects the daydreaming to an internal transformation and incorporation of social messages. To develop this idea further would require filling out what is meant by "*part* of the I" and how that part is incorporated, and then specifying theoretical relationships between daydreaming and internalization/externalization processes in general.

Easier to track are the ontological changes in the self and its social encounters over successive periods of daydreaming. As we have suggested, the microlevel processing of material in relation to life goals holds promise as a way of extending the analysis of micro-macro connections. At this point, it is sufficient that Pereira and Diriwächter's treatment of daydreaming, with some of the extensions we have proposed, justifies submitting experiences of daydreaming to microgenetic analysis. We wish to emphasize the person's ontological development and how it might be affected by microgenetic change, although the microgenetic-ontogentic connection is difficult to demonstrate in empirical studies (see Valsiner & Lawrence, 1997).

In summary, daydreaming is a form of mental activity that warrants serious empirical analysis, at least because of its frequency in people's everyday experience. More, it fulfils some purposes in people's lives, in linking events over time, and assisting them to review what has happened and prepare for what they expect to come. This process, although occurring exclusively in the private world of personal consciousness, has definite links to the social and phenomenal environment. Daydreaming episodes evolve temporally in the immediate experience at one small part of the whole of a person's life. Yet, although they may be fanciful and unfettered by reality, they are imbedded within a person's ontological experience. Clearly this short account of daydreaming processes deals with something that goes beyond off-task, undirected thinking.

Given that daydreaming is a process imbedded in people's everyday and life-long experiences, it has psychological significance in terms of how it emerges and how it is elaborated in a person's internal constructed monologues and imaginary dialogues. It is this complex and personal process that Pereira and Diriwächter set out to "capture" with their empirical investigations. They focused on developing ways of investigating daydreaming as it occurred, in order to identify more closely its characteristics and the processes of its evolution.

If the daydreaming phenomenon is to be described in its entirety, then a variety of methods is called for. Singer's (1976, 2003) long-term commitment to theorizing and observing "streams of thought, daydreams, and interior monologues" (Singer, 2003, p. 462) provides that kind of base. Pereira and Diriwächter are not simply addressing a replication or revision of Singer's agenda. Rather, they are focusing specifically on the ongoing, evolving nature of the activity. We add the connection between microgenetic and ontogenetic processes to their developmental perspective. So the purpose is to obtain theory-driven evidence of daydreaming processes, particularly its emergence and elaboration. With Pereira and Diriwächter, we believe that a multimethod approach is most suitable, given the private and stream-like nature of the processing.

CAPTURING DAYDREAMING PROCESSES

Pereira and Diriwächter used two methods to focus on building up a developmental account of daydreaming. The daydreaming journal technique gave them a lead on the complexity and part-whole dimensions of the activity. The reports of reconstructed daydreaming episodes could not, however, yield evidence of the evolving character of a whole episode. If contemporary researchers are to add a microgenetic analysis that can reveal the successive parts of the evolving activity, then some form of online evolving data is needed.

In several respects as they acknowledge, Pereira and Diriwächter are retreading or at least treading in parallel the steps of cognitive researchers who similarly treated problem solving as a complex activity that involves sequenced steps of different forms of mental activity. They refer explicitly to Duncker's (1945) search for the processes by which his laboratory participants constructed solutions to tasks, presenting them with genuine, initially unsolvable problems. Duncker used the think-aloud technique as his way of following his participants' reasoning processes, and it became the premier research tool of the cognitive revival of process analysis in the twentieth century (see Ericsson & Simon, 1993). It is reasonable for Pereira and Diriwächter to borrow this well-used technique, drawing on classical problem-solving microanalyses.

Daydreaming phenomena, however, exert particular constraints on obtaining the immediate, unfolding and dense traces of mental activity that exemplify microgenetic analysis (Lee & Karmiloff-Smith, 2002). The external evidence cannot be isomorphic with the covert processing that is likely to be personally encoded and rapidly executed, and there is no specific environmental task to which the internal processes can be consistently connected. Consequently, any method devised for making covert activities overt entails some risks of imposing further constraints on the evidence of the processing.

The think-aloud method of obtaining online running commentaries of people's problem-solving reasoning has been used extensively in microgenetic studies of phenomena that represent a range of different problems and the mental activities used to solve them. These phenomena range from purely cognitive to value-laden tasks, for example, tasks involving playing complex games, applying professional expertise, and understanding school-related and learning problems (e.g., Chi, Glaser, & Farr, 1988; Ericsson, 1996; Granott & Parziale, 2002; Perkins, Voss, & Segal, 1991). More closely related to the personal domain, we and others have applied the think-aloud technique to personally-involving and socially-charged tasks requiring internalizing and externalizing activities (e.g., people's processing of sequentially presented information about a young person's shoplifting activities; Lawrence & Heinz, 1997; Lawrence & Valsiner, 2003). This technique is ideally suited to microgenetic analyses of evolving complex mental processes with distinct components incorporated in a whole activity.

Nevertheless, Pereira and Diriwächter's specific use of the think-aloud protocol brings out some ambiguities in their methodological assumptions and adaptations of an existing research technique. This is not to imply that they simply dipped into a tool-box of available methods and applied them to a new area (see Abbey and Diriwächter, this volume). With a strong commitment to mounting a microgenetic analysis that would provide observations of daydreaming processes as they occurred, these researchers carefully considered their phenomena, their commitment to a process analysis, and their adaptation of a technique in order to bring theory and data to bear on each other.

The ambiguities of their approach seem to lie mainly in their commitment to treating daydreaming essentially as an off-task activity. This represents a significant departure from its standard use in the problem-solving paradigm of asking participants to think-aloud while engaged with a demanding task. Typically, the task directs the problem-solver's attention and keeps the verbal commentary on track with her attempts to accomplish that specific task. The verbal stream, then, is focused and constrained by the need to move along with the development of the solution process. This channeled focus cuts down on the possibility of editing, and gives the verbalized stream the shape and form of a verbal report running along with the task-directed problem-solving operations.

Ericsson and Simon (1993) provide a thorough conceptual and empirical base for distinguishing the flow of task-directed, online, thinking-aloud verbalization from other forms of verbal report. At other levels of reporting (immediate retrospective explanation, as in the post think-aloud interviews, or accounts of accumulated personal views, as in the journals), the person is given additional tasks to guide their verbal reporting. They may be asked to identifying particular stimuli in the environmental array or to interpret their mental activities over time. For these activities, the attention of the person is significantly moved from the production of the problem solution which they are expressing as they work when thinking out loud.

Benjafield (1969) was able to distinguish the shape and content of think-aloud from immediately retrospective forms of verbal report. He asked one group of students to verbalize while working on solving a tetrahedron problem and another to report on their problem-solving immediately after solving the same problem. The think-aloud reports were expressed in the present tense, used more indefinite referents, were elliptical in form and gave more complete records of the problem-solving operations. Benjafield interpreted the differences as evidence of the think-aloud technique's ability to tap into the students' mental processes by which they planned, organized and executed moves as they were working on the problem.

It is the on-task focus of the think-aloud protocol that makes it dense and idiosyncratic. The general aim is to get as close as possible to the task-focused activity, without eliciting editing or explanation from the research participant. The protocol is designed to provide a descriptive running verbalization expressing the covert processing.

By presenting their participants with a boring, undemanding, visually-presented task, Pereira and Diriwächter were following the Antrobus and Singer (1964) experimental paradigm, by updating the original use of a blinking light to a more complex visual display of vector graphics on a computer screen. However, Pereira and Diriwächter simplified and short-ened the presented non-task. Antrobus and Singer did not actually use their presentation as a non-task. They asked their participants to free-associate while watching the light and recording their responses by press-ing a button when the light intensified. Their sessions took over 90 min-utes.

By making their adaptation non-engaging and boring, Pereira and Diriwächter were expecting that people's think-aloud verbal reports would yield evidence of daydreaming processes unrelated to the visual observation task. That their technique revealed daydreaming as it occurred is now established. The verbal protocols from P106 and P119 show the environmental triggers (referring to the computer in both instances) and changes in participants' daydreaming, in the take-up of triggered information (e.g., P106's reference to desks and chewing gum; and P119's reference to his grandmother).

The ambiguities center on the form of the protocols presented by Pereira and Diriwächter, their method of analysis, and the details they seem to omit from the report of their approach, that we believe, would help the reader to better assess its suitability for observing daydreaming phenomena. Investigators of online problem solving, ourselves included, have trained their research participants to generate think-aloud running commentaries on their task-directed thinking. Such training need not be exhaustive, because according to Ericsson and Simon (1993), the process of thinking aloud is natural. People often talk themselves through difficult activities. However, by training research participants to keep focused on the task and keep up their verbal stream, it is possible to get close to the mental activities in real time.

By using an undemanding, essentially visually-oriented "non-task" of attending to vector graphics (i.e., "watch and report on" them, p. 179 this volume), the researchers were giving their participants mixed instructions.

While visual processing can be verbalized, the change in modality requires another step (Ericsson & Simon, 1993). This added to the burden of generating verbalization that already had multiple focuses. Asking their participants to "speak any thoughts aloud" (p. 170 this volume) was explicitly designed to yield verbalization of *anything* the participant was thinking during the 7 minute experiment. Yet it would seem that without concentrating on an engaging, single task the participants had no need to keep moving along with an online stream of verbalization. They were working in a cluttered field, and were able to attend to the content and presentation of their reports of their daydreaming. Undirected processing imposes no constraints on the style of verbalization.

In one sense, of course, unconstrained processing is exactly what Pereira and Diriwächter wanted. The participant could say "anything," because the researchers were operating from the assumption that any off-task thought would involve daydreaming. On the other hand, the researchers wanted the verbalization to be as close as possible to the actual daydreaming processes, and not to include any "cleaning" of that process for an audience. If the excerpts are verbatim transcriptions of their participants' think-aloud commentaries, then it would seem that these participants had opportunity and time to edit their verbalizations as they expressed them.

In the P119 protocol, for example, the following semantically complex utterance occurs, "Someone else, I think it was my step-dad, told me that I could call the Board of Higher Education, since they sent me letters saying that I had the loan and now they won't give it to me." There seems to be explanatory material for the audience here. We would expect a think-aloud commentary to identify the "step-dad" by name. The "since they sent ... the loan" construction seems to be another explanatory gloss. Perhaps to clear-up any misinterpretations we may be making, it would be useful to include the running time and the researcher's coding of the expressions in the transcribed protocol.

That there are just a few instances of the "um, "uhu," "er" fillers or pauses suggests that the transcription itself may not be a verbatim record. These "interjections" in the stream of verbalization are usually indicators of pauses in concentrating on the task. Daydreaming is self-talk, and think-aloud is meant to be the covert expression of that self-talk. One would expect unexplained references to events and unformed expressions and sentences. While the extracts from P106 move back and forth between the visual display and her daydreaming, the longer protocol from P119 has a narrative flow and cohesion that would be unusual in a verbatim think-aloud protocol. Either these features have been edited out of the transcripts for analysis, or they are online evidence of the shape of the protocol in response to the non-engaging, undirected and free nature of the experimental activity. This is an important point.

The former, transcription possibility makes it more difficult to determine the individual units or monads in the ongoing flow, thereby detracting from the ability to model the evolving process. That modeling process is important for showing the emergence of the daydreaming episode in relation to environmental triggers and personal concerns, as Pereira and Diriwächter demonstrate with protocols from P106 and as they had already pre-figured in the modeling of the journal data.

The latter possibility of the shape of the verbatim think-aloud protocol is more significant. P106's protocol, for example, has the present tense, the interrupted focus (e.g., the movement from the graphics to the writing on the desk) and some of the pauses (e.g., "people, like, put their gum under the desk"). However, it also seems to contain explanatory comments (e.g., "I can't quite describe"). Second-level interpretation of the protocols would be facilitated if the researchers presented a full, segmented protocol with its pauses, referents and asides intact. The two extracts of P106's daydreaming episode are used as examples of the parts of the model, without showing the flow of the whole daydreaming process.

CONCLUSIONS AND DIRECTIONS

We have critiqued Pereira and Diriwächter's adaptation of a well-used technique for observing problem-solving processes. With no other candidate technique readily available, they have made a good initial adaptation. What could take the technique further in the service of the microgenetic agenda, given the suitability of daydreaming as an evolving process? We agree that the think-aloud verbal commentary has value in this personalized area, and we open up the discussion with some suggestions for extending microgenetic investigations of daydreaming.

First, if Pereira and Diriwächter are going to use the think-aloud protocol as their primary data-base, they need to give more details of their procedures for obtaining those commentaries (e.g., fuller details of training, conditions and instructions), and also their techniques for transcribing and then submitting the commentaries to microgenetic analysis. There are indications of their analytic techniques in the identification of $\underline{A}$ to $\underline{H}$ moves in the P119 protocol, and in the modeling of the extracts of P106's daydreaming. A verbatim transcription of an entire think-aloud session would reveal the form, shape, and flow of the verbalization. Making their technique more public would be a useful move on from this initial presentation, for instance, by laying out the protocol in a monad-by-monad form, with analytic comments (and possibly timing).

The use of additional and different experimental tasks may yield converging evidence of the evolving nature of daydreaming without some of the constraints on the verbalized stream the environmentally-presented "non-task" imposes. Some standard and novel methods of investigating daydreaming may be adaptable to microgenetic concerns. For example, Klinger's (1990) two-channel, intrusion method has potential for pinning down any relations between environmental triggering and personal concerns. In a series of experiments, it would be possible to compare when and how triggers are taken up and modified, in relation to previously obtained personal concerns of research participants. While Klinger's task was quite demanding, it did use only the verbal modality and appears to be amenable to training people to verbalize on-line. Its adaptation is worth exploring.

More importantly, we believe it may be useful to develop an experimental paradigm in which daydreaming becomes the explicit task presented to the participant. This is a tall order, but suppose the researcher works with a participant over several sessions, as Duncker (1945) did to investigate problem-solving strategies. Multiple sessions and multiple techniques would be used to converge on describing and modeling daydreaming processes.

In an early introductory session, the participant's task would be to generate a set of personal concerns, similar to Klinger's (1990) task. Alternatively, the early sessions could be given over to developing daydreaming journals over a period of time, since Pereira and Diriwächter have shown that these journals can bring to the fore current concerns. The researcher then would have a set of a participant's prominent issues and interests to search for in actual daydreaming sessions that follow some time later. Later again, the researcher would talk with the participant about daydreaming, much in the form Pereira and Diriwächter used in their follow-up questioning of their participants' personal theorizing about their daydreaming. The existing interview material provides a nice check on any contamination of the theorizing on later daydreaming, identifying any order effects.

Now in an actual daydreaming session, the investigator would explain to participants that their task in the session is to do some undirected, free thinking: daydreaming. It will be noted that here we are removing the "off-task" element. Instead, we suggest that the researcher train the participant in the activity of freely filling a blank space in time with anything that comes to mind. Such an instruction is not far from what Pereira and Diriwächter did, but removes the non-task. The task now is to just think and verbalize whatever occurs and flows through consciousness. Training in free-thinking and in verbalizing would required, but we envisage no problem in training a cognitively aware person to think and talk concurrently. This retains the problem solving, on-task approach, taking the technique outside the realm of monitoring and editing one's thought.

It is not an impossible task, as we found in a preparatory thought experiment. One of us lay down quietly in a darkened room with the eyes shut, and just allowed her thoughts to roam wherever they would. Such a technique is often linked to relaxation exercises, in which the person progressively relaxes all parts of the body, then relaxes the mind by allowing it to roam wherever it will. Pilot work would involve asking research participants to follow this procedure with a tape recorder to capture a running commentary.

One advantage of this approach is that it treats the participant as a partner in the research enterprise and not an uninformed and manipulated subject. In line with that perspective, it may be useful to add another experimental session once the protocol is transcribed. to capture the participants' own understanding of their processing, drawing on their privileged access. This session would yield a form of reflective, negotiated analysis of the original daydreaming protocol. We believe this multisession, multimethod approach would yield data on daydreaming that happens in an uncluttered field, and may have a different form, shape and context to this first round of daydreaming think-aloud protocols generated so creatively by Pereira and Diriwächter.

Finally, with our specific interest in the personal function of daydreaming, we would welcome introducing an longitudinal component into the multiple sessions approach. By introducing a over-time element, such as that Bartlett (1932) used so productively to capture and recapture people's memories of stories, it may be possible to track development in the relationship between daydreaming and ontological experience. For instance, the persistence of concerns in the face of different environmental triggers, or changes in those concerns may get us closer to the microgentetic-ontogenetic connections that are so difficult to trace. This direction for further studies lies outside of Pereira and Diriwächter's current interests, but it is triggered by the creativity of their approach.

REFERENCES

Antrobus, J. S., & Singer, J. L. (1964). Visual signal detection as a function of sequential variability of simultaneous speech. *Journal of Experimental Psychology, 68*(6), 603-610.

Bartlett, F. C. (1932). *Remembering: A study in experimental and social psychology.* Cambridge, MA: Cambridge University Press.

Benjafield, J. (1969). Evidence that "thinking aloud" constitutes an externalization of inner speech. *Psychonomic Science, 15*(2), 83-84.

Bennett, A. (1998). *The complete talking heads*. London: British Broadcasting Corporation.

Chi, M. T. H., Glaser, R., & Farr, M. J. (Eds.). (1988). *The nature of expertise*. Hillsdale, NJ: Erlbaum.

Duncker, K. (1945). On problem solving. *Psychological Monographs, 58*(5), Whole No. 270.

Ericsson, K. A. (Ed.). (1996). *The road to excellence: The acquisition of expert performance in the arts and sciences, sports, and games*. Mahwah, NJ: Erlbaum.

Ericsson, K. A., & Simon, H. A. (1993). *Protocol analysis: Verbal reports as data, (*Rev. ed.*)*. Cambridge, MA: MIT Press.

Giambra, L. M. (1974). Daydreaming across the life-span: Late adolescent to senior citizen. *International Journal of Aging and Human Development, 5,* 115-140.

Granott, N., & Parziale, J. (2002). *Microdevelopment: Transition processes in development and learning*. Cambridge, MA: Cambridge University Press.

Klinger, E. (1990). *Daydreaming*. Los Angeles: Jermey P. Tarcher.

Langens, T. A., & Schmalt, H.-D. (2002). Emotional consequences of positive daydreaming. *Personality and Social Psychology Bulletin, 28*(12), 1725-1735.

Lawrence, J. A., & Heinze, V. (1997). Analyses of adolescents' constructions of a shoplifting event as internalization/externalization processes. In B. Cox & C. Lightfoot (Eds.), *Sociogenetic perspectives on internalization* (pp. 45-73). Hillsdale, NJ: Erlbaum.

Lawrence, J. A., & Valsiner, J. (2003). Making personal sense: An account of basic internalization and externalization processes. *Theory and Psychology, 13*(6), 723-752.

Lee, K., & Karmiloff-Smith, A. (2002). Macro- and microdevelopmental research: Assumptions, research strategies, constraints, and utilities. In N. Granott & J. Parziale (Eds.), *Microdevelopment: Transition processes in development and learning* (pp. 243-268). Cambridge, MA: Cambridge University Press.

Mandler, G. (1985). *Cognitive psychology: An essay in cognitive science*. Hillsdale, NJ: Erlbaum.

Miller, G. A., Galanter, E., & Pribram, K. H. (1960). *Plans and the structure of behavior*. New York: Holt, Rinehart & Winston.

Perkins, D. N., Voss, J. F., & Segal, J. (Eds.). (1991). *Informal reasoning and education*. Hillsdale, NJ: Erlbaum.

Singer, J. L. (1976). *Daydreaming and fantasy*. London: Allen & Unwin.

Singer, J. L. (2003). Daydreaming, consciousness, and self-representations: Empirical approaches to theories of William James and Sigmund Freud. *Journal of Applied Psychoanalytic Studies, 5*(4), 461-483.

Valsiner, J., & Lawrence, J. A. (1997). Human development in culture across the life span. In J. W. Berry, P. R. Dasen, & T. S. Saraswathi (Eds.), *Handbook of cross-cultural psychology. Basic processes and developmental psychology* (Vol. 2., 2nd ed., pp. 69-106). Boston: Allyn & Bacon.

PART V

EARLY DEVELOPMENT OF
SUBJECT-OBJECT RELATIONS

CHAPTER 9

PRODUCTION OF SIGNS AND MEANING-MAKING PROCESS IN TRIADIC INTERACTION AT THE PRELINGUISTIC LEVEL

A Task for Sociocultural Analysis— The Case of Ostension

Christiane Moro and Cintia Rodríguez

INTRODUCTION

Most researchers agree to recognize the qualitative progress in terms of development that access to the production of signs (whether verbal or nonverbal) constitutes for a child. Signs play a key role in communication, in the construction of thought and reality for the child. Concerning nonverbal signs, a great deal of work is still to be done relating to their identification, their genesis and the functions and significations they fill in early development. The present contribution will more specifically study

Innovating Genesis: Microgenesis and the Constructive Mind in Action, pp. 207–227
Copyright © 2008 by Information Age Publishing

the production of ostensions at the prelinguistic level in the context of educational situations organized around the transmission-appropriation of the use of objects by the child.

The Study of Microgenesis in a Sociohistorical Framework

In our research, microgenetic analysis appears to be a major methodological tool for the investigation of the interactive processes where signs, and more specifically ostensions, are produced by the child. Microgenetic analysis reveals the fundamentally interactive nature of cognitive development. Without being exhaustive on this question, we will just point out that "the study of microgenesis is not recent. Siegler and Crowley (1991) mention Vygotsky (published in 1978) who quoted Werner's work in 1925. Piaget's work on the sensori-motor stage (1936/1977) must also be mentioned" (Saada-Robert, 1994, p. 58).

In our work, part of our inspiration comes from the neo-Piagetian studies on cognitive functioning made in Geneva in the 1970s (Inhelder et al., 1992). The microgenetic perspective of the school of Geneva "aims at identifying and explaining the mechanisms of change" in the discovery of new knowledge (Saada-Robert, 1994, p. 59). We nevertheless distance ourselves from the position of the neo-Piagetian school of Geneva insomuch as it remains confined in a subject/object-type epistemology. Our approach, on the contrary, reconsiders early development from a social and pragmatical perspective where signs play a key role.

Our study is grounded in the sociohistorical conception of the elaboration of consciousness as developed by Vygotsky (1934/1997), in the semiotic approach proposed in *Thought & Language* and of which we have, in previous studies (Moro & Rodríguez, 2005a; Rodríguez & Moro, 1999), suggested the extension to the prelinguistic level of development. In this conception, the part played by signs in development is central. As considered by Vygotsky, signs constitute artificial means of action that are appropriated by the child in contexts of social interaction then integrated to the functioning of the psyche, thereby considerably transforming and reorientating the child's possibilities of action, thought and communication. For Vygotsky, the analysis of signs is the only method adapted to the analysis of the human consciousness (Rivière, 1990; Vygotsky, 1934/1997).

As indicated, the nonverbal signs that we are going to focus on are *ostensions*. These particular signs are related to a great variety of phenomena, whether on the level of their expression, of their function or of their signification.

In a first part, we will place the issue of the production of signs with regard to the double sense of communication: *communication towards other people* ("traditional" sense) and *communication towards oneself* (the sense that we are formulating in line with the Vygotskian framework). In a second part we will define ostension according to Eco (1992) as well as to Vygotsky. In a third part we will point out some questions related to our work and the context of our study. In a fourth part we will examine some prototypical examples of ostensions produced by children of 7 and 13 months of age, which come from a longitudinal study, and for which we will propose a semiotic analysis. Finally in a fifth part, we will present a reflection on the implications of the study of signs (and specifically of preverbal signs) for the research on psychogenesis.

Sign-Production, Communication, and Cognition

Before we enter more closely into the definition of ostension, let us point out some aspects of our previous works (Moro & Rodríguez, 2005a; Rodríguez & Moro, 1999). These works bring the evidence of the sociohistorical development of the psyche before language. Concerning the question of the construction of the object through its use, our first studies show that objects are not only to be considered in physical terms (cf. Piaget, 1936/1977) but are also the fruit of conventions that have been socially and historically elaborated. The child thus arrives in a world that is already fabricated (Bruner, 1996; Goodman, 1978), where objects are to be considered as artifacts to be appropriated by the child in their social meanings, that is, as objects to be used, and where the intervention of education is necessary. In order to (re)construct the social meanings of the object—that are not evident from the object itself—the child needs communication with other people (e.g., adults) who intentionally use signs for the transmission of the canonical use of the object to the child, thereby giving him/her the very keys to its use. The child displays intense semiotic activity (i.e., meaning-making) that enables him/her, by making agreements with the other person via the signs that this person produces, to progressively give the object its conventional meanings of use, and to use it according to its social function.

The above mentioned works have demonstrated that the construction of the object is socially and semiotically mediated. Within the framework of these studies, we particularly focused on communication with others and the interpretative processes used by the child to give meaning to other people's signs. Moreover, we were able to observe that, as the child makes progress in his/her knowledge of the social use of objects, he/she appropriates the signs that were initially used by the adult to convey the use of the object to him/her.

It has thus appeared that, during ontogenesis, the child is first of all the interpreter of other people's signs, and only afterwards does he/she progressively institute himself/herself as a producer of signs by his own right.

In this paper, we will concentrate our attention on this second aspect, that is, the production of signs by the child during interaction between child and object, which has two main characteristics: first, the production of signs by the child is closely related to the process of meaning-making; second, this production of signs is to be considered not only in terms of *communicating with others* but also in terms of *communicating with oneself* (cf. Moro & Rodríguez, 2005a; Moro & Schneuwly, 2001; Rodríguez & Palacios, 2007). It is in this double sense of the production of signs that we will examine the use of ostension by the child. Ostension is a sign that is rarely studied by psychologists for itself and which is generally considered as an indexical sign, which it is not. Through some of its prototypical forms, we will show how it is produced in order to depict its significations and functions in communication with others and/or oneself, in situations of triadic interaction where the object plays a central part.

Ostension: Elements of Definition

For Eco (1992), ostension essentially characterizes communication with others. He defines it as "a catch-all sign that works precisely because of its vagueness" (p. 12). Ostension is "a sign that exists only insofar as it has a context" and can have a great variety of meanings. Such a sign makes it possible to establish congruent meanings on a very large scale considering its fundamentally polysemous character. The polysemous character of ostension, which was already underlined by Saint-Augustine (Eco, 1988, p. 56) is remarkably shown in the following text:

> If I wave a packet of "Benson & Hedges" at a friend who is about to go out shopping, the ostension can express either *"get some cigarettes"* or *"get some Benson & Hedges."* In the second case, I would probably add a few denotative conventions such as pointing at the name of the brand on the packet. In other circumstances, it might be necessary to specify and clarify by several means if, for example, when I wave a packet of cigarettes, I mean "cigarettes" or "packet of cigarettes." (Eco, 1992, p. 80)

This polysemy implies a very great flexibility of ostension from the point of view of its meaning. Whereas this can be a problem in adult communication, it is a *major advantage* during the prelinguistic period. Indeed the undefined character of the sign means that, by potentially referring to different levels of pertinence, the child and the adult can come to an agreement of communication without necessarily needing to share the same meanings regarding the world and the objects. This reference to different levels of pertinence allows the progressive construction of shared meanings with regard to the world. The flexibility of ostension can also be seen on the level of the expression of the sign (i.e., of its signifier): still according to Eco (1992), the content is immediately present in the sign, the organization of the content determining (at least partially) the organization of its expression.

In *Consciousness as a Problem in the Psychology of Behavior*, Vygotsky (1925/ 1994) from "the idea of the identity of mechanisms of consciousness and of contact with oneself and [of] the idea that consciousness is, in a way, contact with oneself" (p. 48), reveals the pivotal nature of signs and the fact that signs (mainly linguistic for Vygotsky) are not only oriented towards communication with others, but also towards communication with oneself. This second form of communication (cf. Yakubinski, 1923, quoted by Wertsch, 1985) is, according to Vygotsky, at the source of the constitution of thought and consciousness as a sociohistorical process. With communication towards himself, the child begins to develop reflexive activity. Through a dialogue that goes from himself to himself, the functioning of the psyche is starting to gain autonomy. In this last sense, the sign shifts from the external means of regulation by another that it was, to an internal means of regulation of his own action and psychic functioning, by the subject himself.

Ostension can also be described as a "pivotal sign" in the sense that its origin (most probably) lies in basic abilities that are "engraved in the body itself" (i.e., expression of tone and posture) before becoming a sign that effectively involves the material object. We distinguish between ostension of signs that are more fundamentally engraved in the body or "sketched by the body," using the expression of Feyereisen and De Lannoy (1985, p. 8), and of signs that correspond to ritualized entities such as, for example, gestures of "hand-waving." Following the use of ostension is pointing, an indexical sign that appears around the end of the first year and that Butterworth (2002) qualifies as "distal mean" (p. 17). Intermediate forms of pointing (between pointing and ostension) can also be noted; in these cases, the pointing sign is not produced at a distance but touches the indicated object and, by doing so, presents a distinctly ostension-like character.

Questions and Context of the Study (Situation and Objects)

In a general way, the questions that we formulate through this study are the following: What forms of ostension are produced by a child between 7 and 13 months of age? In which circumstances are they produced? What are the functions of ostensions from the point of view of communication, thought and object? Is there a link between meaning-making and sign-production?

The examples of behaviors of ostension-production that we will examine come from a longitudinal study on the canonical use of the object by children between the ages of 7 and 13 months old. The canonical use of the object refers to the material use of the object, that is, to *what you are supposed to do* with the object. As such, we can consider the use of the object as a sociosemiotic form that is woven out of conventions that the child must appropriate by reconstituting its meanings. It is in a situation of triadic baby-object-adult interaction that we shall examine how the child is brought to make his/her first productions of differentiated ostensions relating to the appropriation and/or differentiation of the use of the object. Observations of triadic baby-object-adult interactions are collected by video-camera at home and duly transcribed. Each session of observation in triadic mode (baby-object-adult) is of 5 minutes duration; The instruction (addressed to the adult) is to "Play with your child as you usually do."

The two objects to be considered in the study are:

1. A truck with six differently-shaped holes in the top (see Figure 9.1) in which can be inserted six blocks of different shapes and colors (a white cylinder; a hexagonal green block; a yellow flower-shaped block; a cubical orange block; a triangular blue block; an oblong red block). The hole where each block is to be inserted matches the shape of the block, so that each block has its particular space. The truck has a skip that can be lifted using a handle on its top-front. The skip also has a back door that can be opened with a little handle at the bottom of the door. On the front of the truck is drawn a smiling face. The canonical use of the truck examined in the following examples is related to the insertion of the blocks in their respective holes;

2. A Fisher Price telephone (Figure 9.2) painted in vivid colors, with a red receiver. It has a traditional front that you have to turn to dial the number. It is set on four wheels and has a string inserted in the front so that it can be pulled and made to go like a car. It has a face painted on its front, with mobile eyes that animate when the phone

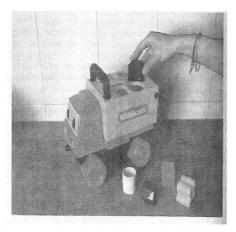

Figure 9.1.   Toy truck.

Figure 9.2.   Fisher Price telephone.

is moved backwards and forwards. The string that goes to the receiver has been extended to make it easier to use by the dyad. The canonical use of the telephone consists in the simulating "Saying Hello." This usage consists in putting the receiver to the ear, using it alternately with one's partner so that it creates something similar to a telephone conversation, with the related uses that are "taking the receiver"; "dialing the number "; "talking on the phone"; and "hanging up."

In the context of our study, sign-production is narrowly related to the interaction with the other person and to the object. With regard to the object, let us specify that a 7-month-old child does not yet apprehend canonical use nor, therefore, its relating public significations; at 13 months old he/she does apprehend canonical use (in the general sense of the word) but he/she must still differentiate the bi-univocal relation between blocks and spaces concerning the truck, and the different segments of usage concerning the Fisher Price telephone.

The following analysis of children's behavior aims at understanding the dynamics of its production by referring it to its contextual elements but also to the processes of communication with others and with oneself and to the cognitive processes (conceived in terms of signification) engaged in the process of production. In this object our study is more particularly based on Peircian semiotics. In Peirce's (1931/1958) conception, the link between the sign (at the starting-point of the process of interpretation) and what the sign signifies (its object) is not immediate, but is mediated by a third element, the "interpretant," referring to an interpretation that puts the sign in relation with its object. According to the interpretation that is produced, the sign can have the value of an icon (the sign refers to itself); of an index (the sign refers to an object other than itself); of a symbol (the sign refers to an object other than itself by virtue of a law). The meaning that is produced (interpretation) gives us access to the inferential processes used by the child in the production of signs, or in other words enables us to render the dynamics of behavior and to give more than just a fossilized description.

Elements of Illustration

In the following examples we will examine how, in the triadic baby-object-adult interaction, the child, *first nonintentionally then intentionally*, becomes a producer of signs. As indicated, the type of sign we are examining more particularly is ostension. At 7 months of age, we observe that it is a sign that is only just emerging and is produced without intention. At 13 months, it appears in many different forms, both directed towards oneself and towards another person (sometimes even halfway between oneself and another person).[1] We will present two related examples, the first illustrating what is meant by "the child as an interpreter of the signs of others in triadic interaction"; the other presenting the production by the child of pointing signs that illustrate the closeness between ostension and pointing (and enable us to suggest the hypothesis of the affiliation between ostension and pointing on a developmental level), an occasion for us to regret that the link between ostension and pointing attracts less scientific interest than that of pointing and language (on this last aspect, see Kita, 2002).

The Child as a Producer of Signs in Triadic Interaction at age 7 Months

> **Observation n° 1 – Nelson, 7 months; Duration of the sequence: 35 seconds**
> **Object: Telephone; canonical use: Saying Hello**
> **Ostension to oneself (initiated with no specific intention)**

The adult rolls the telephone forward and goes "rouuuuuu," makes it climb up Nelson and back down again, then up again going "tourourourourourou ourourourou tourourourourou." Nelson watches the adult's action then follows the adult's action with his hand. Nelson hits on the dial with the receiver and, while he does so, the receiver suddenly ends up (by chance) positioned "the wrong way round" against the cheek of Nelson, who goes "huu." Nelson looks straight ahead for a few moments [in the canonical posture of someone phoning] while keeping the receiver against his cheek. He then turns his eyes once more to the action of the adult (who is still rolling the telephone) and brings down the receiver...

This is an example of ostension taken from the observation of a 7-month-old child, at an age where, as a rule, children are not yet sign-producers as such. The production of signs by the child implies that he has previously engaged an element of "discretization" (Moro & Rodríguez, 2005a; Moro & Rodríguez, 2005b) of the other person's sign. Yet in the present case, we can make a practically "live" observation of the process of differed discretization of the other person's sign, which is established through a cultural meaning to which the child has already been confronted previously. For this reason we can say that here, sign-production does not have an intentional status from the outset.

This ostension is one of the very first sign-productions that we were able to observe from a 7-month-old. It is an age where, as our studies point out, the child is merely the interpreter of other people's signs in the context of the first forms of connexion between the sign and the usage of the object to which it refers (cf. the behavior related in observation n°2). This production of ostension is observed following the fortuitous action on behalf of the child of putting the receiver to his ear (in its approximate form: the receiver ending up next to the child's cheek) whereas the child is making a noncanonical use of the object, following the interest given by the child to the action that was initiated by the adult of rolling the telephone forward and the accompanying verbalizations. This sign can be decomposed into two successive interpretative movements (in French "relations de renvoi" in the sense that is given by Jakobson, 1974) that happen when the receiver is against the child's cheek:

1. A first reaction of surprise, "*huu,*" expressed by the child in relation to his own action. This reaction refers to the child's action itself as such, i.e. to the receiver placed against the cheek;
2. The child's action of *looking straight ahead,* posture of a person who is telephoning and proves that here the child's action relates to the use of the object itself.

During these two interpretative movements (in the sense that is given by Peirce), the child's action is instituted as a *sign* in the emerging process of *communication towards oneself* (cf. Vygotsky, supra). The production of ostension is nonintentional as it happens fortuitously during a noncanon-ical use of the object by the child.

If we now consider the conditions in which this sign is produced, we will note that it happens as a result of the interest that is shown by the child towards his own action (at first) (*reflexive* aspect of the action); an action that progressively refers to the conventional meanings of the object, probably benefiting from other sensations that the child has experienced during the triadic interaction through signs from the other person and in particular through *immediate demonstrations* (cf. observation n°2). This ostension towards oneself is linked to a revivifica-tion of sensations (of a tactile and proprioceptive order) which allows a kind of encroachment of past into present (Alquié, 1979). The sign hap-pens in the context of the beginning of *an autonomous* differentiation by the child of the social meanings of the object, his interest no longer stopping at the action itself (cf. the child's reaction of surprise "*huu,*" which is his first reaction) but extending to the receiver and its use (cf. the child's adoption of the *looking straight ahead* posture of the person on the phone).

The child's own action becomes a sign in a movement that goes from the *icon,* the "*huu*" relating to the action itself, to the *index,* as the posture of looking straight ahead relates to the use of the object. As we can see, the production of signs is narrowly linked with the process of meaning-making. It is the meaning that makes it possible for such a production of signs to be made independently from any intention; it is the increasing complexity of the processes of interpretation that have previously been put into place by the child (cf. illustration n°2) that is at the origin of this sign-production.

The Child as an Interpreter of the Signs of Another Person in Triadic Interaction at age 7 Months

To clarify the distinction we make between interpretation of other people's signs and production of signs within the triadic interaction, let us stop and examine a situation where the child merely interprets another person's sign. On the level of semiotic functioning we can underline that, in ontogeny, the processes of meaning-making precede the processes of sign production.

Observation n° 2 – Nelson, 7 months; Duration of the sequence: 33 seconds
Object: Telephone; Canonical use: Saying Hello
Interpretation by the child of another person's signs

The adult turns the dial ("dials the number"). Nelson lays his hand on the receiver (mechanically absorbed by his interest in the adult, whose action he is watching). The adult turns the dial a second time, seizes the receiver, puts it against her ear and says "helloo hellooo Nelson hellooo hellooo hello hello hellooo Nelson" while from time to time she shakes the receiver that is against her ear. Meanwhile Nelson is sucking at the cord (the one at the front with which you pull the phone). Then Nelson holds out his hand towards the action of the adult, seizes the string (between the telephone and the receiver) and lets go, seizes it again while still watching the adult and smiles. The adult, the receiver still against her ear, says "aaaaah yes yes yes" while moving closer to Nelson. The adult takes the receiver away from her ear and says "do you want to listen?" Nelson lets go of the string then stuffs the cord back into his mouth. The adult places the receiver against Nelson's ear and says "hello helloo hellooo hello helloo hellooo who is it?" For 4 seconds Nelson accepts this immediate demonstration by the adult of the use Saying hello. Except for a quick look at the action of the adult when she places the receiver against his ear, Nelson looks straight ahead for the whole length of the demonstration, in the posture of someone phoning. Then Nelson looks at the receiver and the adult takes it away from his ear while saying "no one there my poor darling". The adult hangs up while Nelson puts the cord back to his mouth.

In such a behavior, the child is the interpreter of another person's signs and not a producer of signs himself in the sense that we have been using. This behavior shows that the child is giving meaning to the other person's action of demonstrating the usage of the object on his own body (*immediate demonstration*). The action of the other person becomes a sign for the child of the social meanings of the object. The process of interpretation put into place by the child shows that he makes a relation between the other person's action (which consequently becomes a sign) and the social meanings of the object. The entry into the conventional meanings of the object can be identified through:

1. The child's 4 second acceptance of the receiver when it is put to his ear by the adult;

2. The child's adoption of the *looking straight ahead* attitude that is characteristic of someone on the phone.

To be more precise, the adult's action of *immediate demonstration* becomes an *indication* (in the hic et nunc) as to the canonical use of the object. The meaning presents the characteristics of an indicative sign in the sense that the adult's action relates to the use of the object "when receiver is held to the ear, accept it and look straight ahead." Another element corroborates our interpretation: Nelson's smile—expressing connivance—when the adult demonstrates the use of the object on himself *(distant demonstration)*; indeed this element confirms that there is a sharing of significations relating to the object and its use between the two protagonists of the interaction.

The Child as a Producer of Signs in Triadic Interaction at 13 Months Old

Unlike the ostension described in example n°1, the ostension we are about to examine presents an intentional character. This ostension shows the complexity of the child's reasoning process during triadic interaction between 7 and 13 months of age. Indeed, in this sequence, the child (Melanie) assesses her own possibilities before taking the decision of handing the object to the adult so that the adult can fulfill the object's most complex uses, which involve first the establishment of a bi-univocal correspondence between the block and the specific space where it is supposed to be inserted, then the action of materially putting the block in the right space and orientating it so that it will fit. Melanie, who does not yet master the bi-univocal correspondence and has come up against the difficulty of the object's uses during previous sequences, resorts to ostension of giving and leaves it to the adult to complete the use for her.

Observation n° 3 – Melanie, 13 months; Duration of the sequence: 22 seconds
Object: Truck; canonical use: Putting inside
Ostension with an instrumental function aiming at getting something done

Melanie is holding the truck with one hand and exploring a hole with the other. Then Melanie drops the truck, which is knocked over while she tries to get her finger out of the hole. She takes hold of a red block. The adult puts the truck back on its wheels. Melanie then looks at the adult who says "Do you know you can put it there put what you've got in your hand over there, using a pointing: touching the adequate spot and putting a finger inside (multiple immediate iconic pointing). Melanie continues to watch the adult's action. Then the adult does a pointing sign at a distance (classic pointing) of the block that Melanie is keeping in her hand. At that point Melanie looks at her hand, which the adult has just indicated while saying "you take it and put it there," thereby doing a further pointing as she touches the adequate spot and puts a finger inside (multiple immediate iconic pointing). Following the renewed action of the adult, Melanie looks at the truck and, after this look, she moves her block close to the truck, then holds it out to the adult. The adult says "do I have to put it in?" while taking the block and directing it towards the adequate space. She says "this," places it on the hole saying "look" and slides it in while ending her action with an "oh."

Let us examine the child's behavior in this sequence more closely, in order to clearly understand the conditions of emergence of *the ostension* of the block that is made in direction of the adult. After a *multiple* (repeated four times), *immediate* (touching the shaped hole), *iconic* (*imitating the downwards movement that is used when putting a block in its space*) *pointing*, a *canonical pointing* (*i.e., made at a distance*) and another *multiple immediate iconic pointing* of the adequate space by the adult, Melanie brings her block close to the truck before holding it out to the adult (*ostension*) so that he can put it in the space, which the adult does indeed. Though not leading to the effective canonical use but only to its beginning point "bring the block close to the truck," this behavior reveals the increasing complexity of the child's abilities of attentiveness, and brings to light the inferential ability that enables the child to progressively make a relation between the different pointings of the adult and the use of the object, a use which is not in itself contained in any of the adult's pointings. This inferential ability can be read practically simultaneously in the various looks the child directs towards the object through the adult's signs. By her gaze, Melanie testifies that she is very closely following the action of the adult on the object and is thus capable of bringing out the meaning of the adult's signs. Melanie looks at the first pointing sign that indicates the correct space. Then she infers the correct meaning of the pointing that indicates the block she has in her hand (whereas it is done at a distance, which is a further difficulty), then that of the renewed pointing of the adequate space by the adult. In response to the meanings of the different signs that are carried by the adult, she moves her block towards the truck, but gives up fulfilling the use of the object by herself—though she masters its general characteristic "if any block put in any hole" (as she has done in other sequences). She hands her block over to the adult so that he can fulfill the use of the object in her stead. The control of attentiveness by the other person's signs is not alien to the remarkable progression of the child's inferences, and proves the part played by attentiveness in the conduct of action. This example illustrates the importance of meaning through the signs used by the adult with a 13-month-old child, and the new semiotic and inferential abilities that are gained at this level by the child. The use of ostension to ask the adult to fulfill the practical part of the action shows a primitive form of representation of the other person's thought. *The child knows that the adult knows.* This is confirmed by the context of the child's production of ostension which happens after intense semiotic and inferential activity.

Observation n° 4 – Nelson, 13 months; Duration of the sequence: 19 seconds
Object: Truck; canonical use: Putting inside
Intentional ostension of the block to oneself

The adult takes the green block. She says "what about this one?" while presenting it to Nelson at the level of his hand. Nelson takes his hand out of the hole where he has put it following the use that was made during the previous sequence, and seizes the block that the adult is holding out to him, as the adult is saying "see" and is about to put the block in the correct space. Nelson's action prevents her from doing so and the block lands on an inadequate space. The adult lets it go. Nelson takes the block while straightening up. The adult nearly simultaneously says "here you put it here here" and does a multiple immediate iconic pointing. Nelson puts the block back onto the previous inadequate space and tries unsuccessfully to fit it in. The adult moves the truck so that the adequate space is next to Nelson. Then the adult does another multiple immediate iconic pointing on the hole while saying "there" while Nelson lifts the block to his face and presents it to himself. The adult eventually leaves her finger in the hole (in a kind of permanent immediate pointing), while (for 2 seconds) Nelson examines his block. The adult says "look" as Nelson puts the block back onto the previous inadequate space. Nelson tries unsuccessfully to force the block into the hole. The truck overturns. The adult says "ah nearly" and puts the truck back up. She then does a multiple immediate pointing as she says "here you put it here," then does another multiple immediate pointing while saying "here darling." The adult does an ultimate multiple immediate pointing while she says "it goes here" and Nelson drops his block.

A detailed examination of the behavior of 13-month-old children shows us that a number of behaviors that are described as manipulating (cf. Piaget, 1974; cf. Saada-Robert, 1978) are in fact directed by signs and in particular by the sign that we have called *ostension towards oneself* and where the child presents to himself/herself an object that he/she lifts to his face, turning it over and examining it. At 13 months old, ostension towards oneself plays an important part in the control of one's own attentiveness, the objective being to carry out the more systematic explorations of the object that are necessary for the action that is in process. Ostensions towards oneself can therefore not be assimilated to simple manipulation of the object or to noncanonical uses as they are made in relation to the canonical use itself. Ostensions towards oneself are made more particularly when difficulties arise in the fulfilling of the action, the child engaging in a sort of organized exploration of the object.

In this sequence, Nelson is brought to make an *ostension toward himself* in the aim of exploring the object after the failure of the practical exercise. As indicated, what we consider as a sign in the context of semiotic activity is usually labeled by the authors (cf. supra) as handling, or is sometimes identified as the carrying out of motor actions with no semiotic character.

Let us examine the sequence and the context in which this sign is produced. First of all, the adult makes an *ostension of the block*, visibly with the intention of carrying out its canonical use. But Nelson takes hold of the block and the usage which was intended by the adult fails, as the block lands on an inadequate space. The adult lets Nelson continue, Nelson straightens up (which indicates concentration) before initiating the process of use. The adult does a *multiple immediate iconic pointing* that Nelson ignores, as he puts the block back on the space where he previously failed and unsuccessfully tries to push it in. The adult moves the truck so that the adequate space is facing Nelson. The adult then does another *multiple immediate iconic pointing* but Nelson ignores it and does an *ostension towards himself* through which he examines his block (for 2 seconds) (probably to try and understand what didn't work previously) while the adult has left his index lying in the hole (in a sort of *permanent immediate pointing*). After this *ostension towards himself*, the child puts the block back into the space he has already tried, unsuccessfully attempts to push it in, and the truck falls aside. Though he is attentive to the ulterior signs of the adult, the child does not act on them, and lets go of his block. In this observation, *ostension towards oneself* is a sign the child directs at himself (i.e., intentionally, in the sense that his action is neither purely coextensive to the interaction, neither due to chance, and that one can suppose the action to be regulated by internal meanings) in an attempt to explore the object.

At the age of 13 months this sign can also appear before use. Here, it enables the child to explore the object following a use which has failed. The production of such a sign testifies of the capacity of reflection of the 13-month-old child in relation with the action, and implies an increasing control of attentiveness by the child himself through signs. Comparing the child's intentional use of the sign as we have it here and its fortuitous use at age 7 months (cf. Nelson, observation n°1 supra), gives an idea of the progress made by the child. In the present realization of Nelson, *ostension towards oneself* is at the service of a vaster action whereas at 7 months old, it identified with the action itself as a whole.

Observation n° 5 – Justine, 13 months; Duration of the sequence: 7 seconds
Object: Telephone; canonical use: Saying Hello
Ostention directed at another person, with a declarative function

[Justine, pulling the telephone behind her with its cord, comes back into the field of vision of the camera]. Justine dashes past the adult, making a detour so that the adult doesn't catch her. Justine says "daddy.... The adult says "well then" while Justine shakes the receiver in the air on the side opposite to the adult (but watching the adult as she does so) and says "a-te-e-duuu." Then Justine lifts the receiver up to her shoulder. The adult [who is trying to prevent Justine from getting out of shot again] says "don't you want to come and play let's say hello" then she takes hold of Justine who lowers the receiver [having kept it at her shoulder for 3 seconds].

In this example, we will show that the function of the ostension that is produced by the child is to bring the adult to share her interest in the object and, furthermore, to show what the object is for. Here communication is used for the sake of communicating, and differs from its instrumental function of getting something done as seen in example n°3. This is to say that here ostension has a declarative function in the sense that its goal is to bring a piece of information concerning the object; a characteristic which, though in another mode of expression, makes it comparable to what happens in language.

In this example of conduct the sign produced by the child, an ostension, has a declarative function (the child shakes the receiver in the air while saying "*a-te e-duuu*") in a form of "exhibition" of the (previously constructed) meanings of the object destined to the adult. It is an exchange of information about the object (the child does not use the object). The receiver of the Fisher Price telephone clearly refers to the "real receiver" of the real telephone. By her verbalization of "*daddy*"—the father is not there —which happens before the ostension of the receiver to the adult, the child expresses to the adult that, with the receiver, they can *pretend* to call Daddy *who is not there*. Through this exhibition of the significations of the object, the child means to show the adult that *she knows what game they are playing with the receiver* (which is confirmed by the canonical use that the child makes of the object later in the sequence that we are not studying here). Furthermore, the child knows—as is confirmed by the study of other sequences—that the telephone-toy is not the real object as you cannot hear anyone in the receiver, and what is more she uses the receiver in alternation with the adult, which is a characteristic of the fictional use of the object. Through this ostension the child shows that *she knows that the adult knows*, that is, that they share the meanings that concern the object; in doing so she expresses the connivance between herself and the adult.

Observation n° 6 – Justine, 13 months; Duration of the sequence: 10 seconds
Object: Truck; Canonical use: Putting inside
Production of pointings that touch the object

Justine takes hold of a block. A says "theeere square put the square there darling" with immediate pointing [touching the adequate shape. Justine, who is following the action of the adult, puts down her block on the indicated spot then takes it away. Justine taps twice (with the block in her hand) on another space, saying "euh dae?" (interrogative tone). The adult says "yeees the square there" while doing an immediate (touching the adequate space), iconic pointing [i.e., indicating the movement that must be done to fit the block into the adequate space). Justine renews her interrogation towards the adult by tapping (with the block in her hand) on a space that is close to the adequate shape then tapping (still with the block in her hand) on the adequate space and saying "there?" (interrogative tone). The adult does a multiple [repetitive], immediate [touching the space], iconic pointing [i.e., indicating the movement to operate to put the block in its space] of the adequate space, saying "here here pumpkin noooo here." Justine then takes her block away and brings her hand back saying "hee."

Through this example, we would like to show another aspect of ostension, its propensity to modify the expression of another sign that appears later in ontogeny, in this occurrence *pointing*. On a prelinguistic level, *canonical* pointings of an object at a distance are very rare, either from the child or the adult. Pointing is traditionally compared to language, rarely to the signs that precede it. Through this example we wish to show the link that exists between *ostension* and *pointing*, which suggests (this would have to be proved by further studies) some form of genetic continuity between the two types of signs.

At 13 months of age the child disposes of the general meaning (close to canonical where the truck is concerned) "if block then put into any space," a meaning which is the fruit of previous social elaboration. Helping herself with the signs that are pointings, she endeavors to construct more precise meanings of the object in the aim of finding the space that exactly fits her block. With the help of repetitive pointing and by successively touching the two potential spaces (the one being adequate, the other inadequate) where she can fit the block, the child tackles the construction of her knowledge of use but also, correlatively, progresses in the knowledge of the meaning of the pointings produced by other people.

The child's production of pointings happens as follows: after the child has seized a block, the adult indicates to her where to put it by doing an *immediate pointing* of the adequate space. The child operates a first adequate semiotization of the adult's pointing, puts the block down onto the indicated space but immediately removes it. It is then that the production of pointing signs (noncanonical, that is, repetitive and touching the space) intervenes, the child using this indicative sign to question the adult: she taps twice on another space with the block she has in her hand, while saying "*euh dae?*" This succession of actions seems to indicate that the meaning of pointing is not yet stabilized, a meaning that goes hand in hand with the construction of more precise significations of the object where a bi-univocal block-space correspondence is required. The adult answers "*yeees the square there*" while doing an *immediate iconic pointing* of the adequate space. The "*yeees*" expressed by the adult, and whose function is more phatic than acquiescent (concerning the spot of introduction of the object), does not seem to reduce the child's doubts as she renews her questioning of the adult, again using pointing (tapping now on the correct space with the block in her hand) then pointing and language "*there?*" The adult answers with yet another *multiple immediate iconic pointing* of the adequate space. But the child gives up. The indicative signs combined with language that are intentionally produced by the child during the interaction in the goal of learning more about the object, though they do not bring the child to fulfill its practical usage, enable her to question the adult with great precision as to the adequate space in which to fit the block. By her questioning, the child testifies of the fact that she is trying to amend the general meaning of which she already disposes, "if block then put into any space." She does so by the use of a pointing sign where signification and sign, in a way, answer each other and become genuine psychological tools at the service of the dialogue with the adult, and with herself. Here the production of signs is obviously intentional. In this example, we can establish that the reference to the object in the *immediate pointing* used by the child presents certain characteristics of *ostension*, regarding the reduction of the distance between the sign and the object it refers to. However, unlike ostension, pointing enables the child both to "have a hand" in her own progress regarding the construction of knowledge on the object in the given situation, and to keep the initiative in terms of communication with the adult.

Microgenesis Analysis and Production of Signs in Early Development: Elements of Conclusion

In conclusion, what is proposed here is a microgenetic analysis of baby-object-adult interactive processes, which shows, within the sociohistorical framework, how the child becomes a producer of signs while appropriating the canonical uses of the objects in educational situations. Through prototypical examples of ostensions, we can observe that before production of genuine linguistic signs, the child, through the production of signs such as ostensions, displays an intense semiotic activity. We more particularly show that communication and representation are narrowly linked through the pivotal character of the sign, which can be directed either at another person or at oneself and, in this second case, permits the advent of precocious forms of reflexive activity.

Ostension, as one of the first signs produced solo by the child, enables us to go back to the sources of the activity of representation. In our study, the representation appears as fundamentally linked with the active and communicative character of the sign. As it is shown, this ability immediately presents a social character and concerns the functioning of the psyche in its whole (attentiveness, action, cognition). We have also shown the important part played by meaning of a public type in the very process of production of ostension; for example at age 7 months (cf. observation n°1), the discretisation of the sign of ostension itself is relative to the activity of meaning-making that is being done by the child.

Our analysis highlights the fact that ostension has many functions varying from communication to representation (notably through the process of the construction of meaning). We can observe that ostension, in addition to its instrumental function of getting something done, can also have a declarative function (commenting, sharing ideas, communicating information on an object) that implies a primitive form of representation of other people's thoughts. Last, combining the process of communication with oneself and the pivotal characteristic of the sign, ostension when turned towards oneself allows the subject himself to regulate his/her own action.

These various elements plead in favor of a study of human behavior through signs and meaning, implying the necessity of exploring nonverbal signs, so as to attempt to go to the source of human consciousness and of reflexive activity which, along the course of ontogeny, shall become a predominant process. In this kind of study, microgenetic analysis constitutes a fundamental tool of investigation to approach cognitive development.

NOTES

1.   For lack of space and in order to concentrate on behaviors that are very much differentiated from a developmental point of view, we will not mention the observations we made of children at 10 months of age (which was also part of the study) and will focalize on the 7th and 13th months. Let us observe however that, at 10 months old, such ostensions as those examined in literature appear but are analyzed as signs, cf. Bruner, 1983); These ostensions are more manifest in the alternate use of the receiver by the child and adult and in the framework of routines or formats. A few rare ostensions directed towards oneself are also observed in relation to communication at 10 months old, in a similar form to those we have chosen to illustrate at 13 months old.

REFERENCES

Alquié, F. (1979). *La conscience affective* [Affective consciousness]. Paris: Vrin.

Bruner, J. S. (1983). *Le développement de l'enfant. Savoir faire, savoir dire* [Child development. Action development]. Paris: PUF.

Bruner, J. S. (1996). *L'éducation. Entrée dans la culture* [The culture of education]. Paris: Retz.

Butterworth, G. (2002). Pointing is the royal road to language for babies. In S. Kita (Ed.), *Pointing where language, culture, and cognition meet* (pp. 9-33). Mahwah, NJ: Erlbaum.

Eco, U. (1988). *Sémiotique et philosophie du langage* [Semiotics and philosophy of language]. Paris: PUF.

Eco, U. (1992). *La production des signes* [The production of signs]. Paris: Le Livre de Poche.

Feyereisen, P., & De Lannoy, J.-D. (1985). *Psychologie du geste* [The psychology of gesture]. Liège, Belgium: Mardaga.

Goodman, N. (1978). *Ways of worldmaking*. Indianapolis, MN: Hackett.

Inhelder, B., Cellérier, G, Ackermann, E., Blanchet, A., Boder, A., De Caprona, D., Ducret, J.-J. & et al. (1992). *Les cheminements de la découverte de l'enfant: Recherches sur les microgénèses cognitives* [Child process of discovery: Researchers in cognitive microgenesis]. Neuchâtel & Paris: Delachaux & Niestlé.

Jakobson, R. (1974). *Coup d'œil sur le développement de la sémiotique* [Glance at semiotics development]. Bloomington, IN: Research Center for Language and Semiotic Studies.

Kita, S. (Ed.). (2002). *Pointing where language, culture, and cognition meet*. Mahwah, NJ: Erlbaum.

Moro, C., & Rodríguez, C. (2005a). *L'objet et la construction de son usage chez le bébé. Une approche sémiotique du développement préverbal*. Berne, Switzerland: Peter Lang.

Moro, C., & Rodríguez, C. (2005b). L'éducation et le signe comme conditions de possibilité du développement psychologique. Un questionnement qui transcende les frontières disciplinaires [Education and sign as conditions of possibility of psycholgical development: Beyond disciplinarily]. In G. Chatelanat, C. Moro, & M. Saada-Robert (Eds.), *Unité et pluralité des sciences de l'éducation. Sondages au cœur de la recherche* [Unity and plurality in educational sciences research] (pp. 61-87). Berne, Switzerland: Peter Lang.

Moro, C., & Schneuwly, B. (2001). Réflexion duelle sur le rôle du signe à l'étape préverbale du développement et retour sur la thèse vygotskienne de la double racine de la pensée et du langage [Reflections on the role of sign at prelinguistic level and the Vygotskian thesis of the two roots of thought and language]. In J.-P. Bernié (Ed.), *Apprentissage, développement et significations* [Learning, development and meaning] (pp. 77-91). Bordeaux, France: Presses Universitaires.

Piaget, J. (1974). *La prise de conscience* [Self consciousness]. Paris: PUF.

Piaget, J. (1977). *La naissance de l'intelligence chez l'enfant* [The origins of intelligence in children]. Paris: Delachaux & Niestlé. (Original work published 1936)

Peirce, C. S. (1958). *Collected papers.* Cambridge, MA: Harvard University Press. (Original work published 1931)

Rivière, A. (1990). *La psychologie de Vygotski* [The psychology of Vygotsky]. Liège, Belgium: Mardaga.

Rodríguez, C., & Moro, C. (1999). *El mágico número tres. Cuando los niños aún no hablan* [The magical number three: When children still do not speak]. Barcelona, Spain: Paidós.

Rodríguez, C., & Palacios, P. (2002). Do private gestures. *Infant Behavior & Development, 30,* 180-194.

Saada-Robert, M. (1978). *Les modifications du déroulement de l'activité observable comme indices d'un changement de significations fonctionnelles* [Changes in activity as a clue for changes in functional meaning]. Thèse de doctorat, Université de Genève.

Saada-Robert, M. (1994). Microgenesis and situated representations. In N. Mercer & C. Coll (Eds.) *Teaching, learning and interaction* (pp. 55-64). Madrid, Spain: Infancia y Aprendizaje.

Siegler, R. S., & Crowley, K. (1991). The microgenetic method: A direct means for studying cognitive development. *American Psychologist, 46,* 606-620.

Vygotsky, L. S. (1978). *Mind in society. The development of higher psychological processes.* Cambridge, MA: Harvard University Press.

Vygotsky, L. S. (1994). La conscience comme problème de la psychologie du comportement [Consciousness as a problem of psychology of behavior]. *Société Française, 50,* 29-51. (Original work published 1925)

Vygotsky, L. S. (1997). *Pensée et langage* [Thought and language]. Paris: La Dispute. (Original work published 1934)

Wertsch J. V. (1985). *Vygotsky and the social formation of mind.* New York: Harvard University Press.

Yakubinski, L. P. (1923). *O dialogicheskoi rechi* [On dialogic speech], Petrograd: Trudy Foneticheskogo Instituta Prakticheskogo Izucheniya Yazykov.

CHAPTER 10

CHALLENGING QUESTIONS IN THE STUDY OF EARLY SEMIOTIC ACTIVITY IN CHILDREN

Selma Leitão

The chapter by Moro and Rodriguez (this volume) addresses a doubtlessly critical topic in understanding the different meaning-making processes that occur throughout the course of ontogenetic development of children. Whatever the nature of these processes may be, meaning construction is based on the use of signs—the interpretation and production of words and other signs of a nonverbal nature (images, gestures, etc.). If we, like Peirce (1974), understand that a sign is something that under a certain aspect or to some extent means something else to someone, it is possible to conclude that anything can acquire semiotic value. The role of signs in the make up and functioning of intellectual life is the central issue in the theory put forth by Vygotsky (1930/1987) as well as contemporary theorists who adopt a historical-cultural perspective in understanding the genesis of the human psyche (Valsiner, 2000; Wertsch, 1985b; Wertsch, del Río, & Alvarez, 1995). A key postulate of this theoretical framework is that characteristically

Innovating Genesis: Microgenesis and the Constructive Mind in Action, pp. 229–240

human mental processes can only be understood through the comprehension of the signs that constitute such processes. Relying on this axiomatically assumed premise, the chapter by Moro and Rodriguez touches upon a series of theoretically and methodologically challenging points.

From the theoretical perspective, Moro and Rodriguez affirm the existence of intense semiotic activity in children in early phases of their (pre)linguistic and cognitive development. The study focuses on the semiotic activity of ostension, a phenomenon that the authors state is as yet largely unexplored in psychological research. Ostension is investigated in both directions: ostension toward another and ostension toward oneself. The authors give the latter a central role in the genesis of the reflexive activity of children. The reference point they use in attributing a reflexive dimension to ostension is the Vygotsky (1925/1994) proposal, which states that awareness and reflexive activity develop as the child becomes capable of establishing forms of communication with his/herself. The authors argue that ostension toward oneself would qualify as one of these forms of communication. Although this is a theme that remains underexplored in the chapter, the suggestion of reflexive activity in early phases of development appears to be a particularly interesting contribution of the Moro and Rodriguez study.

From the methodological perspective, Moro and Rodriguez support their arguments with the microgenetic analysis of videographic records of adult-child interactions in situations designed for the transmission-appropriation of socially established (*canonic*) uses for culturally produced objects. The use of microanalytical procedures allows the authors to obtain accurate descriptions of the emergence of ostension in child-adult interaction. It also permits them to draw parallels between semiotic activities in children at different ages. There are multiple issues that Moro and Rodriguez seek to address in their empirical study: the types of ostension children produce between the ages of 7 and 13 months; the circumstances in which they are produced; the functions the ostensions serve; and the relationship between the production of signs and meaning construction.

My aim in this commentary is to discuss aspects of the Moro and Rodriguez study that seem to be particularly puzzling—as well as challenging. Three aspects are addressed: [1] the role of vocalizations and verbalization in the ostension episodes analyzed; [2] the conception of psychological subject, subjacent to the Moro and Rodriguez study; and [3] the perspective from which Moro and Rodriguez assign meaning to children's ostensions. It is my hope that the discussion of these aspects may offer a broader context for further investigations into ostension as an early semiotic activity in children and its impact on the development of strictly human psychological functioning.

THE LINGUISTIC EMBEDDEDNESS OF NONVERBAL SIGNS

This first issue that arises in reading the More and Rodriguez study regards the role the authors award, if any, to utterances and other types of vocalizations (henceforth generically referred to as verbal components) in the development of the communicative and cognitive processes analyzed. The ostensions discussed in the chapter do not emerge in a linguistic vacuum. In drawing attention to components of this type, obviously one cannot ignore the specific purpose of the study, which the authors clearly define. Moro and Rodriguez's interest is in the analysis of ostensions (defined as nonverbal signs) produced in situations of interaction on the prelinguistic level. In my point of view, however, considering the specific focus of the study does not impede an inquiry regarding the role of verbal components in the structuring of the phenomenon investigated. The issue seems to gain relevance above all when we observe that verbal components are constitutive parts of all the communicative situations discussed in the chapter. Vocalizations permeate throughout the action adults perform in an attempt to demonstrate and transmit the socially established uses of the objects in question to their children. Less frequent and predictably less extensive vocalizations from the children appear equally in at least half of these cases. The issue raised, therefore, is to what extent it would be pertinent, for analytical purposes, to separate nonverbal actions (namely, the specifically addressed ostensions) from vocalizations and verbalizations in the midst of which those ostensions emerge.

Although the presence of verbal components in the episodes investigated is not a topic explicitly discussed in the chapter, it would be unfair to state that Moro and Rodriguez completely ignore them. In half of the cases presented, verbal components are in fact mentioned as the emergence of ostensions is analyzed. In Observation #1, the authors describe the constitution of a sign produced by Nelson (7 months) as involving a combination of two interpretative movements: vocalization (*huu*) and nonverbal action (*looking straight ahead*). Moro and Rodriguez understand the vocalization as a reaction of surprise on the part of the child regarding the fact that the telephone receiver with which he is playing ends up casually placed near his cheek. The second movement (*looking straight ahead*) is seen as the child's adoption of the posture people typically employ when using the telephone (canonic use of the telephone).

The second case in which verbal components are mentioned in the discussion on the emergence of ostension appears in the analysis of Observation #5. In the sequence of both verbal and nonverbal actions that Justine (13 months) executes, she says *"daddy"* (absent from the situation), shakes the telephone and looks at the adult, who responds to her saying *"well then."* Justine then says *"a-te-e-duuu"* and lifts the receiver of the phone up to her shoulder. Moro and Rodriguez interpret Justine's sequence of actions as a form of "exhibition" for the adult of the meaning of the object that she holds in her hands. The verbalization of the word *daddy* is seen as a way of expressing to the adult that they could pretend that they were calling *daddy* with the telephone.

The third and final case in which verbalizations and non-verbal actions are simultaneously addressed in the analysis on the same sign production is shown in the discussion of Observation #6. Justine places a block in the only space of a toy truck in which the block can adequately fit and immediately removes it. In the sequence, she taps it twice over another space that is inappropriate for the insertion of the block, saying (interrogative tone) *"euh dae?"* The adult responds *"yeees, the square there,"* while touching the appropriate space. Justine taps on a space that is close to the one in which it is possible to insert the block, then taps on the appropriate space saying (interrogative tone) *"there?"* The adult touches the same space the child has selected, while saying *"here here pumpkin noooo here."* According to the analysis Moro and Rodriguez offer, indicative signs and language are combined here and intentionally produced by the child with the purpose of learning about the object. A set of indicative signs and language allows the child to ask the adult about the exact place in which the block should be inserted.

The apparent integration between verbal and nonverbal actions in the above analyses, however, does not eliminate a certain ambiguity regarding the status of verbal actions in the emergence of the ostensions described. There are a number of reasons for this. The first is that only in Observation #1 the vocalization of the child is explicitly highlighted as a constitutive component of the sign produced. In the analysis of Observation #5, no indication is given with regard to how Moro and Rodriguez understand the vocalization the child produces (*a-te-e-duuu*) or the role it may have in the production of the ostensive sign. A second vocalization from the child (the word *daddy*) is described as something that occurs *before* the child produces the ostension with the telephone for the adult. According to the analysis, with this word the child would express to the adult that it would be possible to pretend she was calling *daddy* with the telephone that she has in her hands. Thus, the function attributed to this word seems to be that of a vehicle that enables the expression of a (supposedly preexisting) meaning—and not its constitution. As can be seen, in none of the cases does it become clear to the reader what type of relation there would be between *doing* (ostension) and *saying* (vocalization) in the situation analyzed—whether it is mere concomitance or an intertwining. In the first case, *doing* and *saying* would be seen merely as actions that coincide with regard to the time of occurrence or that immediately follow one another. Contrarily, in the second case, *doing* and *saying* would be understood as actions that combined in a nondissociable fashion in the production of a single semiotic activity.

Ambiguity regarding the status of the verbal components is even more pronounced in the analysis of Observation #6. At the beginning of the discussion on this case, the entire weight of the meaning-making process is placed on the nonverbal action of the child. "With the help of repetitive pointing and by successively touching the two potential spaces (the one being adequate and the other inadequate) where she can fit the block, the child tackles the construction of her knowledge of use" (p. 221 this volume). There is no reference in this comment to the verbal components that permeate the actions of both the child and adult. The split between the verbal and nonverbal seems to be reverted as the analysis progresses: "The indicative signs *combined with language* ... enable her [the child] to question the adult with great precision as to the adequate space in which to fit the block" (p. 222, this volume, stress added). In the conclusion of the chapter, however, the separation between the verbal and nonverbal is taken up again: "before production of genuine linguistic signs, the child, through the production of signs such as ostensions, displays an intense semiotic activity" (p. 222, this volume).

The point that seems pertinent to bring up is whether in all the above cases the ostensions and vocalizations (either produced by the child or directed to him/her) would be more appropriately addressed as components of a single semiotic activity that enables the child to construct knowledge regarding the use of objects. Characterizing the emergence of ostensions as a phenomenon that occurs apart from language does not in fact appear to do justice to the participation of verbal components in the structuring of the interactions in which the child produces them. The decision to isolate ostension in order to study it outside the broader semiotic activity in which it occurs is one that is perhaps more justified by the need to simplify the activity of investigation than by the nature and context of the emergence of the very phenomenon investigated. The split between verbal and nonverbal aspects stressed here appears to become all the more critical when one considers that in the same phase of development in which the child produces ostensions of the type Moro and Rodriguez investigate, he/she is equally involved in intense verbal communication activity, which will ultimately enable the acquisition of language. If we understand language acquisition as a process of increasing linguistic structuring from experience (Rommetveit, 1985), the issue of possible relations and crossovers of processes that enable the production of different modalities of semiotic activity becomes imperative. Addressing this issue will inevitably lead the researcher to deal with the complex relations between action-language-thought in early stages of child development.

In concluding this section, it is perhaps pertinent to recall the methodological critique put forth by Vygotsky (1930/1987) in *Tool and symbol in child development*: "Even in cases when speech and the use of tools were closely linked in one operation, they were still studied as separate processes belonging to two completely different classes of independent phenomena" (p. 13). Further ahead in the same article, the authors propose what to me appears to be a position of great theoretical scope and clear methodological implications: "*the child solves a practical task with the help of not only eyes and hands, but also speech*" (p. 15). The phenomenon that Vygotsky has in mind when they make such comments is the function of speech in the use of tools (practical intelligence) and the more specifically discussed topic is the function of egocentric speech. It is therefore not adult-baby communication that they are addressing. I believe, however, that there is something to be learned from this comment that may also be pertinent in the context of the Moro and Rodriguez study.

Semiotic Activity and the Constitution of the Subject

The second point that moves me to comment is directly linked to the developmental perspective adopted in the study. Like Moro and Rodriguez, I also see the engagement of the child in semiotic activity as a basic condition for the constitution of his/her own psyche. The child's participation in semiotic activity (particularly language) is characterized not only as a process that enables knowledge and the appropriation of culturally created resources, but, above all, as a process of subjectivation that permits the child's passage from *infans* to *subject* (De Lemos, 2000; Sinha, 2000). This passage fundamentally depends upon the communication of the child with a social other as well as the properties of the available systems of signs in this communication and the action of the child with regard to these systems. From this perspective, cognition is understood not as something that precedes semiotic activity, but as the result of collaborative social constructions effected amid processes of symbolic communication. The use of signs is therefore the condition and basis for the constitution of cognition. This statement appears compatible with the view proposed by authors such as Vygotsky (1934/1986), Bakhtin (1929/1984), Vološinov (1929/1996) and others from the so-called "golden era of soviet psychology and semiotics" (Rommetveit, 1992, p. 24), as well as with proposals from contemporary theorists that link contemporary dialogic and sociohistorical approaches (Linell, 2006; Marková, 2000; Wertsch, 1985a; Wold, 1992). The conception of the child that emerges from this theoretical perspective is that of an *infans* on the path of becoming a *subject* through participation in semiotic activity— and not that of a constituted subject who merely expresses his/her possibilities of functioning through semiotic activity.

With this premise in mind, the following question arises in reading the Moro and Rodriguez text: of what psychological subject do the authors speak when referring to the child being observed? How are we to understand the cognitive functioning of the child who interprets and/or produces ostensions? If we accept the interpretations of the child's actions as presented by Moro and Rodriguez, the conception of the child that emerges for the reader appears to be that of an already constituted subject in possession of her/himself. In the first year of life and the beginning of the second, the child is successively described as an interpreter of signs produced by the adult, the agent of intense semiotic activity, possessing intentionality, having complex reasoning processes, inferential ability and the capacity of making decisions and representing someone else's thoughts. He/she is not only capable of identifying mental states in others ("knowing what the other knows"), but also differentiating real from "make-believe" objects. Considering this variety of psychological functioning, the question becomes: how are we to understand the existence of such functioning in a phase of development in which the very production of signs is as yet an emergent possibility? How are we to understand its origin considering the premise that it is the engagement of semiotic activities that enables the emergence and development of consciousness? In what type of prior experience is such functioning constituted?

Questions of Method

As the authors themselves stress, the production of ostensive signs on a prelinguistic level is an as yet unexplored topic in psychological research. It is therefore not difficult to conclude that the inexistence of a consensual (or widely accepted) methodology from which the phenomenon can be addressed is one of the main challenges that researchers face in studying the topic. The lack of an established methodology for the study of a topic often leads researchers to import resources and analytical processes created for the investigation of other phenomena that are considered akin. Without denying the value of exchanges in the methodological field, it is, however, a concern when this importation is done without due consideration of the axiomatic presuppositions and theoretical frameworks to which the imported methods are linked and the purposes for which they were originally generated. Fortunately, this is not the case with the Moro and Rodriguez study. The procedure adopted for the study of ostensions is microgenetic analysis, which is a method that has been seen as a privileged resource in investigating the emergence of new forms of functioning in the historical-social development of psychological functions (Valsiner, 2000). Its application allows the authors to examine details of communicative processes that lead to the emergence of ostensions in situations of organized adult-child interaction with the purpose of the transmission-appropriation of culturally established manners of the use of objects. That said, the question that arises is: to what extent does the microanalysis presented in the chapter make evident to the reader the early engagement of the child in the interpretation and production of different types of ostension?

While the choice of the microgenetic perspective as an analysis method for the emergence of ostensions clearly appears to have been successful, the application of the method to the cases presented offers a certain degree of difficulty to the reader. A central reason that seems to contribute to this is the omission of more precise information on the interpretative processes the authors employ in attributing meaning to the semiotic activity of the children. As polysemy and context dependence are intrinsic attributes to signs, making explicit the perspective from which the authors *establish the meaning* of the signs produced in different contexts becomes an essential part of the analytical procedure. In the absence of such, various aspects of the analytical process the authors employ remain beyond the reader's grasp, thereby making it difficult to trace the path that leads Moro and Rodriguez to the interpretations offered. For instance: on what grounds do Moro and Rodriguez identify the occurrence of an ostension? How do they distinguish ostensions related to the use of the targeted objects from those that are not? What elements establish the current meaning of an ostension (against the backdrop formed by other potential meanings)? What criteria and/or procedures serve as reference for this decision making?

The lack of a more precise elaboration of certain key concepts used in the interpretation of the observations is a second element that imposes difficulties upon the reader in following the interpretative movements of the authors. For instance: how can we conceptually distinguish the action of the child as an *interpreter* from his/her action as a *producer* of signs?

What attributes define *ostension toward oneself* and differentiate it from *ostension toward the other*? From what elements is the canonic aspect related to the use of an object defined? A second look at some of the cases analyzed in the chapter allows an illustration of the difficulties addressed here.

Consider, for example, the analyses of the semiotic activity of Nelson described in Observations #1 and #2. The authors present the first case as a prototypical situation of sign production and the second one as an example of a situation in which the child "merely interprets" the sign produced by another person. The sign produced in Observation #1 is described as a combination of two interpretative movements: the expression *huu*, analyzed by Moro and Rodriguez as a reaction of surprise, and the action of *looking straight ahead*, seen as the adoption of a canonic posture related to the use of the telephone. The production of the sign in this case is interpreted as something that occurs in an unintentional manner and as an example of the communication process of the child with himself. A central issue that arises when one attempts to follow Moro and Rodriguez's steps in the analysis of this case regards the specificity (and possible relations) between the actions of *interpreting* and *producing* a sign. If, on the one hand, interpreting and producing signs are referred to as specific actions throughout the chapter, the characterizations of these two actions, on the other hand, overlap in the analysis of this case in a way that generates ambiguity. Two aspects of the analysis in particular make it difficult to distinguish the two actions. First, the sign *produced* by the child is described as a composition of two *interpretative* movements. Moreover, the process that gives rise to the production of the sign is explained in terms of an increasing complexification of *interpretation* processes in which the child would be previously engaged. Referring to interpretation as a means to describe the sign production process, without any additional elaboration being offered, leads to conceptual difficulties with clear implications for the comprehension of the analytical procedures adopted. A third element that adds to the difficulty in understanding this analysis is the very characterization of the action of *looking straight ahead* as a typical posture when using the telephone. If the action of lifting the telephone receiver to the ear (involuntarily executed by the child in Observation #1) is shown to be obviously related to the use of the telephone, the status of canonic posture attributed to the action of *looking straight ahead* appears far more disputable.

The analysis of Observation #2 (which is presented with the explicit purpose of assisting in the distinction between sign production and interpretation) also does not do much to clarify the issue above. Here, Moro and Rodriguez take two actions of the child as indications that the child relates (interprets) actions that the adult executes with the telephone to the established uses for the object: [1] for 4 seconds, he accepts that the adult lifts the telephone receiver to this ear and [2] looks straight ahead throughout the entire time. Additionally, the child smiles—which Moro and Rodriguez take as evidence of sharing between the child and adult with regard to the signification of the object and its use. The first difficulty in understanding this analysis—when having in mind the analysis of the previous case—regards the way the action of *looking straight ahead* is interpreted in the first and second case. In the analysis of Observation #1, this action appears as a constitutive component of the *sign production* process of the child, whereas, in the analysis of the second case, it is understood as evidence that the child *interprets* the actions of the adult as related to the social significance of the object. The questions that arise for the reader are: What constitutes such an action as evidence of sign production in one case and of interpretation in the other? What contextual elements (or of another nature) allow variations in meaning to be established in both cases? What procedures and criteria allow capturing the interpretative process of the child? From what perspective is this done?

The problem regarding the perspective from which an investigator analyzes a phenomenon is a central issue that has long fueled the so-called *emic-etic* debate in the social sciences. In response to the controversy surrounding the definition of the two terms, Lett (2007) suggests that they should be used as epistemological concepts. The distinction between them concerns the nature of the knowledge that is claimed. The *emic* perspective leads the analyst to adopt a perspective that privileges the interpretations, meanings and understandings that are meaningful to the participants of the cultural system under analysis. This emphasis on the participant's perspective as the criterion for the interpretation of the data has parallels in studies on mother-child interactions (especially in the field of language acquisition) carried out by researchers who adopt a pragmatic perspective. A central premise for researchers who work from this perspective is the possibility of the mother or other adult who interacts with the child recognizing the communicative intentions of the infant to which she responds. The possibility of identifying communicative intentions in the infant transforms the adult with whom he/she interacts into a privileged observer of the child's action. Such a role makes the adult an important "ally" for the researcher in the interpretation of the child's actions. Dore (1979), for example, explicitly suggests that the researcher should anchor his/her analysis of the child's actions on the interpretations of the mother, as she, more than anyone else, is capable of recognizing and "knowing" the child's intentions. This idea, however, is strongly criticized by other authors who draw a sharp distinction between the understanding that the participant of a situation has regarding what occurs in the situation and the comprehension on the part of the researcher regarding the same phenomenon (Carvalho, 2005).

The *etic* perspective, on the other hand, involves the use of analytical categories established by the researcher that make sense to him/her (as well as to other scientific observers) based on the theoretical framework adopted in the study. For instance, the theoretical knowledge of the analyst regarding power relations in society—and not the here-and-now contextualized interpretations of the participants—is what gives the analyst elements for interpreting aspects and nuances in the meanings produced in communication situations between individuals with asymmetrical social statuses.[1]

Nonetheless, rather than defend the adoption of any of these perspectives, what is stressed here is that a reflection on them could offer a useful starting point from which the issues raised in this section can be productively and effectively addressed. The adoption of one or another of these perspectives will naturally depend upon the epistemological and theoretical-methodological commitments researchers make in their knowledge-construction process.

NOTE

1.   For an instigating discussion involving the insider-outsider debate, see the exchanges between Billig and Schegloff, published in *Discourse & Society*, in 1999 (Billig, 1999a, 1999b; Schegloff, 1997, 1999a, 1999b). Although this debate has had a place within a field of study rather more diverse than that on which Moro and Rodriguez focus (that is, studies on discourse), the points addressed are certainly relevant to what is discussed here.

REFERENCES

Bakhtin, M. M. (1984). *Problems of Dostoevsky's poetics*. Minneapolis: University of Minnesota Press. (Originally published in 1929)

Billig, M. (1999a). Whose terms? Whose ordinariness? Rhetoric ideology in conversation analysis. *Discourse & Society, 10*, 543-558.

Billig, M. (1999b). Conversation analysis and the claim of naivety. *Discourse & Society, 10*, 572-576.

Carvalho, G. M. M. de (2005). Aquisição de linguagem e singularidade da fala da criança [Language acquisition and singularity in the speech of the child]. *Inter-Ação, 30*, 279-288.

De Lemos, C. (2000). Questioning the notion of development. *Culture & Psychology, 6*, 129-182.

Dore, J. (1979). Conversational acts and the acquisition of language. In E. Ochs & B. Schieffelin (Eds.), *Developmental pragmatics* (pp. 339-362). New York: Academic Press.

Lett, J. (2007). *Emic/Etic distinctions*. Retrieved January 15, 2007, from http://faculty.ircc.edu/faculty/jlett/Article%20on%20Emics%20and%20Etics.htm

Linell, P. (2006). *Rethinking language, mind and world dialogically: International and contextual theories of human sense-making*. Manuscript submitted for publication.

Markovà, I. (2000). Amédée or how to get rid of it: Social representations from a dialogical perspective. *Culture & Psychology, 6*, 419-460.

Peirce, C. S. (1974). *La ciencia de la semiótica*. Buenos Aires, Argentina: Nueva Visión.

Rommetveit, R. (1985). Language acquisition as increasing linguistic structuring of experience and symbolic behavior control. In J. V. Wertsch (Ed.), *Culture, communication, and cognition: Vygotskian perspectives* (pp. 183-204). Cambridge, England: Cambridge University Press.

Rommetveit, R. (1992). Outlines of a dialogically based socio-cognitive approach to human cognition and communication. In A. H. Wold (Ed.), *Dialogical alternative: Towards a theory of language and mind* (pp. 19-44). Oslo: Scandinavian University Press.

Schegloff, E. (1997). Whose text? Whose context? *Discourse & Society, 8*, 165-187.

Schegloff, E. (1999a). Naivete vs. sophistication or discipline vs. self-indulgence: A rejoinder to Billig. *Discourse & Society, 10*, 577-582.

Schegloff, E. (1999b). "Schegloff's texts" as "Billig's data": A critical reply. *Discourse & Society, 10*, 558-572.

Sinha, C. (2000). Culture, language and the emergence of subjectivity. *Culture & Psychology, 6*, 197-207.

Valsiner, J. (2000). *The social mind: Construction of the idea*. Cambridge, England: Cambridge University Press.

Vološinov, V. N. (1996). *Marxism and the philosophy of language* (L. Matejka & I. R. Titunik, Trans.). Cambridge, MA: Harvard University Press. (Originally published in 1929)

Vygotsky, L. (1986). *Thought and language*. Cambridge, MA: MIT Press. (Originally published in 1934)

Vygotsky, L. (1987). Tool and sign in the development of the child. In R. H. Rieber (Ed.), *The collected papers of L. S. Vygotsky:Scientific legacy* (Vol. 6., pp. 3-68). New York: Kluwer Academic/Plenum Publishers. (Originally published in 1930)

Vygostky, L. (1994). La conscience comme problème de la psychologie du comportement. *Societé Française, 50*, 29-51. (Originally published in 1925)

Wertsch, J. V. (Ed.). (1985a). *Culture, communication, and cognition*. Cambridge, England: Cambridge University Press.

Wertsch, J. V. (1985b). *Vygotsky and the social formation of mind*. Cambridge, MA: Harvard University Press.

Wertsch, J. V., del Río, P., & Alvarez, A. (1995). *Sociocultural studies of mind*. Cambridge, England: Cambridge University Press.

Wold, A. H. (Ed.). (1992). *Dialogical alternative: towards a theory of language and mind*. Oslo: Scandinavian University Press.

CHAPTER 11

GENERAL CONCLUSIONS

Emily Abbey and Rainer Diriwächter

In its focus on methodology, this volume illuminates one portion of a richer, more complex whole: the scientific study of human lives. As explained in the introduction, our understanding of scientific inquiry is one where axiomatic assumptions, theory, phenomena, and methodology are brought together, forming a cycle of inquiry, and where in particular, methods are not merely chosen out of a "tool box" but are deeply influenced by phenomena on the one hand, and theory on the other (Branco & Valsiner, 1997; Diriwächter & Valsiner 2005). Our specific question has been the study of emergent phenomena, one that is relevant for any researcher whose work acknowledges implicitly or explicitly the irreversible temporal foundation of human lives and the need to understand the conditions through which phenomena change with time. We have suggested that a focus on emergence necessitates a keen attention to the process of transformation, for it is only there that one can begin to uncover the conditions through which novelty emerges. In keeping with the notion of science as a cycle, we have further suggested that one cannot study emergence using methods that only afford "snap shot" views of human lives, for these cannot reveal the process of transformation through which the researcher might indeed glean information about the specific conditions that underlie change. In

Innovating Genesis: Microgenesis and the Constructive Mind in Action, pp. 241–252

addition, we have offered that our cyclical understanding of science necessitates that methods themselves be viewed as developing entities, changed in each use. Thus, in this volume five methodological approaches were presented, each influenced by the need to understand emergence, as well as the researchers own phenomenon of interest and theoretical understanding.

CULTURAL LIFE: A MEANINGFUL DANCE

At this concluding point, we now try to emphasize the links between our specific focus on methodology and the broader context of cultural psychology from which our book began. Why must cultural psychology concern itself with emergence, moreover, what is the history of this realization within psychology? The answer begins with an idea that increasingly finds acceptance within psychology: humans are not alone as they go about the process of making meaning. Cultural psychology takes as its focus the sign-mediated relations of the person and the social surroundings, and the reality that the personal and social are inextricably linked (see Valsiner, 2000, on the definition of personal and collective culture). As humans make meaning about their lives, they do so within semiotic demand settings (Valsiner, 2000) where institutions make suggestions that prescriptively present the world not as it *is*, but as they would like it—as it *should be*, offering the person organizing frames for how to think, behave, and through which to make sense of their experiences. Political groups, educational institutions, religious communities and corporations compete with one another, and with the individual, for control of meaning, each offering their own suggestion through which the ongoing stream of day-to-day experiences can be organized. That said, individuals are powerful forces, and they are not drawn haphazardly into one or another suggestion, rather, as social institutions present normative frames for living, the person is able to make his or her own sense out of these suggestions. Kurt Lewin (1951) talks about the *life space* as the person's physical and psychological extension in the environment, and as people go about daily life the life-space continually touches upon different demand settings. The individual internalizes some demands through symbolic representation, and yet such activity is itself not a grantee that he or she agrees with, or acts in accordance with, prescriptive suggestion. Once internalized, people actively engage in autodialogue—talk with one's self about the world of the self (Josephs & Valsiner, 1998)—and through such discussions various shifts emerge. It is possible that the individual accepts completely a given suggestion in unmodified form, however, he or she can also modify suggested meaning in some way, potentially circumventing some aspects of social suggestion according to his or her own situation (see Abbey & Davis, 2003 for examples), or entirely reject these suggestions.

Signs Operate Within Irreversible Time

Semiotic processes of relating with the world are centrally organized by the tension between personal and social spheres of meaning, and this tension ensures a continual fluctuation within meaning, and possible emergence of new ideas at any moment. Yet such a tension is certainly not the only, or even the primary reason that cultural psychology is deeply related to the study of emergence. Semiotic processes of relating with the world are organized by the tension between personal and social spheres of meaning, but most centrally, by the temporal flow of human lives. Time emerges due to our "situatedness" towards a particular event (Diriwächter, 2006). That is, time is a component of the complex qualities of phenomena, indicating our relationship towards "things." Humans live an irreversible stream of experience, where actions, thoughts, and communications occur once only, and are never repeated in just *that* way again. This sense of irreversibility has roots in the Bergsonian distinction between time understood as space—a medium which does not interact with experience—and time understood as duration (*durée*), where temporal ordering infuses each experience with its "once-occurring" position in that order, and in so doing, produces an essence of novelty in human lives that is as continuous as the flow of time. For Bergson (1944), the past endures into itself, building each moment as its own unique form, just as a snow ball continually changes through the ever-increasing snow pack as it rolls (p .4). In irreversible time, humans live a purely heterogeneous stream of experience (Bergson, 1913) as time breathes itself into every moment of their being, where even two views of the same unmoving object are nonidentical by virtue of the fact that the first glimpse, through such endurance, holds a slightly different form than the next (Bergson, 1944, p. 4).

Representing and Presenting Experience at the Temporal Boundary

In irreversible time, signs are used to make meaning, and mediate the relation between the personal and social, yet within irreversible time this activity can be conceptualized in ways that are not always immediately considered. In irreversible time, the swiftness of experiential shifts is magnified beyond what one may superficially appreciate and the person cannot be said to live in an elongated "stable" present, but rather, at the *boundary* of an infinitesimally small here-and-now and unknown future. Under such conditions, any notion of the present as one may commonly mean it can perhaps better be understood as merely a *boundary marker*, useful in delineating what is now known (the past) and through its realization—stipulation of the known—axiomatically introduces the next experiences as part of the unknown future (Matte Blanco, 1975, 1988). Our lives happen within what can be described as a *boundary zone* of the just barely known moment and the unknown future.

Within the boundary zone, the person is tied to the present and future while not being exclusively part of either. He or she can be understood to experience simultaneously competing "demands" (Lewin, 1936, 1951) of the immediately fleeting here-and-now *and* of a not-yet arrived unknown next moment. In feeling these demands, each contextualization of a sign tries to speak *simultaneously* to the immediate here-and-now—a representational sense that is arrived at as meanings from the individual's personal history are incorporated with the demands of the present moment. Given the uncertainty of the future—as in a Bergsonian sense, any outward likeness of the 'next' experience to the present is only superficial—the sign begins simultaneously to make sense out of this unknown next period of being in the world. Here, in its *presentational sense*, the sign draws upon the capacity of the human mind for imagination, and meaning enters into a space of possibility. Here, the person turns to ideas that inherently cannot accurately represent the world as it is, yet that are nonetheless useful (see Vaihinger, 1935) as they provide a vague range of suggestion through which the immediate (and not so immediate) next experiences can be encountered. The usefulness of such an orientation is clear: through these presentational senses the person is literally pre-adapting to what comes next before it is actually known (Josephs, Valsiner, & Surgan, 1999).

Ambivalence of Simultaneous Demands

Given that the future is reliably different from the present, if the imagined sense is to be a useful guide for the person toward this future, it must set for itself a position that is in some way *incommensurate* with the representational sense. Linking to Lewin (1936) and his notion of the life space as the person's physical and psychological extension in the environment, in irreversible time the person can be seen to experience competing forces of the here-and-now and an unknown future—an ambivalence that must be overcome (Abbey, 2006). In this view, actualizing one's futures from within the range of possibility laid out by the presentational sense of the sign is a process of overcoming ambivalence (Abbey, 2006). Human development in irreversible time becomes a process of overcoming the uncertainty of the next moment through organizational tools—signs—that are themselves equally uncertain and open to reconfiguration. In irreversible time, each new contextualization of the sign (i.e., each next representation) bring simultaneously some essence of discrepancy of the presentational kind—another state of ambivalence. In this view, meaning is itself beginning its reemergence simultaneous to its making.

Some Emerging Tensions

The picture of cultural life here sketched is, then, one of constant emergence. Humans actualize their futures from within the range of possibility laid out by the presentational sense of the sign, and here, human semiotic constructions mirror the *durée* of experience which they seek to organize. Human semiotic constructions experience continual shift through the tension of social and personal senses and through the constant *durée* of experience that grantees an ambivalence between the thoughts of the here-and-now and presentations for the future. Human semiotic constructions are not, in all these senses, discrete units of fixed meaning, but rather, ones that are ephemeral, and in a constant motion of emergence. Thus, what emerges is a highly complex and dynamic field, in which the tension of the personal and social, and of the present and future (along with potentially many others[1]) are brought together as the person makes meaning about his or her life (see Figure 11.1). Their acknowledgement leads us to the position in this book that human lives, and the meanings they make of them, are not fixed and steady through time, but are perhaps more aptly understood as ephemeral, and in a constant motion of emergence.

Historical Roots: From Völkerpsychologie to Cultural Psychology

A focus on emergence, such as that necessitated by an ever-shifting stream of experience, is not limited to our modern cultural psychology. An equally strong emphasis on emergence can be found within an early forerunner of cultural psychology, the "forgotten" discipline of

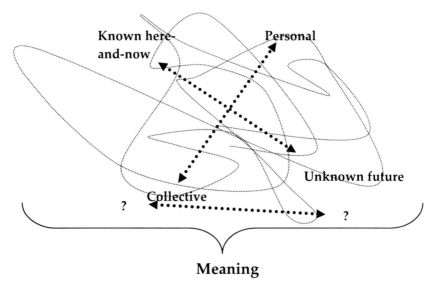

Figure 11.1.   Tensions involved in meaning-making.

Völkerpsychologie, which reached its early popularity when Moritz Lazarus (1824-1903) and his brother-in-law, Hajim Steinthal (1823-1899), formally launched the journal *Zeitschrift für Völkerpsychologie und Sprachwissenschaft* in 1860 (see Diriwächter, 2004). The two scholars outlined a comparative-psychological approach, based largely on Herbartian philosophy, to not only counter the natural philosophers, but also the emerging individualism of the positivists. Their central goal was to study the collective "mental" (*Geist*) life of humans where one aspect (syncretic *Völkerpsychologie*) was to deal with the general requirements of this collective mental live and the other was to apply these requirements. The result over the first 30 years of the journal's existence was a collection of largely nationalistically-oriented writings (Eckardt, 1997) that captured the inherently social nature of humans.

The discipline of *Völkerpsychologie* achieved further fame through the writings of Wilhelm Wundt (1888),[2] who agreed with Lazarus and Steinthal that the discipline of *Völkerpsychologie* was a necessary extension of any individualistic approach:

> Just like it's the objective of psychology to describe the actuality of individual consciousness, thereby putting its elements and developmental stages in an explicatory relationship, so too is there a need to make as the object of psychological investigation the analogous genetical and causal investigations of those actualities which pertain to the products of higher

developmental relationships of human society, namely the folk-communities (*Völkergemeinschaft*). (p. 2)

For Wundt, *Völkerpsychologie* was in essence a social-developmental discipline: social because it predominantly moves within societal dimensions; and developmental because it also needs to examine the different steps of mental development in humans (true psychogenesis).

Whereas the "simple," elementary mental processes could be studied via internal perception (*innere Wahrnehmung*), the higher processes, according to Wundt (1888), necessitated a historical approach. That is, in order to understand higher psychological processes, only historical comparisons – the observation of our "mind's" creations (*Beobachtung der Geisteserzeugnisse*)—could be looked at. Language, mythology, and customs were particularly relevant to psychology as they represented the objectifications of collective mental life. Thus, it was these products that Wundt saw as central to *Völkerpsychologie*. The simple psychological experiences were to be studied experimentally, while the products of the higher processes (which could be seen as having properties of "objects of nature") preceded the folk-psychological analysis. With Wundt, *Völkerpsychologie* was to fill the voids of the limited applicable experimental analyses by examining under a historical-genetic approach complex mental functions which determine both the social dimensions of the mind and the psychic processes.

Yet, the connections between elementary mental processes and the higher, more complex psychological processes were never clearly stated (Diriwächter, 2004). Thus, it became apparent that there was a "gap" between simple and complex mental phenomena—a "missing link" so to speak. Wundt (e.g., 1894) acknowledged this through his notion of creative synthesis (*schöpferische Synthese*) which suggested that any whole of mental configuration is different from a listing or summing up of its parts. Yet, *psychical synthesis* is never created entirely new; that is, out of seemingly unrelated parts. Instead, it merely represents transformed relationships (Volkelt, 1922). For example, the synthesis can be viewed as constant differentiation and de-differentiation of field structures. Hence, Wilhelm Wundt's principle of *creative synthesis* through re-combination of elements does not suffice (Diriwächter, 2008). Rather, the synthesis works between different structured fields; undifferentiated fields transform into more developed wholes (or previous structured fields are transformed into new ones). The starting point of this process is always the higher-level whole. The person's development does not progress from scattered elements to a synthesized whole, rather it progresses from one totality/whole (*Ganzheit*) to another (Volkelt, 1962, p. 27).

Genetic Ganzheitspsychologie—The Second School of Leipzig

It is precisely these totalities, and their subsequent transformations that Wundt's successors at Leipzig would make their core area of research when Felix Krueger (1874-1948) took over Wundt's position in September of 1917; thereby transforming the school into what became known as Genetic Ganzheitspsychologie—the Second School of Leipzig.

The transformed school took upon four central tenets for their core orientation—holism, feelings, structure, and development (see Diriwächter, 2008). Each of these theses highlighted the fact that there is a genetic and functional primacy of the whole over its parts—*that the whole is more (or different) than the sum of its parts.*

It is particularly the "genetic" emphasis of the second school of Leipzig that made their approach truly unique. As Wellek (1954, p. 67) put it: "One has to understand Krueger and 'Leipzig' as inherently developmental-theoretically (*entwicklungstheoretisch*) oriented, otherwise one has not understood anything." As each organism is in a constant state of transformation—never the same as it was just a moment ago—development became a chief preoccupation for *Ganzheitspsychologie* research. As such, psychology researchers need to elaborate on developmental sequences by examining developmental end-states and referring these back to their conditions and the never-ending process of becoming. This major task would illuminate the psychological necessities involved in the development of humans. According to Krueger (1915, p. 177), psychological necessities constitute the core of all we call "culture"—they are the carriers and inner movement which represent the forming forces of every cultural development—hence, cultural phenomena should be examined from the perspective of developmental psychology. In fact, Volkelt (1922, p. 104) mentions that Wundt's (1912, p. 4) use of the term "developmental psychology" (*Entwicklungspsychologie*) in his *Elemente der Völkerpsychologie* was in direct response to Krueger's "lobbying."

But how should one study development? Krueger (1915, pp. 166-171) suggested that the developments of totalities (the transformations of synthesis) are best examined by adhering to the following three guidelines:

1. One should consistently question the developmental changes that occur
2. One should rigorously examine how the developmental changes are dynamically linked and integrated into a uniform whole with qualitatively different, interactive components.

3.   One should be aware of a push, or an overarching "drivenness" of the totalities into a certain direction. Their changes are to be understood genetically and should be based on functional conditions that lead to the laws of occurrences (especially structural laws).

This further requires that we thoroughly understand the components. The components refer to the non-reducible parts of a totality (e.g., human experience), which are necessarily totalities of their own. They stand in relation to each other and cannot be fully segregated from one another—or from the greater totality—without loosing their meaning. Understanding these complex qualities of the whole are an absolute necessity for psychological analysis.

Furthermore, in order to understand the meanings of the complex qualities, we need to analyze the conditions under which they emerge. This approach is always conceptually abstract, and goes beyond the immediate experience, rising analytically over everything that was ever a part of a single psychological experience and could ever be held in its components (Krueger, 1915, pp. 75-80). We need to remember that conditions—especially empirical conditions—are always conceptualized. They are abstracted from compared events of the past, and the terminology we use is bound to the limitations that our language allows for interpretation.

Structural laws, and thus, developmental laws are the precondition of any form of analysis. *The dynamic whole with all its processes is the unit of measurement.* The totality is not just additive, that is, an amorphous unit, rather it is a synthetically, living form, a structure, that cannot be understood without the constant dynamically interacting parts, essential to life, stemming from present as well as past. In this, the *Ganzheitspsychologie* perspective is closely linked with Lev Vygotsky's cultural-historical perspective (e.g., the notion of "minimal gestalt" as unit of analysis).

A New Approach

Much of modern day mainstream research attempts to capture these social and personal interactions via quantitative methodology, thereby often assuming homogeneity of persons past experiences as well as their meaning-making process within a given context. However, our historical past and our integratedness into a greater whole can hardly be quantified, rather must be qualitatively described. *Ganzheitspsychologie* has always been keenly aware of the quantitative approach to psychology. In fact, it was

Krueger, who together with his English friend Charles Spearman (1863-1945), introduced correlations into German psychology (Krueger & Spearman, 1907), where for the first time a "General Factor" to which all correlating achievements can be traced back to was established (a concept that Spearman would later continue to develop).

In this regard, however, Sander (1962) reminds us of an important sentence by Goethe, "Measurement and numbers in their nakedness dissolve and ban the living spirit of observation" (p. 374). The nature of scales, such as those that measure constructs like "personality" (e.g., the dimensions introversion/ extroversion), allow for nothing more than that which is measurable, that is, one cannot imagine anything beyond that which goes through the covariation. According to the quantitative approach (e.g., factor analysis), a personality is a finite whole, which can be determined through an exact number of parts. Individual people differ in the number of these parts out of which they consist. The more same parts people possess, the more similar these people are. This portrays a mosaic of elements, independent of what lies outside the person, through a reflex-like system that constructs a finite whole.

For example, Krueger (e.g., 1928/1953) realized that feelings are *qualities* of the whole that develop and are a central necessity of ganzheitspsychological analysis and are most profound when the experience has not been reduced in its nature (e.g., to numbers). Although the structural component of an experience, which must be seen as an organized dispositional whole, is just as important for analysis as the ever-present feelings or emotions, it may never stand by itself without regard to the totality of the experience.

Last, there has been some criticism (e.g., Catán, 1986) that so-called microgenetic studies do not really address actual genesis, or microgenesis as originally conceived, but rather microdevelopment. Certainly, one could label any time-limited study as microgenetic, thereby defeating the original theoretical goals of gaining knowledge on how transformations through developmental sequences (including their connecting, intermediate steps) actually take place. Nevertheless, we believe that any microgenetic orientation is at the same time microdevelopmental in nature. Thus, studies that aim to capture the transformations that occur in the here-and-now are valuable contributions towards our general theoretical understanding of the processes the human psyche undergoes. It is precisely this goal that has fueled the creation of the present volume —to bring back to discourse possible developmental strategies that will shed light on the nature of the often overlooked meaning-creation as it occurs.

NOTES

1. Possibility of other tensions not here explicitly focused on is signified by the "?" in Figure 11.1
2. See Riebert and Robinson (2001) for a review of his life and work.

REFERENCES

Abbey, E. (2006). Triadic frames for ambivalent experience. *Estudios de Psicología*, *27*, 33-40.

Abbey, E., & Davis, P. (2003). Constructing one's identity through autodialogue: A cultural psychological approach. In I. Josephs (Ed.), *Dialogicality in development. Advances in child development within culturally structured environments* (Vol. 5). New York: Elsevier.

Bergson, H. (1913). *Time and free will*. London: George Allen & Co.

Bergson, H. (1944). *Creative evolution*. New York: The Modern Library.

Branco, A. U., & Valsiner, J. (1997). Changing methodologies: A co-constructivist study of goal orientations in social interactions. *Psychology & Developing Societies*, *9*(1) 35-64.

Catán, L. (1986). The dynamic display of process: Historical development and contemporary uses of the microgenetic method. *Human Development*, *29*, 252-363.

Diriwächter, R. (2004). Völkerpsychologie: The synthesis that never was. *Culture & Psychology*, *10*(1), 85-109.

Diriwächter, R. (2006). The wandering soul in relation to time. *Culture & Psychology*, *12*(2), 161-167.

Diriwächter, R. (2008). Genetic Ganzheitspsychologie. In Diriwächter & J. Valsiner (Eds.), *Striving for the whole: Creating theoretical syntheses*. Edison, NJ: Transaction Publishers.

Diriwächter, R., & Valsiner, J. (2005, December). Qualitative Developmental Research Methods in their Historical and Epistemological Contexts [53 paragraphs]. *Forum Qualitative Sozialforschung/Forum: Qualitative Social Research* [Online Journal], *7*(1), Art 8. December 30, 2005, from http://www.qualitative-research.net/fqs-texte/1-06/06-1-8-e.htm

Eckardt, G. (1997). *Völkerpsychologie—Versuch einer Neuentdeckung*. Weinheim: BELTZ Psychologie Verlags Union.

Josephs, I. E., & Valsiner, J. (1998). How does autodialogue work? Miracles of meaning maintenance and circumvention strategies. *Social Psychology Quarterly*, *61*(1), 68-83

Josephs, I. E., Valsiner, J., & Surgan, S. E. (1999). The process of meaning construction. In J. Brandtstatder & R. M. Lerner (Eds.), *Action & Self Development* (pp. 257-282). Thousand Oaks, CA: Sage.

Krueger, F. (1915). Über Entwicklungs-Psychologie: Ihre Sachliche und Geschichtliche Notwendigkeit [On developmental psychology: Its thematic and historical necessity]. *Arbeiten zur Entwicklungspsychologie, 1. Band—Heft 1.* Leipzig, Germany: Verlag von Wilhelm Engelmann

Krueger, F. (1953). Das Wesen der Gefühle. In E. Heuss (Ed.), *Zur Philosophie und Psychologie der Ganzheit: Schriften aus den Jahren 1918-1940* (pp. 195-221). Berlin, Germany: Springer Verlag. (Reprinted from *Archiv für die gesamte Psychologie, 65,* pp. 91-128, 1928)

Krueger, F., & Spearman, C. (1907). Die Korrelation zwischen verschiedenen geistigen Leistungsfähigkeiten. *Zeitschrift für Psychologie und Physiologie der Sinnesorgane, 44,* 50-114.

Lewin, K. (1936). *Principles of topological psychology.* New York: McGraw-Hill Book Company.

Lewin, K. (1951). *Field theory in social science.* New York: Harper & Brothers.

Matte Blanco, I. (1975). *The unconscious as infinite sets.* London: Duckworth.

Matte Blanco, I. (1988). *Thinking, feeling and being.* London: Routledge.

Sander, F. (1962). Das Menschenbild in der neueren Psychologie. In F. Sander & H. Volkelt (Ed.), *Ganzheitspsychologie* (pp. 369-382). München, Germany: C. H. Beck'sche Verlagsbuchhandlung.

Rieber, R. W., & Robinson, D. K. (2001). *Wilhelm Wundt in history: The making of a scientific psychology.* New York: Kluwer Academic/Plenum.

Vaihinger, H. (1935). *The philosophy of "As if."* (C. K. Ogden, Trans.). London: Kegan Paul, Trench, Trubner.

Valsiner, J. (2000). *Culture and human development.* Thousand Oaks, CA: Sage.

Volkelt. H. (1922). Die Völkerpsychologie in Wundts Entwicklungsgang. In A. Hoffmann (Ed.), *Wilhelm Wundt-Eine Würdigung* (pp. 74-105). Erfurt, Germany: Verlag der Keyserschen Buchhandlung.

Volkelt, H. (1962). Wilhelm Wundt auf der Schwelle zur Ganzheitspsychologie. In F. Sander & H. Volkelt (Eds.), *Ganzheitspsychologie* (pp. 15-30). Munich: C. H. Beck'sche Verlagsbuchhandlung.

Wellek, A. (1954). Die genetische Ganzheitspsychologie der Leipziger Schule und ihre Verzweigungen. *Neue Psychologische Studien, 15*(3), 1-67.

Wundt, W. (1888). Ueber Ziele und Wege der Völkerpsychologie [On the goals and paths of Völkerpsychologie]. *Philosophische Studien, 4,* 1-27.

Wundt, W. (1894). Ueber psychische Causalität und das Princip des psychophysischen Parallelismus [On psychical causality and the principle of psychophysical parallelism]. *Philosophische Studien, 10*(1), 1-125.

Wundt, W. (1912). *Elemente der Völkerpsychologie—Grundlinien einer psychologischen Entwicklungsgeschichte der Menschheit* [Elements of Völkerpsychologie—Outline of a psychological developmental history of humanity]. Leipzig, Germany: Alfred Kröner Verlag.

ABOUT THE AUTHORS

Emily Abbey is an assistant professor in the Department of Psychology at Ramapo College of New Jersey. Working from an explicitly present-to-future developmental orientation, she is generally curious about the role imagination plays in guiding the transformation of thoughts and feelings over time. Recently, she has published in the journals *Culture & Psychology, Estudios de Psicologia,* and *FQS: Forum Qualitative Sozialforschung.* Address: Emily Abbey, Ramapo College of New Jersey, Mahwah, NJ, USA.

Valerie M. Bellas (previously Haskell) is a doctoral candidate in clinical psychology at Clark University in Worcester, Massachusetts. Valerie has a research and clinical interest in emotion processing and adult-child relationships. She is completing her dissertation research on teachers' emotion socialization in early childhood classrooms, a project which is funded by the Spencer Foundation for Education. She will complete her clinical internship at Tulane University in New Orleans which includes specialized training in dyadic assessment and treatment for children birth to age five and their caregivers, trauma-based intervention and pediatric consultation-liaison.

Nicole M. Capezza is a doctoral student in social psychology at Purdue University. She primarily studies issues of partner violence, namely perceptions of psychological abuse, victim blaming, and victim coping. She also examines how dating couples respond to relationship threats. She has received several honors and funding awards for her research. Contact information: Nicole M. Capezza, Purdue University, Department of Psychological Sciences, 703 Third Street, West Lafayette, Indiana

47907. E-mail: ncapezza@psych.purdue.edu. Phone: (765) 409-2898.
Fax: (765) 496-1264.

Carla Cunha, MA, is a student of the Doctoral Program in Clinical Psychology at University of Minho (Braga, Portugal) with a PhD scholarship from the Fundação para a Ciência e Tecnologia (FCT—Portuguese Foundation for Science and Technology: reference SFRH/BD/30880/2006). She is also a teaching assistant at the Department of Psychology of ISMAI (*Instituto Superior da Maia*, Maia, Portugal) and a researcher at GEDI (Group of Studies in Dialogicality and Identity), Unidep, at ISMAI. Her current research interests are focused in the bridging between dialogical perspectives, microgenetic change processes, and self-organization in the field of psychotherapy. Mailing address: Instituto Superior da Maia, Avenida Carlos Oliveira Campos, 4475-695, Avioso S. Pedro, Portugal.

Rainer Diriwächter is an assistant professor of psychology at the Department of Psychology, California Lutheran University. His current interests lie with the history of psychology and Ganzheitspsychologie in particular. He has published previously on the topics of Ganzheitspsychologie and Völkerpsychologie and is coeditor—with Jaan Valsiner—of the forthcoming book *Striving for the Whole: Creating Theoretical Syntheses*. Contact Information: Rainer Diriwächter, PhD, California Lutheran University, Department of Psychology, 60 West Olsen Rd. #3800, Thousand Oaks, CA 91360, USA. Tel: 805-493-3442, E-mail: rdiriwae@clunet.edu

Agnes E. Dodds, Medical Education Unit Faculty of Medicine, Dentistry and Health Sciences, The University of Melbourne, Melbourne Vic 3010, Australia E-mail: agnesed@unimelb.edu.au'

Lothar Kleine-Horst studied biology, social work, and psychology. After conceiving—on the ground of *genetic Ganzheitspsychologie*—the first version of the *Empiristic theory of visual gestalt perception* which describes, and accounts for, in addition to others, the now-forgotten actual-genetic facts, he left university without a degree in 1962. In the 60s and 70s, as a freelancer he developed "programmed instructions" on behalf of both the German Federal Republic and a number of large private companies. Since 1980, as a freelance researcher he has written 10 scientific books published by himself (http://www.enane.de) in which he has developed his visual theory further, applied it by accounting for well-known visual facts, and replaced the usual monistic, or dualistic, weltbild by a quadrialistic one in which his Empiristic theory is integrated. He published the qualitative and quantitative results of his visual ESP experiments performed with both naive subjects and a new and more effective research method which interprets and utilizes the actual-genetic pregestalts of the ESP images drawn by the subjects. Furthermore, he provided evidence of both fraud on the domain of visual actual genesis by a number of German psychologists and the covering-up of this fraud by the German Society for Psychology up to the present day. Contact Information: Lothar Kleine-Horst, Formesstr. 31a, D-51063 Koeln, Germany. Tel: +49(0)221-621783, E-mail: l.kleine-horst@arcor.de

Jeanette Lawrence, School of Behavioral Science, The University of Melbourne, Melbourne Vic 3010, Australia. lawrence@unimelb.edu.au

Selma Leitão is an assistant professor of psychology at the Universidade Federal de Pernambuco, Recife, Brazil. She is also a visiting professor at the Graduate Program in Psychology at the Universidad del Valle, Cali, Colombia. She received her DPhil from the University of Cambridge, UK, and has been a visiting scholar at the Francis Hiatt School of Psychology at Clark University, USA, where she performed postdoctoral work. Her research focuses on argumentation and cognition. Address: Universidade Federal de Pernambuco Pós-Graduação em Psicologia Cognitiva CFCH, 8o. andar. Cidade Universitária 50670-901 Recife, PE Brazil Phone/Fax (55-81) 2126-7331

James P. McHale, Department of Psychology. University of South Florida, St. Petersburg Dav 100, 140 Seventh Avenue South, St. Petersburg Florida 33701 jmchale@stpt.usf.edu

Christiane Moro, Institut de psychologie, Université de Lausanne, Quartier UNIL-Dorigny, Bâtiment Anthropole, CH-1015 Lausanne, Switzerland. E-mail: Christiane.Moro@unil.ch

Stacey Pereira is a doctoral fellow in the Socio-Cultural Anthropology program at Rice University in Houston, Texas. She is currently interested in cosmetic surgery tourism in Brazil with regard to the themes of beauty ideals, commodification of the body, and nationalized identity. Contact information: Stacey Pereira, Department of Anthropology, Rice University, 6100 Main Street MS 20, Houston, Texas 77005. spereira@rice.edu

Cintia Rodríguez, Universidad Autónoma de Madrid, Facultad de Formación de Profesorado y Educación, Cantoblanco, ES-28049 Madrid, Spain. cintia.rodriguez@uam.es

Jaan Valsiner is a cultural psychologist with a consistently developmental axiomatic base that is brought to analyses of any psychological or social phenomena. He is the founding editor (1995) of the SAGE journal, *Culture & Psychology*. He is currently professor of psychology at the Department of Psychology, Clark University, USA, He has published many books, the most recent of which are *The Guided Mind* (Cambridge, MA: Harvard University Press, 1998), *Culture in Minds and Societies* (New Delhi: SAGE, 2007) and Comparative study of human cultural development (Madrid: Fundacion Infancia y Aprendizaje, 2001). He has edited (with Kevin Connolly) the *Handbook of Developmental Psychology* (London: SAGE, 2003) as well as the *Cambridge Handbook of Socio-Cultural Psychology* (2007, with Alberto Rosa). He has established the new journal on individual case analyses—*International Journal of Idiographic Science* (2005—www.valsiner.com) and is the editor of *Integrative Psychological and Behavioral Sciences* and *From Past to Future: Annals of Innovations in Psychology* (from 2007, with Transaction Publishers). In 1995 he was awarded the *Alexander von Humboldt Prize* in Germany for his interdisciplinary work on human development, and Senior Fulbright Lecturing Award in Brazil 1995-1997. He has been a visiting professor in Brazil, Japan, Australia, Estonia. Germany, Italy, United Kingdom, and the Netherlands. E-mail: jvalsiner@clarku.edu

Brady Wagoner is completing his PhD in social and developmental psychology at University of Cambridge, with the support of the Gates Cambridge Trust and the ORS award. His main interests are in the study of remembering as a social process, issues of communication and understanding within a dialogical epistemology, revisiting the history of psychology in search of potentially productive theories and methods, classical pragmatism, existentialism, hermeneutic philosophy, and the absurd pursuit of mountain summits. He is on the editorial board of the *International Journal of Dialogical Science* and *Integrative Psychological and Behavioral Science*. With Gerard Duveen and Alex Gillespie he created the *F. C. Bartlett Internet Archive* [Retrieved from, www-bartlett.sps.cam.ac.uk], and is editor of *Symbolic Transformations: the Mind in Movement Through Culture and Society* to be published by Routledge in 2009. Brady Wagoner, Department of Social and Developmental Psychology, Faculty of Social and Political Sciences, University of Cambridge, Free School Lane, Cambridge, CB2 3RQ.

Printed in the United States
204656BV00002B/136-141/P